THE WEST POINT CANDIDATE BOOK

HOW TO PREPARE • HOW TO GET IN • HOW TO SURVIVE

WILLIAM L. SMALLWOOD

BEACON BOOKS
Mesa, Arizona

THIS BOOK WAS PRODUCED WITH THE FULL
COOPERATION OF THE UNITED STATES MILITARY
ACADEMY. HOWEVER, THE AUTHOR IS SOLELY
RESPONSIBLE FOR ITS CONTENT.

THE PHOTOS IN CHAPTER TWO WERE FURNISHED
BY THE WEST POINT ASSOCIATION OF GRADUATES
AND THE INDIVIDUAL GRADUATES WHO APPEAR IN
THAT CHAPTER. THE PHOTOS IN CHAPTER TWELVE
WERE FURNISHED BY MARLENE MOULDER AND
REPRESENTATIVE JACK FIELDS (TEXAS).

ALL OTHER PHOTOS WERE FURNISHED AS A
COURTESY BY THE UNITED STATES MILITARY
ACADEMY. THEY WERE TAKEN BY
PHOTOGRAPHER CHARLES W. KELLEY, JR.

TABLE OF CONTENTS

THE UNITED STATES MILITARY ACADEMY MISSION

The mission of the United States Military Academy is to educate and train the Corps of Cadets so that each graduate shall have the attributes essential to professional growth as an officer of the Regular Army, and to inspire each to a lifetime of service to the Nation.

INTRODUCTION

This book is a "how to" book for those who think they want to go to West Point. It tells how to prepare for West Point. It tells how to get into West Point. And it tells those who get into West Point how to survive after they get there. In addition, it has advice for parents.

The advice this book contains is based upon interviews with nearly 250 persons. They include over 100 who were interviewed at West Point—mainly cadets, but also admissions officials, military supervisors, professors and administrators.

Another important resource was the 82 congressional staffers and panelists who gave advice on all aspects of the nomination process. This is important information because all candidates have to obtain a nomination before they can be offered an appointment by West Point.

But why West Point? Why should a candidate want to go there rather than the Naval Academy or the Air Force Academy?

Most of the cadets were asked that question. Surprisingly, their answers were quite similar. Here are two examples.

Said a cadet from Virginia: "I want to command men, not machines. I want to be a leader and I will be when I graduate. I'll have a platoon of my own—forty men whose lives I'll be responsible for—forty men whose respect I'll have to earn—forty men I'll try to make into the best platoon in the Army. And what would I be doing if I was in the Navy or Air Force? I would be flying a plane or managing a bunch of machinery. And it would probably take me five years to reach a position where I would be leading forty men."

And a cadet from Colorado: "In the Army you take and hold land and I like that. In the Air Force you fly over land but you don't take anything. The Navy is worse—all you see is water. Also, I'm a people person and when I look around here I see statues of leaders—Eisenhower, Patton, MacArthur—when I visited the Air Force Academy the only thing I saw was machines—this plane and that plane. I don't want a career of managing machines; I want to be a leader of people."

Do not let the preceding quotes mislead you. (Marines from the Naval Academy also command platoons.) The words were spoken by partisans—West Point Cadets who have yelled themselves hoarse cheering for Army over Navy and Air Force. The rivalry between the three service academies is probably the fiercest in the country.

The point of asking the question at all—Why West Point?—is to hammer home the most important thing that a candidate should consider before reading this book. That question is: Do you want to be in the Army?

If you select West Point as your college of choice, you are selecting the Army for your way of life. True, at West Point you will learn calculus and physics and essay writing as a part of your academic studies. But you will also learn how to use hand grenades, machine guns and Claymore mines—not only in your military classes and field training, but as a part of your career—or at least for the five-year tour in Army service that is mandatory for all graduates.

So do you want to serve as an officer in the Army? That is actually what you should be deciding as you think about West Point.

If you decide that, yes, I do want to become an Army Officer, then this book is an important resource for you.

Few would argue against the premise that West Point is the best place to learn how to be an Army Officer. But to get there you have to prepare and you have to overcome some unique hurdles getting in. Then, once you get there, you will have to survive a rigorous four-year program that about one-third of each entering class lacks the determination to complete.

Is West Point and the Army what you want? If so, then this is a book, not to read, but to study. It takes a lot of determination to get into West Point and survive there. Prove to yourself that you have that kind of determination. Start by studying this book!

ONE
THE INSTITUTION

The United States Military Academy, better known as West Point, is located on the Hudson River, about 60 miles north of New York City.

The buildings of the institution are clustered on a high bluff on the west side of the river. This is the site where General George Washington had a fort built during the Revolutionary War. The purpose of the fort was to guard the Hudson River and keep British ships and troops from moving upstream. Washington feared that the British, if they controlled the river, would divide the young nation and conquer each half separately.

Besides the fortifications on the bluff, General Washington also had a heavy chain built and stretched across the river as a barrier against ships. This was a monumental task because the chain weighed 150 tons and had to be

A view of West Point and the Hudson River—looking north.

1

floated into place each spring and removed each autumn before the river froze.

The combination of the fort and the chain was successful for no British ship managed to get beyond that site during the war. However, the outcome might have been different had not some colonists stopped and searched a man coming downstream from the fort. They discovered a paper hidden in one of the man's shoes, a proposal from the West Point Commander for selling the plans of the fortifications to the British. The man carrying the proposal was found to be a British officer out of uniform and he was hanged as a spy. The West Point Commander, General Benedict Arnold, escaped to Great Britain but lived the rest of his life branded as a traitor, even by the British.

In 1802 Congress established the U.S. Military Academy on the site where the fort stood. The mission of the Academy was to train officers who would also be engineers for the Army—a goal George Washington had long advocated because of the desperate shortage of engineers his army had suffered during the war.

West Point became the first military and engineering school in the United States. However, its academic standards for the first fifteen years were very loose and the quality of its graduates was lacking.

The academic program improved after 1817, when Colonel Sylvanus Thayer became Superintendent of the Academy. Thayer immediately initiated changes that strengthened the academic standards. Included in his program were two new requirements: (1) every cadet will recite every day in every class, and (2) no class will contain more than 15 cadets. The small class size enabled instructors to quiz each cadet and thereby hold each of them accountable for every assignment.

Together, those requirements have since become known as the "Thayer Method," and to this day they form the philosophical basis of instruction in some of the West Point academic departments.

Thayer served as superintendent for 16 years. During his tenure the quality of education at the Academy improved greatly and soon it was turning out the well-trained engineers the young, growing nation badly needed.

2

Because of Thayer's leadership in establishing high-quality academic standards, he is now officially known as the "Father of West Point."

Throughout the years, West Point has trained most of America's top military leaders. During the Civil War those included Union Generals Grant, Sherman, Sheridan and Meade, and Confederate Generals Lee, Johnston, Jackson, Bragg and Longstreet. (The President of the Confederate States, Jefferson Davis, was also a graduate.) Of the 60 major battles fought in that war, West Pointers commanded both sides during 55 of them—and in the other five battles there was a West Point graduate commanding either the Union or the Confederate forces.

New cadets form ranks in front of the General Douglas MacArthur statue.

3

During World War I, the general commanding the American forces, John J. Pershing, was a West Pointer. Also in that war, Colonel Douglas MacArthur, class of 1903, was decorated nine times for extraordinary heroism while fighting in France. After the war, MacArthur returned to the Academy as its youngest superintendent.

During World War II, West Point again provided most of the key leaders. These included Generals Eisenhower, Patton, Bradley and Clark in the European theatre; Generals MacArthur, Stillwell and Wainwright in the Pacific; and General "Hap" Arnold in Washington who was in command of the Army Air Force.

Two of those wartime leaders went on to become U.S. Presidents. General Grant served two terms, from 1868 to 1876. General Eisenhower also served two terms, from 1952 to 1960.

The West Point of today is no longer just an engineering school—although engineering is still one of its strongest programs. The mission of West Point today reflects the broader needs of our highly technical, highly mobile Army. That Army needs officers with a broad education who will have the ability and desire to keep on learning throughout their professional careers.

The West Point curriculum reflects the mission of the Academy. For example, all cadets take the basic courses that will enable them to master the technological challenges of the Army—courses such as calculus, chemistry and physics. But they also study political science, history, economics, literature, essay writing, geography and computer science— subjects that will give them the skills and intellectual breadth to grow and function in or out of the Army.

The other mission of West Point is less tangible, but more idealistic. It is to inspire each cadet to a lifetime of service to the Nation.

Interpreted narrowly, this means that graduates should be inspired to serve a twenty- to thirty-year career in the Army.

A broader and more literal interpretation is that any West Point graduate who serves in the public sector in any capacity is living up to the West Point mission.

The latter interpretation, however, does not mean that a person can attend West Point for four years and then run for Congress or become a public school teacher. All graduates have to serve a minimum of five years in the Army, and it is hoped that most will want to remain in the Army for a twenty- or thirty-year career.

It is vital that any candidate realizes that West Point is a very demanding military school in addition to being a first-class college.

Because West Point is a military school, the life of the cadet is nothing like the life of a student in a civilian college.

The military training during the first year is, by far, the hardest. It begins around the first of July with a six-week indoctrination period, officially called Cadet Basic Training, but traditionally called "Beast Barracks," or, more commonly, just "Beast."

The purpose of Beast is threefold. First is to teach the new cadets* the traditions, courtesies and basic knowledge of the Army in general and West Point in particular.

You will become an officer but you first have to learn what it is to become an Army recruit.

* "New cadet" is the name used until after Beast and acceptance into the Corps of Cadets. Then they become "Plebes." Second-year cadets are "Third Class Cadets" or "Yearlings;" third-year cadets are "Second Class Cadets" or "Cows;" and fourth-year cadets are "First Class Cadets" or "Firsties."

Second is to train the new cadets the way a new recruit in the Army would be trained. This includes training them to follow orders instantly and without question, teaching them basic combat skills, and pushing them through a rigorous period of physical development.

Third is to put the new cadets in a very demanding environment where they will be forced to learn how to manage their time and to use teamwork to achieve the goals set for them. The demanding environment teaches self-discipline and the teamwork training teaches the new cadets to suppress their individual desires and to work for the betterment of the group. The latter, in turn, develops group pride, an essential characteristic of any effective military unit.

In general, all three goals are designed to teach new cadets what it is like to be a follower—the idea being that they will make better officers when they know what it is like to be a recruit.

Beast Barracks is the first and most concentrated segment of an overall program called the "Fourthclass Development System." What this means is that the rigorous military training conducted during Beast Barracks continues, in bits and pieces, throughout the whole fourthclass, or "Plebe" year.

The military pressure during the academic year is not as concentrated as during Beast. However, with a heavy load of demanding classwork, and the additional pressure of mandatory intramural athletics, the "bits and pieces" of military training continue to be a heavy source of stress throughout the academic year.

The cadets say that every year there are new cadets who report to West Point who believe that once the six-weeks of Beast are over, they are then relatively free to become normal college students. Do not be one of those who is so naive!

According to many cadets, the end of Beast and the beginning of the academic year is the HARDEST part of the year. They point out that during Beast the new cadets outnumber the upperclass cadets who are giving them the training. But, with the beginning of the academic year and the return of the whole Corps of Cadets, the plebes are then

New cadets in their first awkward attempts to present arms. The George Washington statue is in the background.

outnumbered almost three to one—with almost all upperclass cadets eager to bring their own talents to the job of plebe development.

The candidate also should put the fourthclass system into perspective. It is not only a system to develop plebes; it is a system to develop plebes AND to develop the leadership skills of the upperclass.

It is a goal of West Point to turn out officers with the leadership skills needed to function in the Army immediately after graduation. But how do they learn those skills?

They learn some leadership skills during various summer training experiences, which include short stints in the real Army.

But their main experience comes from within the institution through the Fourthclass Development System, which is administered by Second and First Class Cadets.

In other words, the plebes are the "guinea pigs" for the upperclass to use for their "experiments" in learning leadership. However, "experiment" is probably not the best word, because the upperclass cadets must learn to exercise their leadership within the constraints of firm guidelines— as they will when they become officers in the Army.

Thus, there are two dimensions to the fourthclass system. The first is to develop the plebes; the second is to give upperclass cadets the kinds of experiences they need to develop a leadership style that will make them good officers in the Army.

So much for West Point as a college and as a military school. What does a graduate gain after surviving the rugged, four-year experience?

First, each graduate receives a Bachelor of Science Degree from one of the finest colleges in the country.

Second, each graduate is awarded a regular commission in the Army as a Second Lieutenant. Thus, unlike civilian colleges, West Point gives its graduates a job guarantee.

Third, the graduate will have experienced great personal growth—growth far beyond what graduates at civilian institutions will experience.

What kinds of growth? Read what the graduates in the next chapter have to say.

TWO
TEN GRADUATES: WHAT WEST POINT DID FOR ME

You will get an excellent education at West Point. You will also learn the fundamentals of leadership.

Those merits of the West Point experience are well known.

One other merit of the West Point experience is not so well known. That is the profound impact the West Point experience can have on one's personal life.

Many college and university alumni become enthusiastic boosters for their alma maters. With great enthusiasm they tout their institution's educational program, the greatness of their football team or the good times one can have as a Trojan or a Buckeye or an Aggie.

West Pointers are also proud of their education and their football team, and, despite the stern reputation of their institution, they also speak of the good times they have had.

But when they speak about their West Point experience, they always go beyond the traditional merits of their school. Instead of talking about their education or their football teams, they tell of the deeper, more personal influence that the institution has had upon their lives. They speak of personal development that graduates of most other institutions have not experienced.

Every young person who is a candidate for West Point should be aware of these deeper effects of the experience.

Some candidates, of course, can hear all of this first hand—from graduates known by family and friends. But such opportunities are not available to everyone, which is the rationale for including this chapter in a candidate book.

What follows is testimony from ten graduates with a great variety of careers and with a time perspective ranging from six to sixty-two years. So read the following accounts and learn what the West Point experience has meant to these graduates. Then decide if that is what you want to have happen to you.

9

Cadet Garrison
Davidson in 1927.

General Davidson when he was
Superintendent of West Point.

*Lt. General (Ret.) Garrison H. Davidson, Class of 1927.
General Davidson stayed at West Point eleven years after
graduation—six years as assistant football coach and five years as
head coach. During World War II he was the Army Engineer under
General Patton, then remained in the same position in the Seventh
Army under General Patch. He was fighting in Germany when the
war ended. He was Chief of Staff at the Presidio in San Francisco
when the Korean War broke out. During that war he had the major
responsibility for constructing several key defensive lines and
perimeters. After the Korean War, General Davidson served as the
senior Army Officer with Pentagon Weapons Systems Evaluation
Group, then served, respectively, as Commandant of the Army
Command and General Staff College, Superintendent of West Point
and Commanding General of the Seventh Army in Europe. His final
assignment before retiring in 1964 was Commanding General of
the First Army. He lives in Oakland, California and at the time
of the interview he was celebrating his 55th wedding anniversary.*

I grew up in the Bronx section of New York with a father
who had fought in the Spanish-American War. He had a great
admiration for the West Point graduates he had encountered—he
was especially impressed with their integrity. So it was natural

10

for me, after hearing these things and living in New York, to want to attend West Point.

What did West Point do for me? The most important thing every graduate gets is an appreciation for good moral values and an understanding of the necessity for a high degree of integrity. That is number one.

Number two is a very high sense of responsibility along with the discipline to meet that responsibility.

I can't overstress the importance of integrity. I won't denigrate those young officers who came through ROTC or OCS—many were fine young men. However, the West Pointer had lived a life of integrity for four years and there was just naturally a tendency for me to trust them immediately. I should stress that many of the others caught up, but I could clearly see the difference whenever I dealt with young officers. Of course, a few of the West Pointers disappointed me because of their lack of initiative, but the basics were there. They had the values of West Point and the commonality of good character that was recognized regardless of their rank.

And by the way, this was a helluva asset to our country when World War II broke out. This group of West Point officers was an important binding element for the Army. Having those key people in strategic positions gave us confidence in planning and executing our operations.

My advice to candidates is to go to West Point if your number one goal is to achieve the personal benefits that such an experience will provide. What you will learn personally will be extremely valuable throughout your lifetime regardless of what you do.

However, you have to recognize that something as valuable as that is not bought cheaply. You are going to be subjected to rules and regulations and personal deprivations. In other words you have a price to pay but, in my opinion, the price you pay is worth the value you receive from it.

And I do believe that the stress you will encounter in West Point will pay off. For example, I have a letter I received from a young chap in the Vietnamese War. He was a lieutenant right out of West Point and he described his responsibility in a very severe firefight. He described his circumstances and all the responsibility placed on him. He wanted me to know that he attributed his West Point experience for having the ability to meet those circumstances.

There is no question that the West Point graduate is better prepared to meet stress in the early years after graduation than a young person right out of a regular college.

11

There is one other good thing about West Point that a candidate should know. It gives the person an opportunity to have a lifetime career doing physical things as well as exercising your mind. This is important because I believe in the old Greek philosophers who said that you need a sound body as well as a sound mind. In West Point and, later, in the Army you have the best of everything...you have it all...you are constantly being developed physically, mentally and morally.

Cadet Charles "Monk" Meyer in 1937.

General Meyer just before he retired.

Brigadier General (Ret.) Charles R. "Monk" Meyer, Class of 1937. General Meyer lettered three years in basketball, two in football and one year in lacrosse while at West Point, and during his senior year was voted most outstanding athlete—while weighing only 140 pounds! After graduation he was inducted into the National Football Foundation Hall of Fame on the receipt of the gold medal, the Foundation's highest award. In his Army career he served at Pearl Harbor during the bombing, then fought in the New Guinea and Luzon campaigns in the South Pacific. In Korea, he commanded a regiment then went on to become senior advisor to the Fifth ROK [Republic of Korea] Corps. He asked for a combat assignment in Vietnam but, because of his age, was given a support command to "make sure those boys get enough bullets and food." He received many awards and medals including the Distinguished Service Cross, two Silver Stars and two Purple Hearts. His last

12

assignment before retiring was as Deputy Commanding General of Fort Ord, California. He now lives in Monterey, California.

When I got out of high school I could have been a bum— it was during the worst of the depression...I could have gone right or left or up or down...but I had a keen interest in going to West Point and that saved me. I went to two different West Point prep schools and while at the second one, I was invited to a party which turned out to be at the house of our U.S. Representative. I did an extra dance with the congressman's daughter and she offered to introduce me to her father. He liked me and gave me a civil service examination, then a nomination—and that's how I got to West Point.

West Point, in my opinion, is the greatest thing that can happen to a young man. Of course, there are many wonderful colleges and universities but how many of them bring their alumni back to bury? You graduate from West Point and you are in a big wonderful fraternity of men, and now women, who care for each other.

I remember as a plebe we could volunteer to go to the cemetery each Memorial Day and decorate a grave for whomever we chose. I picked the grave of Phil Sheridan, who had been killed two years before in the Yale football game. I remember being so proud to have the privilege and pleasure to do that all four years. What other colleges have students who do that?

The personal development is what is really important. You learn discipline and when you get out, you are a different person than when you went in. I learned self-discipline, I had a better outlook on life, I had goals, I had my country to serve and I had a serious feeling about my responsibilities. I carried those goals all my life—I still punch the clock every day and live out the words of the cadet prayer.

I also had made great athletic friendships that have lasted me all my life.

There is a pride among graduates and I, personally, would trust them more because I know how they have been living. Also, as officers they are trained to hold up better. I don't think that I ever, in heated combat situations, saw a West Pointer turn around the wrong way. Sure, there were a lot of guys who came from civilian schools that were fairly outstanding, but we expected more out of West Pointers. The common expression was, "He is a West Pointer; he had better be good!" It was what was expected.

I know I was so proud of West Point, I haven't taken my ring off. And during the war it was dangerous to wear it—you could

13

get shot if you were captured. But if they shot me, I wanted them to know who I was.

What would I say to a candidate? Well, when I was in Germany my sophomore son came home from school and said—he called me Monk—"Monk, I want to go to West Point; can you give me some advice."

I didn't want to influence him, but when he said that, I was so proud. I told him to study hard every single day, and try to be in competitive athletics because that gets you into the right spirit. Also help in your community and school and learn to serve because that is what it is all about.

I can't say any more to a candidate than what I told my own son—who, by the way, went on to graduate and serve in Vietnam where he was badly wounded while saving another officer.

Cadet Jack Broughton in 1945.

Colonel Jack Broughton in his F-105 "Thud" in Southeast Asia.

Colonel (Ret.) Jack Broughton, Class of 1945. While at West Point, Colonel Broughton played football and, in a unique wartime flight training program, he also completed much of his Air Corps flight training—while graduating in three, rather than four years. After graduation, he served as a fighter pilot in Europe, then in the Korean War. After that, he led the Thunderbirds, the Air Force precision aerobatic team. During the Vietnam War, he flew 104 combat missions from Thailand as Vice-Commander of a wing

14

*of F-105 Thunderchiefs—which the pilots called "Thuds." He
retired in 1968 and published* Thud Ridge, *a hair-raising account
of his missions over North Vietnam (out of the two Thud wings
flying out of Thailand, 130 men were killed or captured and 270
planes were lost). Recently, he published* Going Downtown: My
War with Washington and Hanoi, *an account of the frustrations
experienced by a commander in that war. After retirement, he
began working for Rockwell International. He now lives in
Lancaster, California.*

I was a senior in high school when Pearl Harbor was bombed.
That was on a Sunday and the next morning at seven o'clock I
was waiting at the Navy Recruiting Office. When I got in, a crusty
old petty officer said, "Son, how old are you?" I said, "I'll be
seventeen next month." Then he said, "What year are you in
school?" I replied, "Sir, I am a senior." The guy then looked at
me and said gently, "Son, you go back and finish your senior year.
Then come see me."

After that, getting into the service was all I could think about.
And as I considered all the options, I decided that I wanted to
fly. At that time they were beginning to wave the college
requirements for Air Corps cadet training. But with the war on,
West Point had initiated a new program where you could get a
college education and learn to fly. That appealed to me very much
and I began doing everything I could to get myself a nomination
and an appointment.

I had two paper routes at the time and I used some money
I had saved to go to Washington D.C. to talk to our congressman.
I told his staffer that I would take either West Point or the Naval
Academy because either could lead to pilot training. But she told
me to stick to West Point— that it would be my best opportunity.
Then the congressman took me to a session in the House and on
the way began asking me about my father. I told him he was a
drapery-hardware salesman. I don't think he was impressed,* but
he said he would do what he could for me.

Luckily, the son of a wealthy local guy declined his
appointment and the alternate couldn't pass the physical. I was
third on the list so I got a telegram to report for a physical and
two weeks later I was on my way to the Point.

I felt it was a tremendous challenge and that appealed to
me—I have always enjoyed taking on challenges.

I was immediately impressed with the institution. I quickly

---

*Years ago it was common practice for congressmen to give nominations as political
favors to wealthy or influential constituents. That practice has almost vanished—see
Chapter 10.

learned to respect its history. Also, the stories I heard about the wartime leaders who had attended West Point were a great inspiration to me. I developed a great desire to become an outstanding leader like them.

But I had a terrible problem. I had to struggle violently with the academic classes, especially math. I didn't have a good academic foundation and knew almost nothing about studying. I lived each day in fear of being thrown out. However, I always managed in some way to squeak through the classes with a 2.0 average.

What did that experience do for me?

For one thing it reinforced the drive that I had in high school to be a part of an elite team. If I was going to be on a football team, I wanted it to be the best football team. If I was going to be in a squadron, I wanted it to be the best squadron that ever existed. In other words, West Point greatly strengthened my desire for perfection.

West Point also taught me that I could overcome obstacles. I mentioned the first two years and how I struggled with academics. But by hammering at that obstacle I was able to overcome it. By the third year I had learned how to study and academics were no problem at all.

Learning how to study was basically a lesson in time management. What I really learned was how to analyze tasks and decide what needed doing and what to disregard.

I also learned the importance of carrying on when you have a responsibility. Because of the Thayer Method, we had to stand up and recite in every class, every day, including Saturdays. And it didn't make any difference if you had a headache or your shoulder had been ripped up in football. You knew you were going to get graded every day and if you were not prepared, you would get in trouble and eventually flunk out.

All of these lessons paid off when I became a pilot. For example, I didn't want to be just any fighter pilot—I wanted to be the best.

This drive for perfection was very helpful when I took over as leader of the Thunderbirds because that work demanded nothing less than perfection.

When I was a commander in Thailand, that same drive made me want to have the best wing that ever flew. But also I aspired to become the kind of leader that I had learned about at West Point. Like those leaders, I wanted to do the job—I wanted to get airplanes and bombs to the target. But also I learned that a good leader looks after his men. So my drive was to do the job and get as many guys back as I could. That was my focus day after

16

day; do the job as best as possible and get the most men out.

As a leader, West Point molded me in many ways. After learning to manage my own time, I became very intolerant of those who were not efficient—those who couldn't get a job done on time. And after my West Point training, when I learned to be neat and presentable, I had little patience for those who were sloppy.

The West Point lessons in efficiency really paid off in Thailand. Even though I was the Vice-Wing Commander and could have been an administrator, I tried to fly every mission. But that didn't eliminate the administrative chores. They were always piling up while I was out flying. But they were not a problem. Paperwork, efficiency reports and handling inspectors and visitors were the kinds of administrative headaches that drove some commanders crazy. But they were easy for me because I had learned how to do things efficiently.

West Point also left me with a lifelong desire to keep improving myself. When I was leading the Thunderbirds, I could have easily thought of myself at the peak of my flying ability. But with my inner drive, I kept improving and became a much better pilot. By the time of my last missions over North Vietnam, I could do anything that was possible with my airplane. I peaked at that time, with my flying, with my shooting and with my bombing— and this was twelve years after I had led the Thunderbirds.

What advice would I give candidates?

Just remember that the West Point experience will be just as important in the business world as in the military, should you decide to get out. Since I have been out in the business world, I have seen an awfully lot of people who can't organize themselves and direct others. The business world badly needs people who can lead and who can get jobs done on time.

I also want to stress that even though I have been talking about myself, what I am saying applies to most of my classmates. Anybody who goes to West Point and is able to graduate probably has the leadership training that is needed in the business world as well as in the military.

Colonel (Ret.) William De Graf, Class of 1950. Colonel De Graf graduated from high school in 1943 and enlisted in the Army. Because of his outstanding record in high school ROTC, he was sent to college for two semesters where he won a competitive exam for West Point. However, he failed the physical exam because of sinus problems and was sent to infantry training and, in October 1944, to Southern France. By the following January, one week after his 19th birthday, he was given a battlefield commission. He was wounded in March while fighting on the Siegfried Line and at the

Cadet William De Graf in 1950.

Colonel De Graf just before he retired.

end of the war in Germany, he again failed a physical for West Point. However, he was given a third opportunity and passed. He was sent to a prep school and then to West Point where he lost his rank of First Lieutenant and became a lowly Plebe. He adapted well. He rose to become a regimental commander and graduated number one in his class. Just after graduation, the Korean War broke out and he began a new combat career as a platoon leader. Later he was sent to Purdue to get a Masters Degree in nuclear physics and then to West Point as a professor of electrical engineering. Later he commanded a battalion and ended his career in the White House as a special assistant for nuclear policy. He retired in 1974 and became a top business executive for Science Applications International. He lives in Alexandria, Virginia.

West Point did many things for me. Above all, it instilled a strong sense of duty and service. Some of those feelings had been instilled in me at home—my father had been a National Guardsman. But West Point built upon what I had, and I left there with a very strong commitment to duty, honor and country.

West Point also helped make me into a rounded person. I received a good engineering education—that was the institution's traditional strength. But I also studied language, economics and history, all of which broadened me. I also learned to solve

18

problems logically and that skill helped me in the business world as well as in the Army.

The stress on physical development was also very important because it developed in me a personal commitment to stay in good physical condition. West Point's emphasis on individual sports such as handball, squash and golf were especially important because it introduced me to activities that I have continued to enjoy.

Another big thing that West Point had was excellent role models. When you are young, you are always looking at your superiors and trying to decide who you want to emulate. After World War II, the Tactical Department at West Point was full of men who had been outstanding combat leaders. They were a great inspiration to me.

One of the most important parts of the West Point experience is the lifelong bonds you make with your classmates. There were 671 of us and, because we took the same classes in those days and the classes were constantly mixed, I knew all 671 of them. We were very close then, and today, after forty years, we are still very close.

Those bonds mean a lot during an Army career. You are always having to pack up your household and move. But when you get to a new post, there are always classmates there to pick you up and provide transportation, to give you food to get by, and to help you get settled. I never served anywhere without classmates throughout my whole career. For example, in Korea there were five in my battalion and when I returned to Camp Roberts in the States, the man at the next desk had been an usher at my wedding.

Sometimes these close bonds are spoken of derisively as the "West Point Protective Society," meaning that West Pointers look out for each other at the expense of officers trained elsewhere. I don't agree with that; there are many fine officers who have come through ROTC and up from the ranks. And in the Army you want to serve with the officers who do the best job regardless of their background.

I think the proper terminology for our fraternity should be the "West Point Assistance Society." Our role is to help each other when there is a need, which is only an outgrowth of the close feelings we have for each other.

An important part of this bonding is the way the wives become a part of our fraternity; they are almost as active as we are. And if they are widowed, we don't just forget about them. They continue to be a part of us and we remain very concerned about their welfare.

What would I tell a candidate?

I can't help being biased. But if you really want to be good at something, you do what you have to do to become that way. For example, if you want to become a good doctor, I think you should go to the best medical school that you can get into. Likewise, if you want to become a good Army Officer, you should try to get into the best officer training school you can find. In my book that would have to be West Point, and I don't think there are many who would argue with me about that.

Cadet Denis Mullane in 1952.

Mr. Denis Mullane as Chairman and CEO of the Connecticut Mutual Life Insurance Company.

Mr. Denis Mullane, Class of 1952. Mr. Mullane served in the Army Corps of Engineers after graduation and ended his career as a company commander in Germany. After resigning his commission, he joined the Connecticut Mutual Life Insurance Company as a commission agent. In that first job he compiled a record of outstanding sales and soon he started advancing rapidly through management positions. He became president of the company in 1976, just twenty years after joining it. In 1983 he advanced to the position of Chief Executive Officer and in 1985 he added the title of Chairman. Mr. Mullane serves on several corporate boards. In addition, he has had a long career of public service leadership. He was recently elected President of the West

20

Point Association of Graduates in recognition of his many years of service with that organization.

I was ideally suited for West Point because I had a lot of idealism in me that I had picked up from my family and my high school.

My grandparents were all Irish immigrants but, unlike most of their contemporaries, they would never allow themselves to be called Irishmen. They insisted on being called Americans because they had a great love for this country. Their love and pride were instilled into me early.

Then I went to a Catholic boys high school where I became immersed in an atmosphere where we were constantly reminded of our duty to live a life of service to our fellow men.

West Point simply took those basic beliefs that I had acquired at home and in school and strengthened them.

But West Point did much more than that. The most important thing I learned was how to be a leader. Currently there are numerous books on the market that tell how a leader should be concerned about the people under him, and how a good leader should help his people become all that they can be. Well, I learned all of that at West Point back in the late 1940s.

Contrary to the common opinion about military leadership, it is not simply a process of ordering people around as a result of one's authority and rank. At West Point I learned that you can only be a good leader when you earn the respect of those under you, and one of the ways you earn respect is by looking out for those for whom you are responsible.

I remember as a plebe having to memorize General Scofield's speech [it is still required], the essence of which was that in wartime you are going to have to lead citizen soldiers rather than career soldiers and that to lead citizen soldiers you have to have respect for them, and you have to gain their respect before you can lead them into battle.

So, West Point gave me a twenty-year head start on leadership skills and philosophy. And, absolutely, what I learned about leadership at West Point has been an important factor in my success as a leader in the insurance industry.

Another thing I learned at West Point was time management. Like all plebes, I could never find the time to do all the tasks that I was assigned. But I learned self-discipline, and with that I was able to assign priorities to tasks—in exactly the same way I have to sort through tasks as the CEO [Chief Executive Officer] of this company.

21

My son, who graduated from West Point in 1980, summarized the whole concept well when I first asked him what he had learned about time management. He said, "Dad, that's easy. To be successful at time management all you have to do is keep 37 balls in the air until you know which 20 will crash quietly."

Another thing everyone learns at West Point is the importance of personal integrity. I know West Point doesn't have a corner on that—there are other fine institutions where integrity is stressed. But the honor code is an important piece of the life at West Point and anybody who has graduated from there cannot help being affected by living under it for four years.

Like the values of service and love of country, I also went to West Point with a strong belief in the importance of personal integrity. My dad always said, "Son, if you commit murder or arson, I'll stand by you, but if you tell a lie, I have never had a son." That is about the way they felt at West Point, too.

There are two other benefits of West Point that I didn't learn about until after I graduated.

One is the spirit of fraternity that exists among West Point graduates. The friendships that have continued over the years have meant a lot to me. Even though I did not remain in the Army, I have remained active with graduates and it was very rewarding to me when I was elected president of our association.

The other benefit is the prestige one derives from being a West Point graduate. That has been very beneficial to me in business. Of course, I won't say a West Point degree is any more prestigious than a degree from Harvard, but it is certainly equal to it.

How does it help? I think there are certain things taken for granted about a person who has graduated from West Point. It has been my experience that people tend to assume you must be pretty good if you made it through there. Being a West Pointer tends to give you a little edge because it is presumed that you will do a good job until you prove otherwise.

On reflecting over what I have said, I think I should add one more thing that West Point did for me. It gave me a lot of self-confidence, which has also contributed to my business success. Really, self-confidence goes hand-in-hand with time management. Using my son's example of the balls in the air, time management teaches you to let some of the balls fall, while self-confidence enables you to let them fall and to feel that you made the right decisions.

Judge Eugene R. Sullivan, Class of 1964. Judge Sullivan served in the 3rd Armored Division in Germany, as an instructor in the Army Ranger School at Fort Benning, Georgia and with the 4th

Cadet Eugene Sullivan
in 1964.

Federal Judge Eugene Sullivan in his judicial
robe.

Infantry Division in Vietnam. He resigned his commission in 1969
and went to Georgetown Law School where, during his senior year,
he was an editor of the Georgetown Law Journal. After receiving
his law degree, he entered private practice. But after one year, he
chose to enter public service where he advanced through several
highly responsible positions, including General Counsel of the Air
Force. In 1986 he was nominated by the President and confirmed
by the Senate as a Federal Appeals Judge. He is now a judge of
the United States Court of Military Appeals.

In high school I did very little to distinguish myself. I was
not a varsity athlete; I was not in student government; I was just
average in academics; and I didn't get into West Point until I had
taken a year of college.

But when I got to West Point, my life changed. The changes
began after we were told that we were the cream of American
youth and that everybody at West Point was equal regardless of
background. I believed them because I could see that they were
telling the truth. I came from a modest background—my father
was a police sergeant in St. Louis. Yet, in my company there were
several who came from wealthy families and there was a son of
a general. But we all had equal status—we had the same clothes,
the same shoes, and we all had to do the same chores.

Another thing that inspired me was the "can do" attitude that permeates the school. For example, I decided that I wanted to earn a letter as a varsity athlete and with that "can do" attitude, I did it. I played lacrosse and won a star for my letter when our team beat Navy.

The most significant thing that happened to me was my election to the Honor Committee during my sophomore year. I served on that Committee for three years and the experience of serving as a jury for honor violations triggered a strong interest in justice and the law. Although I came out of West Point wanting to be a tank general like General Patton, I realized after a few years that what I really wanted was to be a lawyer. There is no doubt that my three years on the Honor Committee started me on the path that I have followed for the past twenty years.

West Point also gave me a whole new degree of confidence. That confidence has lasted because it was forged in fire at West Point and tempered later in Ranger School and in Vietnam. That confidence enabled me to believe that I was as good as anyone else and if I worked hard I could be better than most.

That confidence did a lot of things for me. When I was in Germany, I saw a beautiful Danish model and fell in love with her at first sight. Without the confidence that I gained at West Point, I doubt if I would have had the nerve to approach her, let alone think that she might want to marry me—which she did.

That confidence also helped me as a ranger instructor, which was a real test, mentally and physically. But I had learned there is no obstacle that cannot be overcome if you put your mind to it. You just have to dedicate yourself to the task and put in a lot of hard work. Failure is not a ranger word. You learn to do anything you set your mind to—like walking through jungle and swamps for three days without sleep. As a ranger you do your mission and you get back. And through the tough times you remain loyal to your fellow rangers; if they need help, you help them. Exercising leadership as a ranger was a rewarding experience and I found that remaining loyal to your associates is as important in civilian life as it is as a ranger.

Confidence also helped me when I decided to go to law school. Confidence made me believe that I could be a top student and become an editor of the law journal—and I accomplished both. Also, the hard work paid off because during my senior year, I was selected for a prestigious assignment as a Federal Law Clerk for the 8th Circuit U.S. Court of Appeals—and that led to a position with one of Washington D.C.'s best law firms.

24

But it is hard to go through West Point without becoming a believer in the importance of service to your country. I think that influence was a big factor in my leaving a potentially lucrative private practice and taking a series of public service legal positions. I was much happier as a public servant and I enjoyed the work even when I had to spend nights and weekends on some jobs. I didn't make near the money I could have in private practice, but making money has never been a strong driving force—perhaps I also got that from West Point. You will never make the kind of money to have a millionaire's home on Malibu Beach while serving your country. But it is certainly an exciting life and, if you only have one life to live, why not live it to the fullest?

Would I be different if I had not gone to West Point? There is no question about that. I would have been less confident of myself. I would be less of a "can do" type of person. I know I would not have achieved anything like what I have achieved in the legal profession.

I'm sure West Point caused me to set higher goals for myself. In St. Louis I would have been more content with a boat on a lake and membership in a Friday afternoon bowling league. I would probably be more money oriented. Also, it is very doubtful that I would have gone to law school because I would have missed the experience of serving on the Honor Committee.

I guess I can sum it all up by saying that West Point made me want the world rather than the outer limits of my city.

Mr. Joseph Anderson, Class of 1965. Mr. Anderson was born and raised in Topeka, Kansas and became interested in West Point after receiving a congratulatory postcard from the Admissions Office when he was selected to represent Kansas at Boys' Nation. At West Point, he played football until suffering a knee injury and during his senior year he was a battalion training officer. After graduation he went to Airborne Ranger School and then to Vietnam as a platoon leader in the First Cavalry Division. While leading search and destroy missions, his platoon was accompanied by a French film crew for six weeks and their work ended up as a film documentary called "The Anderson Platoon," which won worldwide acclaim and an American Oscar and Emmy as the Best Documentary of 1967. Three years after returning to the U.S., Anderson returned to Vietnam as a company commander and after that tour, was sent to UCLA where he earned two Masters' Degrees in preparation for a teaching assignment at West Point. He taught there for three years, then spent a year at the Command and General Staff College and another year as a White House Fellow. In the latter assignment he worked for the Secretary of Commerce

Cadet Joseph Anderson in 1965.

Mr. Joseph Anderson as a General Motors vice president.

and while there, decided that he wanted a new challenge in private industry. He joined General Motors and advanced through operations (car manufacturing) as General Superintendent, Production Manager and Plant Manager. He was sent to Harvard for an advanced management program and is now head of a business unit with 4,000 people, 650 million-dollars in sales, and plants in the U.S., Canada, Mexico, Spain and Korea.

The first thing West Point did was make me aware that there is a bigger world out there—a world beyond Kansas.

Between my sophomore and junior years they sent me to Germany where I traveled and visited a lot of historic places. Then, the next summer, three of us volunteered for a Peace Corps-type project in Africa. We went to a remote, primitive village in Uganda and built a small community center.

Those trips, along with all my military travel and things like the study of comparative government at UCLA, greatly increased my exposure and understanding of the world.

West Point also gave me opportunities that most others of my race did not have at that time. When I grew up, the elementary schools in Topeka were still segregated. And, although I had better opportunities in the integrated junior and senior high schools, West Point was a vehicle that allowed me to move upward into a significantly more challenging social, economic and professional status than was available to my friends and contemporaries.

West Point also affected me at the personal level. I grew up in a solid, stable home with the typical mid-America type of parents who were religious and who had a strong sense of values. But the whole moral and ethical dimension of my being was strengthened at West Point.

West Point also deepened my middle-America values, and the words Duty, Honor, Country became very important elements in my personal fiber. Today, when people interact with me, they learn quickly that my word is my bond. In my company they know that when Joe says he is going to do something, they can take it to the bank.

Another important thing West Point did was to build my self-confidence. By learning to overcome the obstacles that were thrown in front of us, I learned that you can go far beyond what you ever perceived as your capability. This self-confidence was extremely important in ranger training and, later, in Vietnam.

Actually, the lessons in self-discipline and self-confidence that I learned at West Point were really a set of survival skills that allowed me to take on a succession of uniquely different assignments. There was a direct carry-over from adapting and surviving at West Point to adapting and surviving while in that Uganda village, while putting out trip flares and claymores [anti-personnel mines] in Vietnam, while teaching at West Point, while working as a White House Fellow and now, while managing a business unit of General Motors. All of those experiences were drastically different, but West Point gave me the self-confidence I needed to adapt and be successful at all of them.

People often say to me, "You have so many different responsibilities being the head of a GM business unit—you are responsible for engineering, manufacturing, acquisitions, financing and joint ventures on a global scale." They say, "Aren't you overwhelmed and intimidated by the complexity and all the responsibility?"

I say, "Yes, it is difficult and the learning curve has been steep, however, it is not much different from what I had to do at West Point or when I was taking on various assignments in the Army."

What would I tell a candidate who is considering West Point?

I would say, first, that West Point will give you an excellent, excellent education.

Secondly, it will help develop or reinforce the personal values that are extremely beneficial wherever you are committed—be it military, government, industry or academia.

Thirdly, it will give you the skills and self-confidence that will enable you to interact and relate with fellow members of any organization. You will definitely have that ability because it is a necessary part of survival at West Point—you can't get through West Point without it.

Cadet First Captain
Richard Morales in 1976.

Major Richard Morales, Army Physician.

Major Richard Morales, Jr. Class of 1976. Major Morales grew up in New York State just a few miles from West Point and applied there because of the academic and physical challenges that it offered. He played varsity soccer and lacrosse and was captain of the '75 team that went to the NCAA soccer playoffs. He was Regimental Commander in charge of Beast Barracks and was then appointed First Captain (the highest ranking officer) of the Corps of Cadets. He graduated in the top five of his class academically and was selected for a Rhodes Scholarship. After a year's study at Oxford, he trained at Infantry and Airborne Schools and commanded a platoon in Italy. Then he applied and won a scholarship to the Yale School of Medicine. He is now Staff Anesthesiologist at Letterman Army Medical Center and an Assistant Professor of Anesthesia, University of California, San Francisco.

28

I think that the West Point experience is unique in three ways when compared with schools of comparable quality such as Harvard, Brown and Stanford.

First, West Point offers a unique environment where students will develop a strong sense of self-confidence.

The institution builds this confidence by giving innumerable challenges to each cadet. The cadets see each challenge as an obstacle, but putting it in perspective, each challenge is an opportunity because the accomplishments that flow from the challenges cause the individual to develop a true sense of achievement. After successfully meeting all of those challenges for four years, the graduates cannot help but feel a sense of confidence and be ready for whatever they may encounter in the future.

The second thing West Point does is create an environment which gives cadets the strength to become disarmingly honest. Let me explain what I mean by that.

I think most professionals are very conservative in initiating change or in upsetting the status quo. So, when they have an opinion that needs to be expressed, they either keep it to themselves or they express it very cautiously.

I think most West Point graduates have more courage than other professionals when expressing opinions. Because of their four-year experience living with the Honor Code, I think West Pointers are more willing to risk the security of their positions by giving honest, straightforward answers and opinions. And, because the recipients of those opinions expect this kind of honesty from a West Point graduate, they tend not to suspect a hidden motive, and they tend not to react defensively.

Of course, honest opinions can make people uncomfortable, especially when colleagues and superiors are not used to hearing them. That is why being honest takes courage, and why West Pointers are different because they, for the most part, have that courage.

The third thing unique about West Point, when compared to non-military schools, is the attitude you gain when you lose your freedom. What you gain from the loss of freedom is a true respect for its value.

Those who have lost freedom and then regained it are more ready to defend it in the future. Also, they are more enthusiastic when it comes to defending the rights and freedom of other people.

In my own case this respect for freedom has carried over into my attitude toward the defenseless, and the people who are being brutalized by economic and social forces in our society. Because

I know what it means to be without rights and freedom, I am more sensitive to those within our society who do not enjoy all that they deserve.

Of course, there is a negative side to the loss of freedom at West Point. I think that sometimes there is too much suppression of the individual. However, I believe that the errors which occur on the negative side are more than made up on the positive side. The net result is a deep appreciation for freedom and I believe that this is a very valuable attitude for a graduate to carry into society.

In addition, I think there is a side benefit that results after individuals at West Point have experienced the loss of their freedom. They learn there are common goals which are more important than their individual goals and this has a tendency to inspire some West Point graduates to become involved in public service.

Let me try to put that into a personal perspective. Since I graduated 13 years ago, I have met many outstanding individuals. These include outstanding medical clinicians, but they also include top leaders from the realms of business and public service. But, of all the outstanding people I have met, the individuals who continually impress me as being the most concerned about affecting change for the betterment of many people rather than themselves, are the West Point graduates. As a group they stand out far more than any other group of individuals that I have met.

I would like to add one more thing to these comments. I am afraid that when readers of this book see that I graduated high in my class and that I went to Oxford on a Rhodes Scholarship, they will think, "Oh well, this guy is tremendously gifted and that's why he was so successful."

I want the reader to know that my contemporaries in high school might not have predicted the success that I have achieved. I had some identifiable talents in high school but I'm not sure many, including myself, recognized them.

My success can be attributed to two things. First, I put in a whole lot of hard work.

Second, West Point gave me many opportunities to grow as an individual. This, in turn, allowed me to develop the talents that I had, and it greatly increased my desire to excel and go beyond what I ever dreamed that I could do.

Therefore, in conclusion, I would say this to any candidate. Make sure that you want to experience this kind of personal development and that your desire to go to West Point is a personal, rather than a family decision. The development you will experience requires a strength that has to come from within—it can't come from your family, or your teachers, or from anyone else who might want you to succeed.

Cadet Andrew Burke in 1978.

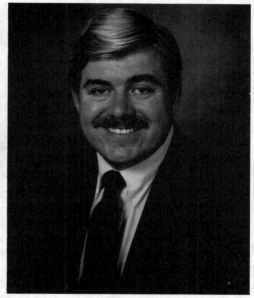

Mr. Andrew Burke today.

Mr. Andrew Burke, Class of 1978. Mr. Burke was born at West Point because his father (Class of 1932) was there as Staff Judge Advocate—his last tour in the Army. From there they moved to Long Island where Mr. Burke excelled in high school athletics and was active in student government. He won an ROTC scholarship, but after one year of college, he managed to get a nomination and appointment to West Point—following a brother who graduated in '58. After graduation he trained as an artillery officer and commanded a detachment in Germany. Then, after several stateside assignments, he got married and decided that a job in industry would be better for the family that he wanted to raise. He was immediately offered three jobs with Fortune 500 companies and chose to work for the Garrett Corporation. He advanced rapidly through several high-level sales and marketing positions while Garrett's parent company, the Allied Corporation, merged with the Signal Companies, forming the huge Allied-Signal Aerospace Company. Now Mr. Burke's title is Sales and Marketing Manager, East Coast Helicopter Programs.

Like most high school seniors who made the transition to West Point, I had a rough shock waiting for me. We had all been

31

tops at something—in our squad we had an all-state football player, an outstanding gymnast, a star hockey player and I was a pretty fair high school fullback—and, of course, we all had a tendency to think a great deal of ourselves.

In addition, I went there thinking I knew all there was to know about West Point. After all, I was born and baptized there, and, because of my father and brother, I grew up being closely associated with the place. During summers I went to West Point Boys Camp and then I worked at the Camp as a counselor. I thought for sure I knew what to expect when I got there, and I didn't even come close!

The problem that so many of us had was that we were not used to taking criticism, especially when we were also staring rejection and possible failure right in the face. Until you experience it, you cannot realize how deeply you are affected when, suddenly, you can't do anything right—you can't shine your belt buckle right, you can't shine your shoes right, you can't polish your brass right, etc. Then there is the memorization that is required, which you can never do fast enough, so you're told—and I'll put it politely—that you're dumber than a wedge.

Suddenly, those who were used to nothing but achieving excellence were getting nothing but criticism and were living with the real fear of failure. That sudden change was too much for many of them and they quit—they couldn't take the pressure and the criticism.

And those of us who stayed soon realized that we were no longer near the end of the bell-shaped curve like we were in high school. We realized that we were lucky to be in the middle of the curve and just running with the pack.

The point of saying all this is to explain how those difficult first weeks at West Point taught me two things: humility and fortitude.

The lesson in humility taught me that I had weaknesses as well as strengths. However, by identifying those weaknesses early in the plebe year, I had all of the rest of the time to build on them and learn how to compensate for them.

Because I learned my limitations, my ego doesn't get in the way now that I'm in a company with thousands of engineers. Even though I am an engineer, too, I don't hesitate to call on another one if there is something I don't understand. That makes me a more effective manager, and I can thank West Point for the humility I have brought to all my jobs.

Fortitude is the ability to keep on functioning when you are subjected to criticism, or exhausting work or any another type of stress. We all developed fortitude because we were forced to reach down deep and use strength that we didn't know was there. Knowing that I have this kind of strength in reserve has given me confidence that I could not have learned in any other way.

I also learned how to solve difficult problems rather than just beating my head against the wall. I learned how to break problems down into pieces and to apply analytical thought processes to each of them separately. This ability has carried over and helps me every day as I analyze problems and make decisions. I especially appreciate this West Point training when I see others attacking problems haphazardly or making decisions based upon emotions rather than reasoning.

West Point is a competitive environment and because of that, I think the graduates who come out of there tend to be more aggressive than those from other institutions. I know I am definitely more aggressive because of my tour there, and I am also what you might call "street smart" because I had to learn how to survive. All this pays off when you get into a job like I have where quick decisions have to be made under a lot of pressure.

Another thing West Point did was cause me to set higher goals for myself. I push myself more than I would if I hadn't gone there and I think my standards are much higher than they would have been had I gone to another college. Right now, should I lose my job and have to become a garbage collector, I can guarantee you that I would soon be the best garbage collector on Long Island.

That attitude—call it a drive to succeed—was instilled in me at West Point. It's the kind of attitude that makes you always want to be the best and to do the best job.

But it has another side. We don't always succeed at what we try; we sometimes fail. But, if you can look back and honestly say, "I did my best—I gave it my best shot," then you have nothing to be ashamed of.

I also learned some important things about leadership at West Point. I remember as a squad leader during Beast Barracks how it was when the first women were entering West Point. A lot of my classmates were skeptical that they would do well and to insure that they got a fair break during Beast, I asked to have some of them assigned to my squad. I felt I could be neutral toward them.

Well, I got three of them [out of 12] and I felt that I did a good job. I tried to be a good example and I tried to be fair. But I didn't realize how good a job I had done until a year later. Now realize that I hadn't had anything to do with the cadets in that squad after those weeks in Beast Barracks. Yet, they all came to me during June Week [the week of graduation] and presented me with a plaque and a sword in appreciation of the way I had treated them.

That shocked the hell out of me, but it convinced me that even though people dislike the event they are going through, they will respect you as a leader if you are fair when you are building their fortitude and pushing them to their limits.

I think I can summarize my feelings by saying that even though I was not the most gung ho cadet, I will always be close to West Point because of what it has shown me of my true potential. West Point steered me in the right direction and gave me confidence that I never would have achieved at another school. Now I'm always ready to look adversity in the eye and work against it. I'm a little like the typical Irishman who was not the brightest bear in the woods, but West Point taught me how to match my weaknesses with my assets, and, because of that, I am a lot better person.

Cadet Mary Finch
in 1983.

Captain Mary Finch in her flight suit.

Captain Mary Finch, Class of 1983. Captain Finch grew up in Tucson, Arizona and after graduating from high school in three years, she applied to West Point. However, because her SAT math scores were borderline, she accepted an offer to spend a year at the West Point Prep School, after which she received her appointment. At West Point, she competed on the gymnastic team and during her senior year was captain of the Dance Team (head cheerleader). She also went to Airborne School during one of her summer breaks. After graduation she completed helicopter pilot

34

training at Fort Rucker, Alabama, then flew UH-1 (utility) and OH-58 (observation) helicopters in Germany with the First Armored Division. She returned to the U.S. and attended Intelligence School. She also married a graduate (Class of 1977) who moved to West Point for an assignment in the Admissions Office. She opted to join him and enrolled in a new graduate program designed specifically for West Point Tactical Officers. She is now beginning her first year as a Company Tactical Officer.

When I was in high school, I was good in athletics and academics, but didn't have a lot of confidence as to where I stood in relation to others. When I went to West Point, I learned a lot about myself. I found out about my weaknesses and mainly about my strengths. I also found out how far I could push myself, physically, mentally and emotionally.

But the experience was also frustrating because I developed a heightened awareness of what prejudice can do to hurt people.

West Point is traditionally a male institution and it is very oriented toward combat arms—from which women, by law, are excluded. Of course, I had encountered some prejudice in high school about women being unequal but I laughed it off. But then, all of a sudden, I met cadets at West Point with that attitude and they were threatening my ability to survive. They were endangering my future!

That made me much more sensitive of prejudicial attitudes, not only toward women, but toward race, religion or anything else. Now that I'm back as a Tac Officer, I still see prejudice. It isn't evident in a bad or gross way—cadets would get into a lot of trouble if it were—but because I know the kind of pain it can cause, I am determined to fight it—not just for women, but for the betterment of West Point in general.

When I got out of high school, I was thinking about going to a junior college. Now, looking back, I can see how much different my life would have been had I gone there. I know I would always have wondered about myself—what I could have done, and what I could have been. I know that I would not have the confidence that I have now—confidence, for example, that, tomorrow, I could go right down into New York City and get a job if that is what I wanted.

I wouldn't know my limitations, either. Now I can look at something new and give it an honest assessment. I can evaluate it in terms of my strengths and my weaknesses. And I have enough confidence in my judgement now that if I think it is something I can do, I will go for it and I won't let people or the job intimidate me.

I know also, if I had not gone to West Point, I would have been satisfied with much less of myself. Now I love challenges. For example, I almost had to fight my way into Air Assault School and I made it through there even with knee problems. I know I wouldn't have taken on anything like that if I hadn't had the West Point experience.

West Point gave me strength because it was hard. And if I die tomorrow, I will have achieved more and been pushed to my limits more than people who are twice my age. I feel good about that and I have to give West Point the credit for making all of those opportunities possible.

HOW TO
PREPARE

THREE

MENTAL PREPARATION IS MOST IMPORTANT

Before pilots take off in an airplane they go through a printed checklist. This is a list of items in the cockpit that must be checked—items that are critical for the safe flight of the airplane.

The checklist is so important that few pilots would think of relying on their memory because something critical might be forgotten. Methodically, they read and check each item even if it is their thousandth takeoff in the same airplane.

This chapter is also a checklist for those thinking about going to West Point. It is a checklist of the ways your mind has to be prepared if you want to survive there.

Read this chapter like a good pilot reads a checklist. Think carefully about each item and make sure that each applies to you before you proceed to the next item. If you can complete the checklist, you will have an excellent chance of surviving at West Point—if they let you in.

If you fail to complete this checklist, you will not crash and burn—as a pilot might. But you will be setting yourself up to become a statistic if you do manage to get admitted.

About one out of every three who enroll at West Point fail to survive. And, according to the cadets and the staff, it is primarily the one-third who go there unprepared mentally who become the dropout statistics.

CHECKLIST ITEM NUMBER ONE. The first thing you must do to prepare yourself mentally is to find out who it is that wants you to go to West Point. Is it your father or your mother? Is it your high school coach? Is it an uncle or your grandfather?

If you want to go to West Point for any of the above, forget it. You are almost certain to fail.

When the West Point cadets were asked why their friends and roommates did not make it, the most common explanation was something like the following:

38

"My roommate really didn't want to be here but it had been the dream of his father for him to go to West Point. When my roommate first got here, he, too, thought he wanted it. But then, when it began to get rough, he realized that it wasn't something that he really wanted. He kept trying, but his heart wasn't in it. Eventually he got kicked out because of grades, although he really didn't have an academic problem. He was smart enough. He just didn't have the desire to study and do all the other stuff. He was here for somebody else."

You may be thinking, "Oh, this will never happen to me." But do not be too sure of it. The author interviewed several who either dropped out or were expelled from West Point and the other service academies. One of the common denominators of their stories was how they had come to believe that their parents' desire was also their own desire.

YOU have to want it for yourself when the upperclassmen start your development. Those who go for some other reason rarely survive.

Cadets say that it is almost impossible to survive if you do not have a strong, personal desire to be at West Point.

Ex-cadets, who resigned or who were expelled, say the same thing. For example, a young man from West Virginia realized during his first year that the military was not something he wanted. However, because of his respect for his parents, who were very proud of his selection to the Academy and who wanted very much for him to graduate, he kept struggling. He made it through three years but was finally expelled during his senior year—mostly because he ran out of motivation. He did not want anything to do with the military and just could not force himself to make the necessary effort to continue.

So look closely at this first item on the checklist. Clearly identify the person who wants you to go to West Point.

If you are certain that it is YOUR idea and not the idea of someone else, go on to checklist item number two.

CHECKLIST ITEM NUMBER TWO. You must think seriously about WHY you want to go to West Point.

Are you going for the glamour and prestige?

Certainly not! That is what most candidates will say.

But think about it again after you read about Mark Smith—who is not a real person, but who is a composite of several young men and women known by the author.

Mark was the number three student in his class of 224; he was captain of the football and baseball teams; and he was highly respected by his coaches, teachers, counselors and principal.

One day near the end of Mark's junior year he happened to be speaking with his counselor about his plans after graduation. The counselor mentioned Mark's high score on the SAT and his good academic record. "You might be able to get into a school like Dartmouth or Cornell. And, of course, you know that the service academies like West Point and Annapolis are looking for students like you."

It was just a casual remark but the sound of West Point had an exciting ring to it. It was something Mark filed in the back of his mind.

Later, during the summer, there were conversations at home about college. Mark mentioned that his counselor had encouraged him to set his sights toward a prestige college. But his parents looked worried whenever the subject was mentioned, and Mark knew it was because of finances. His father had a good job but he did not make a lot of money. Also, Mark had a brother and sister close behind him who would be wanting to go to college, too.

But West Point was also on his mind and when school started in the fall, he stopped his baseball coach in the hall and mentioned it to him, just to get his reaction. Surprisingly, the coach was very encouraging. "You might be able to play baseball there and you'd get a great education," he said.

So Mark began thinking more about West Point and after a few days he went to his counselor and mentioned his interest. The counselor was enthusiastic and immediately gave Mark the West Point Catalog to read. He also mentioned Mark's interest in West Point to the principal and another counselor as Mark was leaving the counseling office. The principal smiled and patted Mark on the back. "You would do great there," he said.

Mark felt good that his coach, his counselor and his principal felt so positive about him being a good candidate for West Point. At the dinner table that evening he mentioned it to his family. His father was also very positive. "I'll tell you this," his father said, "if you can get in and make it through, you've got it made in this world as a West Pointer."

That did it for Mark. He had always felt confident in his ability. And he had always wanted his family, teachers and coaches to be proud of him. He realized that by going to West Point, he could have everything he wanted: a top-quality education that would not cost his family anything; an opportunity to earn a prestigious degree; and, most important, an opportunity to make everyone proud of him.

Then one of his uncles who had heard about what Mark was thinking cornered him. The uncle had served in the Army in Vietnam and he was not impressed with the military. "Why do you want to go into the Army?" he asked.

Mark could not give a good answer, mainly because he had never even thought about the Army itself. But after his uncle had finished talking with him, he began to wonder if he was making the right choice. After all, West Point meant going into the Army and was that what he really wanted?

But now there was strong momentum behind him. His counselor had already arranged a conference with the local West Point Field Force Representative. So Mark met with the officer and, with his counselor, teachers, coach, principal, parents and even some of his friends thinking that his going to West Point was a neat idea, he had to show them that he had the right stuff. So in the interview with the officer he put on his "game face" and made a favorable impression.

One thing that could be said about Mark was that he was no wimp. He was tough, confident and determined. If getting into West Point was a difficult challenge, he was more than ready to tackle it. In fact, the thought of failing to get in never entered his mind. He was a winner, not a loser.

So, despite all the admissions paperwork and hurdles, Mark slugged through the process just the way he was battering through his opponents lines on the football field that fall. And his hard work paid off. First he got a congressional nomination, and then an offer for an appointment.

He made it! And with the achievement came congratulatory letters and a personal telephone call from the U.S. Senator who nominated him. This was heady stuff for a 17-year old and Mark felt very proud of the achievement.

Then came the publicity. There was an announcement on the morning bulletin at his high school. Later in the day his achievement was a news item on the local radio. Later in the week his picture and an announcement were in the weekly newspaper.

Throughout the rest of the school year Mark could feel that he was somebody special—that he was destined for a glory that the lesser mortals in his class could never hope to achieve.

Then, at graduation, his achievements were cited. Hundreds attending the ceremony cheered as he marched across the stage and received his diploma. And it was not just polite cheering. Mark, through his athletic exploits, had brought recognition to their town and with their applause the townspeople in the audience were trying to repay him. With their exuberance they were telling him that they were proud of him and were sure that when he went away to West Point, he would continue to bring glory to their town.

Mark was riding a wave of popularity now. During the two weeks before he left for West Point, he received the well wishes of his townsmen everywhere he went. Even the man whose son he had beaten out for the first-string fullback position two years before came up to him at the post office, shook his hand and wished him well at the "Point."

Days later he was on a plane for New York, alone and

apprehensive. His concern increased when he arrived at LaGuardia Airport and began meeting others who would be in his class. Immediately he saw that he was not nearly as big or as well muscled as most of the others. Nor, he felt, did he feel as worldly as the others looked. All of them seemed to know exactly where they were going and exactly what was going to happen to them. For the first time in his life he felt inferior. And on the bus ride up the Hudson, he sat by himself and began to doubt himself.

Then his fate was turned over to the West Point upperclass cadets. And over the next several days he could do nothing right. He would make his bed and it would be torn up. Then he would be yelled at. He would make his bed again and it would be torn up again and he would be yelled at again.

Every day there was immense pressure put upon him—pressure to do far too many things in the time allotted. Failure was guaranteed, as the upperclass had planned it.

In addition, there was, what seemed to him, endless nonsense to memorize. But he could never do it fast enough to please the upperclass.

Long days followed short nights and the physical and mental pressure increased. And he became depressed. He missed his home, his family and his friends. Also he knew that the upperclass were watching him closely, sensing that his motivation was declining.

But what was he to do? He could not bring himself to think of quitting and going home. The humiliation would be too much to bear. There were simply too many people counting on him.

So he struggled on and made it through Beast Barracks. But then a new hurdle was thrown in front of him. The classes were nothing like those in high school. The professors gave long assignments and they expected him to recite the next day. No one wanted to spoonfeed him like his teachers in high school.

He fell behind in math first, and his professor told him during a private conference it was because he was putting too much time in on his military responsibilities. That was a tendency of all plebes, said the instructor.

So Mark concentrated on math at the expense of his

military responsibilities. And he got himself into more trouble. Not only were the upperclass cadets on him, but he also flunked a chemistry test because he had not studied for it.

And then an English paper was returned with an "unsat." The same day he failed to work a math problem that he was called upon to put on the chalkboard for his class. And that evening he was called before his company commander and chewed out for having a dirty rifle for the third time since he had joined the company.

The trials of Mark Smith continued over the next few months. Desperately, he juggled the little free time he had in the evening between long, demanding academic assignments and the demands of the upperclass. And after the lights were out, when he laid his tired body on the floor (he did not dare sleep on his bed—he knew he could not make it well enough to please the upperclass cadets in the short time he had in the mornings) he agonized over his predicament.

Of course, the questions that crowded his mind more frequently were the ones he should have answered back when he was thinking about going to West Point. Why did I come here? What am I going to get out of all this if I do make it?

There is no point in dragging Mark's story out any longer. On Christmas vacation Mark went home and saw his friends who were enjoying campus life at the colleges they were attending. They told of parties, of dances and girls and fun. And, sheepishly now, he admitted to his friends and his family that he had made a huge mistake—that West Point was nothing like he expected and that training to become an Army Officer was something that he really was not interested in pursuing.

He wanted to quit and that is what he did.

End of story—not of Mark Smith, for he went on to a community college nearby, became a baseball star and is now very happy as a high school coach in a town just a few miles from his home.

But it is the end of the story so far as this item on the checklist is concerned.

So here is that question again. Are you thinking of going

to West Point because of the glamour and prestige that it will give you?

If so, forget West Point. Thousands of Mark Smith's have tried that over the years and they did not make it. And the reason they did not make it was because they did not have clear-cut goals. There was nothing at the end of the long, dark tunnel that they were willing to sacrifice so much to achieve.

If you are thinking about going to West Point, the second item on your checklist is to make sure you are going FOR THE RIGHT REASONS. Make sure that your goals are clear—that there are things you want very much when the four years at West Point are over.

What are the right reasons for going to West Point?

There are several, including the desire for personal development. But the MAIN ONE should be that you want to become an Army officer and you want the best leadership training that is available.

This does not necessarily mean that you should want to be a career officer, although that is what the Army would like. But you should want to be an Army officer for at least five years, for that is the length of time you will have to serve if you graduate and receive a second lieutenant's commission.

Of course, if the country is fighting somewhere in the world at the time your five years are up, do not expect that you will be allowed to resign.

So if you are even thinking of going to West Point, burn it into your mind that what you are really thinking of doing is going to a four-year officer training school that just happens to give you a college degree in the process.

Are you willing to put in four long, hard years in order to serve as an Army officer for at least five more years? If this is truly something that you want to do, proceed to checklist item number three.

CHECKLIST ITEM NUMBER THREE. Before applying to West Point, you should acquire some basic knowledge.

You should learn all you can about the Army and what you will be doing as a junior officer if you have to fight in a war. (You will most probably be either a second or first lieutenant for most of the five-year obligation.)

You can learn a lot about the Army and what war can be like for a junior officer by reading certain books. The Department of Behavioral Sciences and Leadership at West Point has listed such books, both fiction and non-fiction. Some of them, which a professor in the department felt would make good reading for candidates, are listed at the back of this book.

Candidates are being briefed by an admissions officer. Visits to West Point are strongly recommended.

The Department of Leadership also recommends a few videos that give a realistic view of what military service and combat are all about. Those, too, are listed.

Another good way to learn what it is to be an Army officer is to talk with some of them. Almost every community has such persons and most would be pleased to discuss their experiences with you. Of course, when they reminisce about their experiences, they will have a tendency to describe the good things and avoid the bad things. But do not let them do that if you can help it. You want an honest picture.

If the officers you speak with have been in combat and will talk about it, ask them how they handled their fear. Ask them how they managed to continue when those around them were being wounded and killed. Ask them to tell you what it takes to be an officer in combat. Then, when you go home and think about West Point, ask yourself if you think you have the potential to do those things. If you doubt yourself, it is better to do it now than when you are leading a platoon of men in combat. (Female candidates do not have to worry about this problem; by law females are excluded from combat assignments.)

Besides learning about the Army, you should also learn as much as you can about West Point.

Reading this book is a good way to begin.

But you should also talk with cadets who are going there. Check with your counselor and find out who the West Point Field Force Representative* is in your area. This is an official representative of West Point whose job is to counsel candidates like yourself. Telephone that person and explain that you are thinking about applying. Then ask if he or she can arrange for you to meet some cadets during their summer or Christmas vacation. That is a routine request. Field Force Representatives want to provide this service because they want candidates to know as much as possible about West Point.

An even better alternative is to visit West Point. Between September and April, Monday through Friday, a tour, including talks with cadets, can be arranged by the Admissions Office if you are at least a high school sophomore. To arrange such a tour, you must contact the Admissions Office at least two weeks before your visit.

For seniors who are applying to West Point there is a visitation program that allows you to stay with a cadet and see the kind of life they lead. For more information on this program, contact your Field Force Representative or the Admissions Office.

*If your counselor does not know a Field Force Representative, call 1-914-938-4041 or write: Cadet Public Relations Council, Admissions, USMA, West Point, NY 10996-1797.

Are you willing to do all the things that have been recommended to give you knowledge of the Army and West Point? If so, go on to checklist item number four.

CHECKLIST ITEM NUMBER FOUR. How do you react when you encounter a problem or a situation that is very difficult?

Would motivation make a difference? Would it matter how much you wanted to solve the problem or overcome the challenge?

Of course it would. That is why items number one and two are on the mental preparation checklist. To overcome the challenge of West Point you have to want it for yourself, and you have to know why you want it.

So much for motivation.

There is another factor that is involved in solving problems and overcoming challenges: determination.

How determined a person are you? In the past have you given up when faced with difficult challenges?

Only you can answer that question. However, to pass through the fourth and final item on the mental preparation checklist you must be certain that you can make yourself into a determined person.

This does not mean that you simply say to yourself, "Yep, if I go to West Point, I'm going to hang in there and do whatever I have to do to survive."

Survival at West Point requires a more heroic level of determination. You must program your mind to believe that NOTHING you will face is worth quitting for. When you are being yelled at, when you are homesick, when you are depressed, when you are so tired you can fall asleep standing up and you still have three hours homework to do, your mind must reject any thoughts of giving up.

Under worse conditions than you can possibly know about now, the message that must come through is: There is NO WAY I am going to quit. There is absolutely nothing they can do to me here that will make me quit. I will keep going no matter what happens. Period. They might kick me out, but I will never leave of my own free will. NEVER!

Can you program that message into your mind? Can you keep it there and will it be strong enough to drive out all

New cadets the afternoon of their first day—R-Day. Look at their apprehensive faces and picture yourself in that crowd. At this point will you have the determination to endure the next ten and one-half months?

the pleasant thoughts of quitting—thoughts that will creep into your mind almost any night you lay awake worrying about your fate?

Does this mean that you should not quit under ANY circumstances?

Not at all. If, after a year at West Point, you truly believe that you made a mistake going there, by all means you should quit.

BUT UNLESS THERE ARE EXTREME CIRCUMSTANCES, YOU SHOULD NOT QUIT BEFORE THAT.

By sticking out the first year you prove to yourself and everyone who has supported you that you do, indeed, have the right stuff—that you have what it takes to survive what is by far the roughest year at the Academy.

So sticking out the first year is very important for the long term good health of your ego.

But sticking out the first year is also important for a practical reason. By completing the first year at West Point you will earn a full year of college credits. These can be transferred to another college and you can continue your education as a college sophomore.

But what, you may ask, can I do about it if I do not have the ability to stick it out?

The cadets who were asked that question have a favorite answer that you should probably also program into your mind. The cadets say that you must believe that IF THEY LET YOU INTO WEST POINT, YOU HAVE THE ABILITY TO MAKE IT THROUGH THERE.

In other words, the Academy will not let you in if you do not have the ability to survive.

But what they cannot control is how much determination is in each cadet's soul. Only you know that quantity.

Do you have enough determination to survive the challenge of West Point for at least one year?

If so, you are mentally prepared for the Academy. Your next task is to deal with more practical kinds of preparation—preparation that is discussed in the next four chapters.

FOUR
HIGH SCHOOL PREPARATION: THE MYTH AND THE FACTS

You are in high school and you are taking college preparatory courses. In addition you have earned mostly "B's" and "A's," and your scores on the SAT or ACT tests are very good. So, when you graduate you should be able to do well at West Point. Correct?

Probably not during the first year.

What you and your parents think is a good high school education may not be a good education at all. At least it probably will not hold up well at West Point or at any other service academy.

One would have to have listened to hundreds of cadets and midshipmen from the three service academies to appreciate how poorly most high schools are educating students for collegiate academics. The author has pages and pages of notes, all saying about the same thing. Here is a typical comment:

"I graduated fourth in my class with a 3.8 [grade point average] and had a 1220 on my SAT. I took advanced everything and thought I was really going to be prepared for academics. It was the military stuff that had me worried. Well, after I got here, the academics were a shock. I went into the first semester finals with less than 2.0 in math and chemistry and just over 2.0 in English. I was scared out of my mind and almost had a heart attack before the scores were posted. I squeaked by—barely in math and chemistry, and ended up with a 2.3 in English. If I hadn't nearly killed myself studying for the finals, I might not even be here right now."

Here is another account. It was told by the mother of a young lady who is now a graduate of the Naval Academy:

"Our daughter went to one of the most famous public high schools in the country—a few years ago it was written up in magazines and its reputation was the pride of the area. Our daughter was a very hard worker and an outstanding student. She graduated near the top of her class and at the time she had won more honors than any other graduate. In addition she won first place in the nation as a debater.

"So it was a real shock to us when she called home crying, saying that she wasn't going to make it. And when she came home for the first time, she ran into my arms, crying, and saying, 'I'm flunking, I'm not going to make it and I don't know what else to do.'

"But she struggled on—I don't know how many times she went before the Academic Board, but each time, because of her determined attitude, they gave her another chance. And that's how she got through. It was just raw determination. By the way, she went back to her high school and told her counselor what a great disservice the school was doing in preparing students. 'If I was at the top of the class and I find myself flunking,' she said, 'you are not preparing students for college.'"

Have these two examples gotten your attention? Do you think you also might be going to a school that is not preparing you properly?

You do not have to speculate about it. You will know in just a few moments—right after you visit two classrooms and see two different teachers in action. You will certainly recognize one or the other, and then you will know whether you are or are not getting good academic preparation.

First, we are going to visit a chemistry class taught by a teacher whom we shall call Mr. Easy. It is in Room 314 of Prestige High School, and the assignment for yesterday is still on the board: Read pages 142-146 in the textbook—acid-base reactions.

We are in the back of the room as the bell rings and it is time for class to begin. After taking roll and listening to the morning bulletin, Mr. Easy says, "All right, class, today we are going to discuss the assignment that you had on acid-base reactions. But before we do that, let's review the concept of pH just so we will have that clearly in mind as we discuss those reactions. Now you remember that we started with water and hydronium ions..."

As we watch Mr. Easy, he gives the students an excellent review of the pH concept. Then, using overhead trans-

transparencies as well as very clear chalkboard diagrams, he spends a little more than half the period explaining acid-base reactions. While he is doing so, several of the students are taking notes. Most of the others are listening carefully, and, from the lack of questions being asked, they seem to understand everything he is saying.

Mr. Easy finishes his explanation of the assignment, then goes into the storeroom to get some flasks and chemicals. He then brings them out to his demonstration table and, with just a few drops from a pipette, he changes a solution from acid to base, then back to acid again.

There are a few minutes left at the end of the period and Mr. Easy puts the next day's assignment on the board and tells the students they can use the time left to work on that assignment.

We continue to watch Mr. Easy for several more days and see that the pattern of teaching is almost the same every day, except the day before a test. On that day he spends the whole period reviewing everything that might be on the test. And it is a good review. Even an observer who knows very little about chemistry should be able to pass the test.

Now, let us move down the hall to Room 316 of Prestige High School, to Mr. Tough's chemistry class. He, too, starts his first period class by taking roll and listening to the morning bulletin. Then, he says to his class (the students had the same assignment as those in Mr. Easy's class), "Take about five minutes to look over your assignment while I finish grading some of yesterday's quiz papers."

All but one of the students already have their books open and are reading furiously. The one exception, a new boy who transferred in from another school, has his hand up. "Yes, David," Mr. Tough says, recognizing him.

"I didn't understand any of that stuff," says David. "I don't think its fair for you to test us on it."

Mr. Tough replied, "I'm sorry that you're having trouble, David. But don't worry. After the quiz I'll explain it once, twice or even three times. You will understand it when you leave the class today."

That reply did not please David. "But what good will that do?" he complained. "I'll get a bad grade."

Mr. Tough was patient. "I'm sorry about that, David. But your grade in here should reflect how well you can do the assignment on your own. I wouldn't want to spoonfeed you the material and then give you a quiz. That would only show how well you were able to parrot back what I have told you. That would be like training you to mimic a tape recorder. And what good would that do you? If you leave school and can only mimic a tape recorder, you are sure to lose because the tape recorder will always win. Do you understand?"

David was not pleased and he did not want to understand. But he opened his book and began turning the pages.

A few minutes later Mr. Tough told the class to close their books and take out a sheet of paper. Then, before giving them a question, he reviewed the concept of pH, which they had covered the previous day. After that he gave them one essay question and let them have ten minutes to answer it.

When the time was up, he randomly collected one-fourth of the papers, then asked, "Now, who can do the best job of explaining the answer to this question for the rest of the class?"

Several hands went up and Mr. Tough selected a girl from the first row. "Okay, Laura, go to the board and take a shot at it. And David, you listen carefully, and when you don't understand something, you stop Laura and make her go over it again. Okay?"

David's expression was not pleasant but he listened and watched as Laura explained the answer and drew diagrams and chemical equations on the board. When she was finished, Mr. Tough asked the rest of the class to comment.

Several remarks were made. One student caught an error. Another more clearly explained a point that Laura had passed over briefly. Then Mr. Tough asked for a volunteer to come forward and answer another question about the assignment. Again, the class critiqued that student's presentation.

Then Mr. Tough asked how the acid-base reactions could be demonstrated. There were several ideas, and after the class decided on one, Mr. Tough went to the storeroom and brought the materials to his demonstration table. "Okay, Mike, this was your idea. Why don't you come up here and let's see what you can do." As Mike came forward, Mr. Tough added: "The rest of you watch and be ready to comment if you have any suggestions."

After the demonstration, which did not go as well as the one done by Mr. Easy, there were about fifteen minutes of the class period left. At that time Mr. Tough said, "Okay, it is my turn now. It's spoonfeeding time. I'm going to tell you how an expert would answer the three questions we have discussed today. And, David, you listen carefully. I'll bet I can explain the answers so you will understand them, but if I don't, stay after class for a minute and we'll talk about it. Okay?"

Mr. Tough then proceeded to lecture, covering quickly the items the students had already learned from the earlier discussions, and concentrating on the less well understood concepts. He also explained how Mike's demonstration could have been more effective.

Mr. Tough's class was observed for several more days and the pattern was about the same. Every day he gave a written or oral quiz; then he had the students discuss several questions. And always, near the end of the class period, he would give a short lecture and explain what the students—at least some of them—did not understand.

Now let us discuss the two teachers and their methods—first, Mr. Easy.

There is no doubt that Mr. Easy is a dedicated chemistry teacher. From his knowledge, preparation, presentations and attitude, it is clear that he wants all his students to understand chemistry. Moreover, it is clear that Mr. Easy will work as hard as necessary to make sure that they do.

And Mr. Tough?

He, too, seems to know his subject. In addition, he is well prepared, he presents the material clearly and he appears as dedicated as Mr. Easy in wanting his students to learn chemistry.

So the two teachers are similar in the ways most teachers are evaluated.

Yet, there is a world of difference between the two when it comes to what their students learn.

Mr. Easy's students learn chemistry, period.

Mr. Tough's students learn just as much chemistry. But they learn many other things.

They learn how to study on their own. This means that they learn to read the difficult chemistry text. It means that they learn how to rank the material in an assignment according to its importance. It also means that they learn how to take concepts that they have already learned and apply them to new material.

Mr. Tough's students also learn how to express themselves. Every day they practice verbal expression, including recitations in front of the class. They also get lots of writing experience.

They also learn two other things not associated with chemistry or communicative skills.

They learn accountability. When Mr. Tough gives an assignment, they know that he will hold them accountable for it the next day. So studying gets to be a habit and homework, instead of being a distasteful chore, gets to be something that is done every day—a task almost as routine as brushing the teeth.

Most important, Mr. Tough's students develop an independent attitude. Throughout the year Mr. Tough has poked fun at his lecturing, treating it as a remedial measure for those who could not (or would not) comprehend the lesson on their own. He calls it spoonfeeding, deliberately putting a derisive label on it so the students will take pride in needing as little of it as possible. Mr. Tough very much wants his students to be like those of a good swimming teacher—students who can look at him at the end of the year and say, "Thanks, Mr. Tough. Now I don't need you any more. If I want to learn something, I can do it on my own."

And Mr. Easy's students? They were spoonfed everything they learned. For one complete school year they had no opportunity to learn to study, no experiences expressing themselves, no opportunities to learn accountability or to develop an independent attitude. In terms of the latter, they were worse off than when he got them. After a year of spoonfeeding, they had a more teacher-dependent attitude than they had at the beginning of the year.

In short, Mr. Easy seems like a good teacher, based upon the normal criteria that are used to evaluate a teacher's performance. It is only when one looks critically at what he does and does not do for his students that his shortcomings become obvious.

Now, the important question. Who do you have for your teachers? Are they like Mr. Easy or Mr. Tough?

The cadets at West Point were almost unanimous in describing most of their teachers as being like Mr. Easy. The typical comment was: "All you had to do in my high school was pay attention in class—I hardly cracked a book. If you just pay attention and listen in class, it was easy to get good grades."

The problem for the cadets is that many of their professors at West Point are like Mr. Tough. And they are proud of it because they are practicing a tradition that goes all the way back to the Father of West Point, Sylvanus Thayer.

A math professor criticizes a cadet's solution. Such criticism is difficult for those who were spoonfed in high school.

If you will recall from Chapter One, when Thayer was Superintendent of West Point, he laid down two academic rules: (1) Every cadet will recite every day in every class, and, (2) There will be no more than 15 cadets in any class.

Those two rules were implemented in order to teach accountability, which is of paramount importance for an officer.

The reason for the small class size was so the instructor would have enough time to get around to everybody. In cadet terms, it is relatively easy to escape a "hit" in a large class; in a small class there is very little chance of the "bullet" missing.

Professors at West Point now use the term "Thayer Method" to describe the teaching practice that has evolved through the years. Some departments stick fairly closely to the original doctrine. The math department, for example, believes that students should be prepared to put any assigned problem on the board whenever they get to class.

Other departments are more flexible, depending much upon the individual professor's philosophy. However, there are still many professors who believe in giving "writs"— written quizzes—daily or on a short-term basis.

The title of this chapter is "High School Preparation: the Myth and the Facts." Now it is time to address that subject directly.

It is a widespread myth that students who elect "tough" academic courses such as advanced math, chemistry, physics and English are being prepared for rigorous colleges like West Point and the other service academies.

The facts, as elicited from hundreds of cadets and midshipmen, are to the contrary. Most plebes suffer academic shock at all of the service academies. This mainly is because they were not held accountable in their high schools and therefore never learned to study. But added to that problem is the Fourthclass Development System, which deliberately places plebes under great demands and rigid time constraints JUST AT THE TIME WHEN THE PLEBE HAS TO LEARN HOW TO STUDY.

So what should you, the candidate, do about all of this. First, evaluate your own academic preparation. If you are going to a high school where your teachers have been holding you accountable for assignments, congratulate yourself and thank your teachers. You have lucked out. You are going to a good high school and, if you take the right courses (a subject discussed in a later chapter) and do well in them, you should not expect much trouble with the academics at West Point.

However, if most of your teachers are like the Mr. Easy in this chapter, you are probably a spoonfed cripple and you are going to have to do something about it, either now or when you are in the pressure cooker as a plebe at West Point.

What can you do? That is the subject of the next two chapters.

FIVE
THE PROFESSORS SPEAK:
WHAT YOU CAN DO TO
PREPARE

The professors who teach plebes know how well high schools prepare students for rigorous academic study. They see the results every day they walk into their classrooms. They see the strengths of the plebes, and they see their deficiencies.

The strengths can be summed up in a few words. The professors see most plebes as bright, eager young men and women who are competitive and who have a strong desire for high achievement. The professors truly believe that the West Point admissions process brings in some of the nation's most well-rounded, outstanding high school graduates.

The academic deficiencies of plebes show up mostly in three of the classes that are required: math, English and chemistry.

Several professors who teach those classes were asked to comment on those deficiencies. Also they were asked to give advice to candidates who would like to come to West Point better prepared academically. What follows is a selection of their comments.

COMMENTS FROM THE MATH PROFESSORS

Generally, the math professors agreed that plebes have two major deficiencies and several minor ones that are significant.

One of the major deficiencies is the lack of knowledge on how to solve problems. Said one professor:

"I think their biggest problem is their inability to solve problems. Many do not know how to read the problems. Of course, they can read the words, but they don't know what to look for in the problem when they read it. They have to learn how to read systematically; then go about solving the problem using five basic steps.

"First, they have to read the problem and see what is given.

"Second, they have to read and figure out what is being asked for—what they need to find out.

"Third, they need to know how to formulate and assign variables to the things they don't know; then write out the equation for what they are trying to find.

"Fourth, they solve the equation. They have to manipulate it in such a way that they derive answers for the variables.

"Fifth, they have to draw a conclusion.

"Clearly, it is the fourth step that they are best at. It seems that high schools teach them to do the manipulations. Their hangup is that they come to us thinking that because they know how to do those manipulations, they know everything they need to know. It takes quite a while for many of them to adjust their thinking to the problem-solving mode."

Another professor commenting on the same problem added the following recommendation:

"If a high school kid wants to get better at problem solving, one thing to do is read the book *How To Solve It* by Polya [a $7.95 paperback]. It is an old classic that is still available. It is easy to read—high school students can get a lot smarter at solving problems if they will practice Polya's advice."

While discussing the typical plebe's lack of problem solving ability, the retired head of the department attributed much of the deficiency to the lack of experience solving problems in high school. Then he told an anecdote to illustrate his point:

"A high school math teacher was visiting West Point and as a part of her visit, she sat in on one of the plebe math classes. As the class was ending, the professor asked the plebes if there was anything they would like to say to the teacher. Nobody said anything for a moment, then one plebe spoke up. 'Ma'am,' he said. 'I would like you to go back to your students and make them do problems, make them do problems, make them do problems!'"

There was strong, emphatic agreement by all the professors on the second major deficiency of the plebes. Said one professor:

"They come in here with horrible study habits. In math they haven't done meaningful homework assignments. In high school they were brighter than their peers, and if they just listened, they could get by without studying the book. They were taught by the numbers. They learned algorithms [procedures for solving specific kinds of problems] and not much about formulation. When they are taught that way, there is not much incentive to read the book."

Said another professor when commenting about students who rarely have read their math textbooks:

"I remember one day this plebe came in and he was actually in tears. He was a big guy, and he looked me in the eye through those tears and said, 'Sir, I've never had to read a math book, and I don't know why I can't do it now.'"

The headache for the plebes is the math department's adherence to the Thayer Method. When they give an assignment, they expect the plebes to devote, on the average, about two hours doing it. Then, when plebes come to class, they are expected to recite, usually by taking a position at the chalkboard and explaining the solution to a problem.

But to do that they HAVE TO READ THE MATH TEXTBOOK to learn how to solve their problems.

Rarely do high school students have to do that. In most high schools the math teacher explains the new material, works an example problem or two, then assigns homework problems that are exactly like the examples. Thus, there is no need to read the textbook. All the students have to do is remember how the teacher solved the problems and then repeat those same manipulations.

Plebes with this background are frustrated in their math classes at West Point. They crave the old ways of their high school teachers. They want to be spoonfed, and many of them fight the idea of digging into their math textbook until it is almost too late—until they are making "D's" or "F's."

Then what?

Patiently the math professors sit down in "additional instruction" (AI) sessions, one on one, and teach the plebes

The small classes enable the professors to hold each cadet accountable each day. If you are not prepared, you must be ready to "take the hit."

how to read the math textbook. One professor explained how they go about it:

"The typical plebe opens the text, skims the author's explanation of the new material, briefly looks at the author's example [the problem the author works to show how the new material is set up into a problem and solved], then goes to the assigned problems and wants to charge ahead. But then they bog down because they don't know enough to solve them.

"Their biggest mistake with this approach is that they do not adequately study the author's example. They rush this part. But it takes time—sometimes lots of time. They should study each step in the author's example, and they should understand how and why each step is done.

"Also, they don't realize that as the author goes through the text, he tends to skip steps in his examples— steps that were explained earlier. So what happens is that the typical plebe, who has not studied those examples carefully, goes through a hundred pages of text and then cannot study the examples even if he wants to—because he does not understand the steps the author has omitted. Thus, he is really behind.

"So what we have to do in AI is have them slug through the author's examples with us; then if they don't understand a step, we have to go back in the text—sometimes a hundred or two hundred pages—and we have to learn the steps that the author later omits.

"Of course, we always give them advice at the beginning of the year. We tell them, 'Study the author's example carefully and don't try to do any of the problems until you have done that. Test yourself. Cover up each step in the author's solution and see if you can do it yourself. Then you'll know.' Unfortunately, not many heed that advice. They're too used to the spoonfeeding and they think they're good at math—they plunge ahead—and they fall behind."

In addition to the plebes' lack of skill in problem solving and their poor study habits—both major deficiencies, the professors also cited certain minor deficiencies. These are in subjects that are not taught at West Point—the precalculus subjects that were supposed to have been mastered in high school. Said one professor:

"They are consistently weak in basic algebra skills. One in particular is algebraic substitution—where variables stand for something else. When we use algebraic substitution in five or six different ways, they think we have five or six different techniques. Also, many do not understand the basic properties of numbers and what the rules are for adding, subtracting, dividing, raising to powers and exponentiating.

"A second deficiency is a weakness in trigonometry. In this category the first thing that comes to mind is their lack of understanding of what a function is—the concept of the function is essential in calculus. Another deficiency: few really understand what a unit circle is or how to use it to solve problems—it is a nice tool.

"A third deficiency is a weakness in geometry—two and three dimensional geometry. Sometimes it is the basic things like what are cylinders, what are spheres. Also, many do not know the basic formulas for areas, volumes, perimeters, or, worse, don't know how to derive them."

The retired head of the department agreed that students

lack basic knowledge and skills, particularly of algebra and trigonometry. "They understand the ideas of calculus without too many problems," he said, "but because of their deficiency of rudimentary algebra and trig skills, they can't do the problems."

The math professors were also concerned about the bad attitude plebes have about math. One said:

"Many already hate math when they get here—for some reason somebody has done it to them. That is a real problem for they think of math as a hurdle that they have to get over, not as something useful. It would help greatly if they would come in here with the attitude that math is not their enemy—that it will help them by giving them valuable tools to use for problem solving in other courses."

What can candidates do about such deficiencies?

One bit of advice was heard over and over: Do not bother taking a course in calculus unless it is a very good Advanced Placement course. Their reasoning is as follows.

Too many cadets come in with a "home grown" background in calculus, either taught by a teacher not well prepared, or by a teacher who has not taught the course rigorously.

"This creates a problem," said one professor. "They think that since they have had calculus, they can coast along on their background. Invariably they get behind and in big trouble. In fact, some of the cadets who have the most trouble are those who have had calculus in high school."

If you are qualified and an Advanced Placement course is available, by all means take it, say the professors. But the reason why you should take it is so you can come to West Point and validate (skip and get credit for) it. This way a good student does not have to waste time taking it over, and it gives that student the option to take other classes.

By far the most important thing candidates can do to prepare for math at West Point, say the professors, is to get a strong background in the precalculus courses: advanced algebra, trigonometry, solid geometry and analytical geometry. THOSE ARE THE REALLY IMPORTANT COURSES, say the professors, not calculus.

COMMENTS FROM THE ENGLISH PROFESSORS

Plebe English at West Point consists of a one semester course in composition and a one semester introduction to literature. In interviews with the plebes, they cited problems with the composition course and did not mention the literature course.

Four professors who teach the plebe composition course were interviewed and asked about the kinds of problems experienced by plebes. They were also asked to give advice on what high school candidates could do to better prepare themselves. The following is a digest of what they said.

The director of the composition course started his interview with a positive statement—which he put in the form of a disagreement:

"I disagree with most of the cover stories such as you see in Time Magazine—stories of how Johnnie can't write. And I'm not speaking only of West Point students. I didn't find that [lack of writing ability] at other schools. I have recently taught composition in a community college and in the Harvard Expository Writing Program.

"It is not true that students come to college and can't write. They can write good sentences over and over, and they can, for the most part, write coherent paragraphs.

"What many cannot do is string the paragraphs together into an essay; they can't focus on an idea and play around with it in an interesting, intellectual way. But that's okay; my major task is to teach them to do that. That's what we do in the plebe composition course."

But the plebes do have some problems and those that relate to English are the traditional ones—grammar and spelling. Here are some comments about those problems.

"Students coming here have to realize that we cannot take the time to teach grammar," said one professor. "We issue them a grammar handbook* and we give them a list of abbreviations that are keyed to it. When we read a paper, we simply put in the abbreviation wherever the grammar error occurs. Then it is up to the plebes to use the handbook

*The McGraw-Hill College Handbook by Richard Marius and Harvey Weiner.

66

In West Point classes the cadets have to be prepared to "stand and deliver."

and find out on their own how to correct the problem. We also say, 'If you need help, come see me.'"

The types of grammar errors they see most often? Another professor answers that question:

"There are two of them. The comma splice is one. [Two independent clauses that are joined by a comma instead of a semicolon or instead of being separated into two sentences.] The other is the sentence fragment. We also see agreement problems [between the subject and its verb] but they are easy to solve. The others point to a problem below the surface—usually that [the plebe] doesn't know sentence structure well enough to use it competently."

Another professor cited the plebes' lack of reading while they were in high school as a problem. He said:

"I was shocked the first time I asked my class, 'What is the last book you read?' There was a significant pause while they searched their memory—this was at the beginning of the year. I then said, 'I mean within the last year, while you were in high school.' But most of them could not remember any book they had read.

"After that I began to ask the question more often— with the same results. Then I began asking the question to visitors who come here from high schools. You would think they would be reading something, but most can't remember anything. Very few read the newspaper other than the sports page. Their knowledge of current events is lower than it should be and a lot of this reflects in things they write."

The same professor felt that the plebes are not as good as they appear on paper—meaning that they received better grades in high school than they deserved.

"This is just my opinion," he said, "but I think some of these kids come from schools where the teachers do a lot of baby sitting—where if the kid shows up and smiles and behaves, he [or she] will get a good grade—his behavior is rewarded.

"I get kids who come in after receiving a paper with a "D" or "F" and say, 'Sir, I was valedictorian and never received anything but an "A."' I don't think kids like that were ever graded objectively. I think attitude and manners went a long way in getting them their good grades in high school. But that little edge they got in high school for being a good person is lost here—this is their first experience where being a good person doesn't help them."

The professors were asked to give advice to candidates who want to come better prepared. They all recommended that candidates do more writing. Said one:

"Write often and keep a journal. In that journal don't think about an audience and don't write everything that happens to you every day. Write things that make a difference to you—something that has some emotional impact about it—something that jars you into being. I like to think of what Joan Didion [a novelist and essayist] said about keeping a journal. She said, 'I don't write what happened to me; I write what it felt like.'"

"Get as involved with writing as you can," said another professor. "Get on the school newspaper staff or the annual staff. Enter essay contests. Ask about a literacy program, even if it is at a community college, and get in one if you can."

Said another professor:

"If I could recommend one thing, it would be to work on the school newspaper. There will always be somebody to proof and read your work. And when your writing hits the street, people are going to respond to it."

As part of the composition course, the plebes have to read essays as well as write them. The critical thinking involved with the reading bothers a lot of plebes according to another professor.

"They are used to simplistic thinking," said the professor, "and we give them essays with complex issues— issues for which there are no answers, and issues that are outside their experiences and culture. Advise them to be prepared for questions that don't have answers—and to realize that is what college is about. Technical skills are not all they get here.

"Also advise them to get some mind broadening experiences before they come here. Volunteer to help with the homeless—something where they see another side of life. A foreign exchange program would be good—anything to broaden their insight and perception."

A final recommendation will be expanded in a later chapter but it should be mentioned now. This is the recommendation to learn to type so the keyboard of a computer is familiar territory.

After the first assignment or two, which may be handwritten, all others have to be done by word processing on the plebe's own computer. Plebes can save themselves hours of frustration by learning good keyboard skills before they get into the fourthclass pressure cooker.

COMMENTS OF THE CHEMISTRY PROFESSORS

A full year of chemistry is required in the first year and, according to the plebes who were interviewed, it is their second hardest course—after calculus. Three of the chemistry professors explain why.

"The major problem," said one professor, "is their weak math-science background in high school. They are not well grounded in mathematical operations and analytical processes. And those plebes who come in here without

Chemistry students learning the Second Law of Thermodynamics. Note the calculators on each cadet's desk. You are advised to be proficient with a good calculator before you arrive.

having taken chemistry are very disadvantaged—they're not familiar with laboratory skills, and the pace of instruction will seem somewhat overwhelming to them.

"In addition," continued the professor, "many of them are deficient in problem-solving techniques. They don't do well reading a problem and analyzing what is being asked for and what concepts or operations have to be performed to arrive at the answer. We really feel that this is a skill that should have been learned in high school math and science classes."

Another professor, the plebe chemistry director, blames the problems on the way the plebes were taught in high school. She said:

"Here, under the Thayer System, we expect them to read the material, understand the basics and be able to apply that material when they come to class. They don't like that—when we give an end-of-course survey, they say that they want us to pre-teach the material and let them work the problems after we have explained how to do them. But that isn't the way we do it here—they have to understand it [their assignment] to a certain degree.

"It [the Thayer System] is a way of learning that is going to be very helpful when they get out into the Army. A lot of times an officer will get into a job that he or she has had no training for, yet the officer is expected to take the material left behind by a predecessor and do that job as well as someone who has been working at it for years. At West Point you are expected to study and learn on your own, because as an Army Officer, that is what you have to do.

"For many of them [the plebes], who have been spoonfed by their teachers for 12 years, it is a big shock to have to learn on their own—that is why young men and women don't do well when they first get into this environment."

The third professor, who graduated just ten years earlier and who was a four-year football letterman, had another opinion.

"In my mind," he said, "it all boils down to poor time management. The course itself isn't so tough—it's just that the plebes haven't learned to study efficiently—they haven't adjusted to having so many things to do during the waking hours of their day. What they have to learn is prioritization—doing important things first—and letting others go until they can devote time to them—in their jargon they have to kiss off some things in order to strengthen their weaknesses while sustaining their strengths. But they don't know any of that when they come here—they haven't been under that kind of pressure before."

The three professors were in general agreement on the advice that candidates should receive. Said one:

"By all means take chemistry or honors chemistry. Also, if it is available, take an Advanced Placement course. If they do the latter, there is a chance they can validate our course and that will give them more academic flexibility. If they don't learn enough to validate, it will still make it much easier on them when they get here.

Learning how to work on your own is an important part of being successful in the chemistry lab.

"However, there is one other piece to that [advice]. If they are weak in science, then don't take the Advanced Placement course. They might succeed but get a "C" or "D" grade, which would hurt them—grades like that don't look good on the transcript. It is better to get a "B" in a regular course than a "D" in an AP course."

Two of the professors mentioned that many plebes experience problems using the hand-held calculators that they are required to purchase.

Said one of the professors: "We're now using an HP [Hewlett-Packard] model but we're changing so candidates should check before they get here if they want to buy one and get in some practice with it. I recommend practice because facility with the calculator is very important right from the outset. They need to understand trigonometric functions and logarithms—many have no idea how to use them, yet, in a good high school math program, they should get all that."

A final recommendation was given by the director of plebe chemistry. She said: "This recommendation has nothing to do with chemistry itself; however, I think it is very important.

"These kids come into our classes in September after seven weeks of CBT (cadet basic training). They are so intimidated by the Fourthclass System that many have lost their natural aggressiveness. In class we always ask them if there are questions but no hands go up. Partly they are intimidated because we are officers and partly they don't want to let their peers know that they don't understand the material. We know that because they tell us in the end-of-course surveys that when we ask if there are questions, we should always assume that there are even when no hands go up.

"My advice to candidates coming in here is to be aggressive from the first day. Our classroom environment is not the same as in the barracks—our job, our duty, is to help them. They are not under rigid discipline in our classrooms; we try to maintain a relaxed atmosphere. But it is hard to get that across when these 17 and 18 year olds have been in a system that tells them there are only four responses* to a question. It's amazing how timid they become in just seven weeks."

*Eight, actually, if one substitutes "ma'am" for "sir." The four responses for plebes are: "Yes, sir!", "No, sir!", "No excuse, sir!" and "Sir, I do not understand!"

SIX
ACADEMIC PREPARATION: WHAT CANDIDATES SHOULD DO

If you have read the two previous chapters, you are now ready to evaluate yourself.

Have your teachers held you accountable for homework assignments? Have you learned to read your textbooks? Do you feel confident in your ability to learn on your own?

What kind of science and math background do you have? Have you taken chemistry and physics courses where the teacher assigned lots of problems—problems that you have had to solve on your own?

Have you taken advanced algebra, trigonometry and analytic geometry? Are you confident of your knowledge in those subjects? Do you really understand functions, logarithms, sines, cosines and tangents?

In your other courses have your teachers made you do lots of writing? And how do you feel about writing? Is it a challenge that you like or, at least, do not mind?

What is your attitude about learning? Do you look forward to the challenge of new academic subjects? Is the act of learning something that you enjoy for its own sake?

If you answered all of the above questions positively, you are in great academic shape.

If, in addition, you want to go to West Point for good reasons, and if you are the kind of person who enjoys physical challenges, you are going to love West Point!

It will not be easy—do not even dream that. But it should not be so difficult that you will lie in bed at night wondering if you are going to be sent home, or if you will have to quit.

And the rest of you candidates—you who are the ordinary mortals—you who have had spoonfeeding teachers— you who have learned your mathematics by rotely manipulating numbers—you who have gotten your good grades by being a good person and by being a good listener in class? Is there hope for you, too, at West Point?

Of course. Most of your classmates will be just like you. Every year about 1000 cadets will graduate, most of whom had been spoonfed cripples—cripples who had never read a math textbook—who had never written a good essay—who had never learned to study and use time efficiently.

So you CAN make it, if they let you in.

What you must decide as a candidate is when and where you want to suffer the pain of changing your ways.

The advice in this chapter is for those who want to do as much changing as possible before they go to West Point.

Your first priority is to select the right classes—if you still have enough time left in your high school career.

Make sure you take all of the precalculus courses that are available. If you are a senior and have already had those courses, and if you are thinking about taking just an average high school calculus class, think again. And evaluate yourself as a math student. If you had some trouble with the precalculus courses, or if you do not feel that you remember much about them, you would be much better off to repeat the courses than to stumble on through calculus. Remember what the math professors said. Get the solid background in algebra and trigonometry and analytic geometry. And forget about calculus unless you are really a good math student.

Take chemistry AND physics, even if they are mediocre courses taught by mediocre teachers. Even a little background in those subjects is better than none.

Many students who like science end up taking advanced biology rather than physics during their senior year. If you are looking at this option, just remember that two semesters of physics are required at West Point and it does not even have a biology department!

High school physics is strongly recommended and, if you have room in your schedule for another elective, take personal typing or an elective in creative writing or advanced composition, or even repeat some math courses you do not feel good about.

A speech class will help you develop poise while on

your feet. Debate is a highly recommended activity, which will further your verbal skills and teach you how to research.

The next recommendation is to learn how to be an independent student.

Independent students have two things that spoonfed cripples do not.

You will become an independent student at West Point.

First, independent students have the skills to learn on their own. They can read the textbook in any subject for which they have a background, and they can learn from it. They have the skills to find out what they DO NOT KNOW. And they know how to ask the right questions. In short, they do not need teachers to stand up in front of them and tell them everything they need to know.

Independent students also have a special attitude. It is a stubborn and not always polite attitude. It is an attitude where a little voice inside says, "Why should I have to sit and listen to this teacher droning on about something that I can read in half the time?"

It is a competitive attitude where the student takes great pleasure in trying to go to class knowing more about the assignment than anybody else—perhaps including the teachers.

Can you become an independent student?

Certainly. If you make it through West Point, you will be an independent student. That is what their teaching methods are all about.

But can you become an independent student before you go to West Point?

Yes, but you will have to generate lots of self discipline.

When your spoonfeeding teachers give you an assignment, you should ignore the fact that the assignment will be thoroughly explained the next day.

You should attack the assignment aggressively. You should psych yourself into believing that if your teacher explains something the next day that you do not understand, then you failed at your homework.

In your math classes you should STUDY, not just read, the new material before your teacher explains it in class and assigns problems he or she works as examples.

And you should look for challenges. If there is an American Legion essay contest coming up, commit yourself to writing the best essay you can write.

If your English teacher requires you to read a book and write a report on it once each semester, read two or three books and take on the challenge of convincing the teacher that you should get credit for the extra work.

Do you detect a tone of bulldog-like pugnaciousness in these recommendations?

If so, you are reading them correctly. Because, without the kinds of pressure that you will receive at West Point, you will have to make up for years of being a passive student with a bulldog-like determination.

And do not think it will be easy to wean yourself from the spoonfeeding you have enjoyed for so many years. Many students find it to be a traumatic experience when they start to break their teacher-dependence.

But that is what you should at least START to do if you are thinking of going to West Point.

And what if you decide to procrastinate? What if you decide as a candidate, "That all sounds good. I know all this is going to happen, but I'm just going to wait until I get there. I'm going to wait until I'm forced to do all that by the upperclassmen and the professors."

Your author's reply is that procrastination is fine, if that is what you want. Thousands of others have gone to West Point unprepared for the academic rigors and they survived.

All the author asks is that when you are in the plebe pressure cooker, do not say that you were not warned, or were not given good advice. If you elect to go to West Point first, and then change your ways, then you will be doing it with your eyes open to the challenge. If you have that kind of awareness, these chapters on academic preparation will have served their purpose.

SEVEN
PHYSICAL PREPARATION

The professor in the Department of Physical Education (DPE) spoke bluntly:

"From my observations—and I've been around here awhile including four years as a cadet—physical conditioning is one of the prime distinguishers of who can make it and who can't. Cadets who end up not being able to cut it physically are the first to resign...during CBT [Cadet Basic Training, or Beast] the ones who do the least number of pull-ups are the ones that are gone...zero pull-ups, two pull-ups, he's gone...under five pull-ups, my guess is he's gone too...seven or eight pull-ups, that's an indicator of success."

Not every person interviewed at the Academy was as adamant about the importance of physical conditioning. However, it was mentioned over and over how cadets can get themselves in trouble when they are not fit.

Trouble starts in CBT when new cadets draw attention to themselves. When they cannot keep up on a run or a road

Your best chance to earn respect as a plebe is to be in top physical condition.

79

march, they are singled out as weak performers. From then on, they are watched closely. Is their motivation as lacking as their physical condition? You can bet that the upperclass cadets will use every trick they know to find out.

Later, during the academic year, each day is a long, rigorous test of endurance. The day starts at 6:15 in the morning and is crammed with classes, drill, fourthclass duties and intramurals. Then, at night, hours of study are required. And who gets through all of this with the fewest problems? Who bounces out of bed each morning most eager for the challenges? Who is least likely to slip into low periods of mental depression? According to the cadets and staff the answer to all three questions is: the cadets who are in top physical condition.

So, for two reasons, you should get serious about your physical preparation. One, so you will not draw unfavorable attention to yourself. Two, so you can tolerate the rigorous lifestyle.

What should you do?

You should develop both your strength and muscular endurance.

It is most important to develop the strength of your abdominal and upper-body muscles. Those are the muscles used to do situps, pushups and pull-ups, which are primarily the exercises that are required.

Carefully planned use of weight machines is a good way to develop those muscles according to the DPE. Planning is stressed so the candidates will get professional help and not just go out and haphazardly begin a program on their own.

Women are sometimes hesitant to use weight machines for fear they will develop large, bulky muscles. This is not the case. The fact is, with moderate, sensible amounts of strength training, women will realize significant gains in strength and, at the same time, tend to develop a leaner, trimmer physique.

At the beginning of CBT, all cadets have to take a diagnostic Army Physical Fitness Test (APFT). (This is the first of many such tests during the cadet's West Point and Army career.) This test will be the first opportunity for cadets

80

to demonstrate their fitness level. Success is very important. The new cadets are literally on stage. The upperclass cadets are watching closely and one does not want to be identified as a weak performer.

What should you be able to do? According to a professor in the DPE, men should be able to do 55 pushups in two minutes, 70 situps in that same time and at least five pull-ups. Note that the latter are done with the palms of the

There are many practical reasons why an Army Officer needs upper-body strength and endurance.

hands outward, with no jerky movements and at a slow to moderate cadence.

Women should be able to do 27 pushups in two minutes, 70 situps in the same time and at least one pull-up.

Running is the best endurance activity to prepare for CBT. According to one of the DPE professors, an incoming male cadet should be able to run two miles in 14 minutes. That is a "C." grade on the APFT.

The female cadet should be able to run the same two-mile distance in 16 minutes and 30 seconds for the "C." grade.

For a "B" grade, women must run the two miles in 15:55; men must do it in 13 minutes.

In addition to developing your strength and endurance, you may also need to practice swimming.

All new cadets are administered a swim test early in the CBT schedule to determine their swimming ability. The test consists of a 160-yard swim for time, and the ability levels are Advanced, High and Low Intermediate, Beginner and Non-Swimmer.

Do not feel badly if you are not a good swimmer and are classified as a non-swimmer. There have been many famous graduates who started out as a non-swimmer, or "rock."

The biggest problem for the non-swimmer is the time that must be spent learning to swim. The skill must be mastered, at least to a survival level. Practice sessions are required and come out of time that cadets find much more enjoyable—the intramural sports time.

When should the candidate begin physical preparation?

That depends, say the DPE professors. A male athlete in good shape should be able to get ready in a month—providing he already has relatively good upper-body strength. On the other hand, a female athlete with little upper-body strength might have to train hard for three to six months—or even longer.

The worst problem, say the cadets and DPE professors, is when a new cadet becomes injured in some way during CBT. Cadets forced to the sidelines draw undue attention to themselves and their lives become much harder.

If you do not like physical competition, you will be a misfit at West Point.

The injuries that sideline cadets most often are blisters and muscle strains—both of which can usually be avoided by cadets who have worked intensely on a conditioning program.

And what if a candidate cannot or will not train intensely? Let the blunt-speaking professor who opened the chapter also end it. He said:

"When cadets are not in good physical condition, it snowballs on them. They are like a snowball going downhill, adding problems for themselves every hour they are here. And let me say, these are not bad kids; they are good kids. They want to serve their country; they are intelligent; they are ready to work hard. But unfortunately they are not prepared for the grind and the stress and they can't cut it.

"My advice to those who are concerned about this? Take your own APFT. Time yourself. See how fast you can run and do pushups and situps, and how many pull-ups you can do. It's no mystery. You can find out on your own if you are ready for this place."

EIGHT
OTHER WAYS TO PREPARE

The ideal time to read this book would be at the beginning of the ninth grade. That way the candidate would have four years to prepare for West Point.

You probably do not fit into that ideal group, so there may be suggestions in this chapter that you haven't time to use. This may cause you some problems, both in getting in or in surviving if you get into West Point.

An example comes under the heading of extracurricular activities (ECA). In school these include sports, band, drill team, clubs, newspaper, annual staff and student government. Outside ECA include church activities, fraternal organizations, Boy and Girl Scouts, Boys' and Girls' State, Civil Air Patrol and community volunteer activities.

The West Point Admissions Committee wants candidates who have participated in several ECA. However, they are even more desirous of candidates who have held leadership positions in the ECA organizations.

One reason they feel that way is because many ECA are service-type activities—activities where the participants volunteer their time to serve their school, their church or their community. Since part of the official mission of West Point is to prepare graduates for a lifetime of service to their country, they like to see candidates who already have that inclination.

A person who will voluntarily serve others has to be a generous person. The Admissions Committee believes that trait is essential in potential Army Officers who must routinely give time and effort beyond what is expected of civilian professionals. As an extreme example, Army Officers have to be prepared to give their ultimate; for the service of their country they must be ready and willing to sacrifice their lives.

A second reason why ECA are rated so highly is because they help teach time management.

At West Point time is a precious commodity. For the cadets, there never seems to be enough time to do everything that needs to be done. When faced with that problem, cadets must learn to prioritize. This means that they must learn to rank their tasks in order, from the most important to the least important.

To varying degrees, students who participate in ECA also have to learn time management. Those who participate in sports and clubs, and who may also be involved in the community, have to juggle time to meet all their commitments and excel at academics at the same time. The Admissions Committee at West Point realizes that, and they believe candidates with those experiences are more likely to adapt to the high-pressure environment of West Point than students who have only excelled in academics.

Another reason ECA are important—particularly leadership experiences—is because the participants have to be conscientious and dependable. If they had been otherwise in high school, their organizations would flounder or fail. The Admissions Committee wants individuals who are conscientious and dependable because those are essential officer traits.

A record of participation in ECA also implies that the candidate has had a variety of experiences in getting along with people. This, of course, is an essential trait for an officer.

In addition, a record of leadership in ECA shows that candidates have been able to earn the respect of their peers. This is additional evidence that they have officer potential. Officers, of course, have to earn respect at all levels—from their peers as well from those over and under them.

Although not strictly classified as ECA, work experiences are also helpful on a candidate's record. If a candidate has worked during the school year and has also participated in ECA, this is more evidence of time management experience. Also, by satisfying an employer, candidates show that they have been conscientious and dependable, and, in most cases, that they have been successful in getting along with people.

To summarize, it is important for candidates to participate in ECA. It is even more important for candidates to demonstrate leadership experience in their ECA.

But what if you are a senior in high school and are just now finding out about this requirement?

That question was asked of some of the staff of the Admissions Office and here is what they suggested.

Make the best use of the time that you have left and describe how you are trying to make up for lost time in the personal statement that you must write.

However, if you do not get an appointment and the lack of ECA participation is your main problem, try to do something about it if you go on to a regular college. Get involved in campus activities. Join clubs and if you cannot be elected as an officer, volunteer for committees and strive for leadership positions. (Also see Chapter 13—Alternate Routes to the Academy.)

There are several other things candidates can do to prepare for West Point that can be considered optional. Primarily they are the kinds of things you can learn that will make your life easier when you become a plebe.

Highest on this "optional" list is a recommendation to learn how to type. Why? Because you will have to use a word-processing program for practically all of your written work. In addition, cadets use their personal computers* for communicating by electronic mail with their West Point friends and professors.

Those cadets who do not have good keyboard skills are at a disadvantage. At the beginning of the plebe year, when the time crunch is at its worst, such a cadet has to waste countless hours hunting and pecking around the keyboard, learning a skill that could easily have been learned while in high school.

It will also help plebes if they have had some experience writing with a word processing program. And do not worry about which program you learn to use. They are similar enough that if you learn one, it is easy to learn another.

All plebes must read the New York Times every morning and be prepared to expound on current events to their upperclass inquisitors. Candidates should start this habit at

*By the time you arrive the cadets will be purchasing "laptops" which are lightweight computers that can be carried to class. At this time you cannot bring one from home, but this policy might change.

You will waste much valuable time if you do not have keyboard skills at West Point.

home, not necessarily reading the Times, but by reading some newspaper.

Such preparation will do two things. First, it will bring you "up to speed" on current events so you will be able to place trouble spots like Lebanon and political issues like the PLO-Israel conflict into perspective.

The second reason for getting a head start on newspaper reading is better told in the words of a plebe who had been telling the author how he once had to get up 30 minutes early just to study the paper. Then he said:

"Now I can look at the New York Times, just the title and a few lines of the article, and I can talk an upperclassman blue in the face about it. Once you build up a basic knowledge, one of them [an upperclassman] can say, 'Let me hear what is going on in Iran,' and, even though you read something about Iran yesterday, if you make it sound good and act like you know what you are doing, you can get by. It is how you say it. Confidence is so important. I didn't have it at first and neither did many others. But it will come fast [when you know what you are looking for when you read the paper]."

Of course, newspapers are not the only source of current events knowledge. News magazines like Time, Newsweek and Insight are excellent sources, and it would be good to develop the habit of dropping by the library once a week to read one of them.

Television news as the sole source of your news is not recommended. You need to develop the habit of reading the news so you can eventually learn to glean enough information by skimming—like the cadet who was quoted. You will never learn that technique if you rely solely on the tube for your news.

Plebes also have to memorize a lot of material from a publication called *Bugle Notes*. This can be purchased in the Cadet Bookstore, or, if you know a cadet or graduate, you might be able to borrow a copy.

Here are some of the things you should learn, say the cadets—and if you cannot use *Bugle Notes*, try to find some other source for this knowledge.

Learn the second verse of the national anthem, The Star Spangled Banner—assuming you already know the first verse.

Learn the words to the Corps anthem, "Alma Mater."

Learn the names and missions of the different branches of the Army.

Learn the names and/or numbers of the helicopters, armor and weapons of the Army and be able to recognize them from a picture.

Learn to recognize officer insignia for all the services.

The cadets also recommended that candidates learn some practical skills that will save them time when they arrive.

High on their list were the skills of shining shoes and brass. Those skills are best taught by someone who has been in the military.

The alternative to learning those skills at home, say the cadets, is hours of trial and error when the hours are precious and the errors are costly.

Their final recommendation was to get an adult family member (probably your mother) to teach you how to clean floors, sinks, windows and mirrors. Said one young man as he laughed about how much he had learned about that subject:

"It was one of my biggest surprises when I got here. I had no idea how to clean things—the female members of my family did that. They have such strict standards here...the mirrors have to be spotless, there can't be any dust. But I finally became an expert on household stuff. Now I like Lemon Pledge because it smells good and it was totally foreign to me how good Windex really is for cleaning glass."

HOW TO
GET IN

NINE
THE FIRST STEP:
APPLYING TO WEST POINT

If you decide to apply for admission to West Point, you must go through a two-step process.

The first step is to make application to the Admissions Office of West Point. This chapter will tell you how to do that.

The second step is to apply for a nomination from all the sources for which you are eligible. For most candidates these sources include the two U.S. Senators of your state, the U.S. Representative of your congressional district and the U.S. Vice-President. You must get a nomination before West Point can admit you. How to get a nomination is the subject of the next chapter.

If you get a nomination, and if West Point decides that they want you in their next class, you will be offered an

Admissions officers discuss a candidate. Only the West Point Admissions Office can offer appointments.

appointment. The appointment is an offer of admission, which you are free to accept or decline.

Contrary to what you may have heard, no one else can offer an appointment to West Point—not senators or representatives and not the Vice-President or President. APPOINTMENTS ARE ONLY OFFERED BY THE WEST POINT ADMISSIONS OFFICE.

Requirements
Each candidate must:
- [ ] be 17 but not yet 22 years of age by July 1 of year admitted.
- [ ] be a U.S. citizen at time of enrollment (exception: foreign students nominated by agreement between U.S. and another country).
- [ ] be trustworthy, emotionally stable, and motivated.
- [ ] be unmarried.
- [ ] not be pregnant or have a legal obligation to support a child or children.

The ideal time to start the admission process is in the spring of your junior year. After you have determined that you meet the general requirements (see chart this page), you should write to West Point* and ask for the candidate information packet. In your letter you should include the following information: (1) Name and address, (2) home telephone number, (3) Social Security number, (4) sex, (5) Name of high school and year of graduation.

If you want to make the above task easier, go into your counselor's office and get a copy of the West Point Catalog. In the back of that catalog there is a page of perforated, addressed postcards and all you have to do is tear one out and fill in the blanks. West Point even pays the postage when you mail it!

From West Point you will receive a packet that includes a Precandidate Questionnaire. You must fill out this questionnaire and return it. However, in the words of one of the Admissions Officers, "Don't just fill it out in front of the television. Look it over carefully before you write anything down. And if you have any doubts, get your parents or someone else to look it over with you. Be accurate because your initial evaluation will be based upon the information that you put down."

*The address is: Director of Admissions, United States Military Academy 606 Thayer Road, West Point, New York 10996-1797

What are the admissions officials looking for in that questionnaire?

The most important thing they are trying to determine is your academic potential. They want to know if you are a candidate who can be successful in the rigorous academic program of the Academy.

They weigh several factors in determining your academic potential. Two of the important factors are your grade point average (GPA) and your rank in class.

Another very important factor is your score on the SAT (Scholastic Aptitude Test) or the ACT (American College Testing Assessment Program Exam).

There are no fixed rules on the scores you must attain; however, the Academy publishes average scores of its entering classes. In a recent class, 84 percent scored above 500 on the verbal part of the SAT, while 76 percent scored above 600 on the math. Using those scores as a guideline you can see that not many candidates got in with less than a total of 1100 on their SAT.

On the ACT, 93 percent of that same entering class scored above 20 on the English part of the test and 84 percent scored above 25 on the math.

Admissions officials say there is always a number of highly motivated candidates who get passed over because of low or borderline SAT or ACT scores. If you are a highly motivated candidate, try not to let that happen to you.

What can you do? Every person who had anything to do with the West Point admissions process stressed that candidates, "Should take the SAT or ACT tests AS EARLY AS POSSIBLE AND AS OFTEN AS POSSIBLE."

There are two reasons for repeating the tests. First, almost everyone does better each time the tests are taken. Second, the Academy evaluates you on your HIGHEST scores— thus, if you should do worse on one of the tests the second or third time you retake it, that score will not be counted against you.

And do not overlook the kinds of help that may be available as you try to raise your scores. There are special books and videos that can be purchased and studied on your own. Also, in many areas there are tutors and specialized classes available that can be used to improve your test-taking skills.

To locate study-aids and other kinds of assistance check with your counselor. He or she will know of some of the study-aids and the counseling office may even keep an inventory of books and videos that students can borrow.

Another option is to check your local bookstore. Many have a complete rack of books and materials with the kinds of study-aids you need.

Still another option is to look in the Yellow Pages of your phone directory under "Tutoring." There you will find the names of organizations and individuals who specialize in helping students raise test scores. However, before you decide to use any of their services, ask your counselor to help you find out if they are reputable. Also, if you can locate students who have used their services, talk to them.

What else besides academic potential will the West Point Admissions Office be looking for on your Precandidate Questionnaire?

They will be trying to evaluate your leadership potential. To do this they will want to see if you have demonstrated that potential in high school. For example, were you elected to any offices in your student body—are you a class president or student body officer? If so, that shows you are the kind of person who will take the initiative to become a leader. Also it shows that you have some leadership potential. Winning an election proves that you were able to earn the respect of your peers, which is a fundamental leadership challenge.

With the same objective, admissions officials will be looking at your record to see whether you were a member of the French Club or its president and whether you were a football player or the team captain. In other words, in your extra-curricular school activities were you a follower or a leader?

Admissions officials will also be looking to see if you are the kind of person who finishes things that you start—that you are not a quitter. Being an Eagle Scout is an example of one good indicator of that quality. Over and over the author heard Academy officials saying, "Eagle Scouts do well here."

The reason, of course, is that the Scout has to work for years to get the Eagle rating. The admissions officials know from experience that such individuals tend to transfer that same determination when faced with four rigorous years at the Academy.

There are other reasons why admissions officials will look beyond your scholastic ability and evaluate your extra-curricular activities. They interpret your involvement in school activities as an indication of a favorable attitude toward service. For example, if you have been involved in a lot of outside activities, that indicates you believe service to others is important—that you are generous with your time—that you are not a selfish person.

Academy officials believe that persons with that attitude are also likely to feel the same way about serving their country—which is what West Point will be training you to do.

Heavy involvement in extra-curricular activities also tells admissions officials that you have learned some lessons about time management. A high school student who, besides attending classes, also has leadership responsibilities in clubs, practices athletics and studies enough to earn good grades, is more likely to adapt to the time-crunching schedule at

All West Point cadets have to compete in some sport.

West Point than a student who has only attended classes and done homework.

A person who has high scholastic ability but has not been involved in extra-curricular activities is often thought of as a "bookworm" or "loner." And those individuals are suspect. Said a congressional panelist who interviews and evaluates candidates: "They may have 1400 SAT scores but that type is not going to make a good leader. That type belongs in Georgia Tech or Stanford."

Of all school activities, participation in varsity athletics is, by far, the most desirable according to admissions officials. In a recent class, 1182 out of the 1400 (approximate) entering cadets were letter-winning varsity athletes. And of all the kinds of athletics, the officials believe that contact sports such as football, soccer and wrestling are the most desirable.

Why the emphasis on athletics, especially contact sports? Ask that question of any West Pointer and you are almost sure to get a lecture on General Douglas MacArthur.

General MacArthur had a tremendous record as a leader during World War I. After the war he was appointed the Superintendent of West Point—the youngest man to hold that position in the history of the institution. One of his first acts was to strengthen the varsity athletic program and to imprint his philosophy about athletics upon the institution—a philosophy that continues to this day. In his own words, "The training on the athletic field, which produces...fortitude, self-control, resolution, courage, mental agility and, of course, physical development, is...fundamental to an efficient soldiery."

True athletes are competitive by nature and that is what is required in officers who can lead others, especially in combat. An Army Colonel who was evaluating a candidate for the Admissions Office told this story to emphasize that point:

"One day I met with a kid who was about six-four and had a strong, athletic body. But when I looked over his qualifications I noticed that he had not participated in athletics. I asked him why and he replied, 'Oh, I'm just not very competitive.' Well, that decided it for me. That kid had no business going to West Point even though he was well qualified academically. Can you imagine a second lieutenant who is not competitive trying to lead a platoon of men up a hill into enemy fire?"

While filling out the Precandidate Questionnaire—or later while involved in other aspects of the admissions process—you may have questions that you would like someone knowledgeable to answer. Is there a way a candidate can get that kind of assistance?

There is, and the assistance is as close as your telephone. All you have to do is make a call to the Admissions Office of West Point. Simply dial 1-914-938-4041 and ask to speak with the Admissions Officer for your area. The Admissions Officers at West Point take thousands of calls each year so they will not be surprised to hear from you.

Ask the Admissions Officer any question you wish but do not leave the line until you have asked this one: Will you please give me the name and phone number of a Field Force Representative who might be available to me?

West Point has hundreds of admissions representatives in their Field Force who function somewhat like college recruiters. Most of the representatives are reserve Army officers who are called "Liaison Officers" or "LOs." But some are West Point graduates—on active duty or retired—and some are just enthusiastic civilians—often with sons or daughters who have been to West Point—who just want to help young people learn about the Academy. In any case, if you speak with a Field Force Representative, you can be sure that person was trained by the Academy to answer the kinds of questions you might ask.

If your Admissions Officer at West Point says there is a representative from the Field Force near you, get his or her name and phone number so you can contact that person. A good, enthusiastic Field Force representative can be a strong ally who can help you in many ways.

Even if you do not telephone West Point, you will eventually hear from a Field Force representative—if you are a viable candidate.

When you return your Precandidate Questionnaire your name will be added to a monthly report that goes out to the Field Force. The representative in your area may invite you to a general meeting of candidates where West Point will be discussed. Or the representative may just call you to get acquainted and find out if you have any questions or need assistance.

Eventually a representative from the Field Force will contact you for an interview, and he or she may want to do it in your home. After that interview, the representative will fill out an evaluation form on you, which will be added to your file at West Point. Keep that in mind. When you first contact the representative, the impression you make is bound to affect the evaluation that will eventually end up in your file.

Each year in August the Admissions Office goes through all the candidates' files and does an initial screening. After that screening, outstanding candidates may be selected for a Letter of Assurance, which is a guarantee of an appointment IF A NOMINATION IS OBTAINED.

Also during the initial screening those candidates who do not appear to have a reasonable chance for admission are dropped from consideration. Typically, those are individuals with 700-800 SAT scores and with few if any extracurricular activities on their record. Such individuals are notified by the Academy and told that their files are being closed. However, they are also sent another Precandidate Questionnaire and advised to submit it if they do anything to improve their status.

If, after the initial screening, you remain a viable candidate, your next hurdles will be the Qualifying Medical Exam and the Physical Aptitude Exam.

The medical exam is free and you will be advised by the Academy when and where to go for it. Medical exams by private physicians are not acceptable; the exams must be conducted by military doctors. However, one exam is good for all service academies as well as for any ROTC program for which you might apply. (If you think you might have a problem with some aspect of your health, check Appendix B of the West Point Catalog. It describes the standards and many of the conditions that cause disqualification.)

The Physical Aptitude Exam (PAE) is often conducted by one or more Field Force representatives in a high school gym somewhere near you. The name is descriptive; it is an exam that determines whether or not you have the physical aptitude necessary to survive at West Point and as a U.S. Army officer.

The PAE consists of four tests. For males they are: pull-ups, standing long jump, basketball throw and shuttle run. For females the flexed-arm hang is substituted for the pull-ups. (See Appendix C of the Catalog for descriptions and the typical range of scores.)

Each part of the PAE is scored by points and according to an Army officer who has administered many of the tests, "A lot of candidates underestimate the difficulty of the tests. I strongly urge candidates to practice both the basketball throw and the shuttle run.

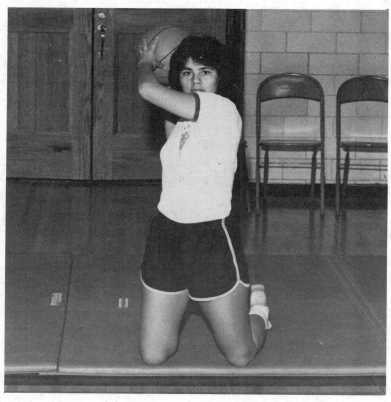

No matter how good an athlete you are, practice the kneeling basketball throw and the shuttle run before you take the PAE.

"The basketball throw is an overhand throw made while on the knees. Candidates can easily improve their scores if they will just practice the technique.

"The shuttle run which is a 300 yard run back and forth between two lines twenty-five yards apart causes problems because they go out fast and just die—they don't know how to pace themselves."

The PAE score is important. It counts for ten percent of the candidate's overall rating and according to one admissions official, "As the candidate pool gets more competitive, the score on the PAE could be the tie breaker."

Each year there is a certain number of candidates who are highly qualified except for certain academic deficiencies. With such deficiencies there is no way they can compete going directly from high school into the rigorous first-year classes at the Academy.

So they are offered an alternative. They are offered a year at the U.S. Military Academy Prep School (USMAPS) in Fort Monmouth, New Jersey. Those who elect that alternative spend a very intensive year mainly studying math and English. All expenses are paid by the Army; they are given a small stipend and, if their progress is satisfactory, they will be offered an appointment for the following year at West Point.*

Admissions officials say that some students are turned off by such an offer, thinking that they will have to waste a year out of their life. That year is definitely not wasted according to those whom the author interviewed both at West Point and at USMAPS.

The year at the prep school gives cadets a running start over those right out of high school because at USMAPS they are forced to develop good study habits. In addition, they are one year more mature, they have outgrown the pangs of homesickness and when they enter the tough fourthclass year, they do so with the support of all the friends they made at USMAPS.

During your interview with the Field Force Representative one of the questions you will be asked is whether or

*Some candidates are also offered the opportunity to attend civilian preparatory schools in a program sponsored by the Association of Graduates. In most cases candidates have to pay their own expenses but scholarships are available for the needy. You cannot apply for one of these prep schools but you can indicate that you would be willing to accept such an opportunity if it is offered.

101

not you would accept a year at USMAPS if it were offered. Think about that possibility now—before you have to answer the question. But remember, a positive answer indicates a strong motivation on your part to go to West Point.

One final recommendation was made by several admissions officials and Field Force Representatives. It is this: DO NOT PUT ALL YOUR EGGS IN ONE BASKET.

That is, do not jeopardize your future by applying only to West Point. If you are interested in serving as an Army officer, you should also apply for an Army ROTC scholarship—your Field Force Representative or Army Recruiter can help you with that. In addition, you should also apply to one or two colleges just so you will have someplace to go if the appointment to West Point does not come through.

Attending a civilian college for one or two years will not prevent you from getting into West Point at a later time—in fact it is likely to make you a more attractive candidate. More will be said about this option in Chapter 13.

TEN
THE SECOND STEP:
GETTING THE NOMINATION

The spring of your junior year is also a good time to begin your quest for a nomination.

But the procedure is much more involved than the application process at West Point. In seeking a nomination you should probably make separate applications to four different nomination sources.*

Your four sources are the two U.S. Senators from your state, the U.S. Representative from your congressional district and the U.S. Vice President. In this book U.S. Senators and U.S. Representatives will be called "congressmen" and their nominations will be called "congressional nominations."

The simplest of all the applications is the one to the Vice President. This nomination is also the hardest to get since there are only five available each year for the whole United States. To apply write to the following address and explain that you wish to be considered for a vice-presidential nomination. You will receive instructions in the mail.

> The Vice President
> The White House
> Washington, D.C. 20501

Getting a congressional nomination can be a lot more complicated because of the paperwork required. Also many congressmen require that candidates go before a panel to be interviewed and evaluated.

How about politics? Do your parents have to have political "pull" in order for you to get a congressional nomination?

That is what many people believe. Some believe that your parents have to belong to the same political party as

---

*If one of your parents is on active duty or is retired from some military service, or if you are the son or daughter of a deceased veteran, you should also apply to a fifth source. You should seek a presidential nomination directly from West Point. The procedure is simple and is explained in the Catalog.

the congressman. Others believe that your parents or relatives have to have helped in the congressman's campaign or contributed money to it.

Thirty to fifty years ago some of those beliefs were true—service academy nominations often were awarded as political favors. However, according to hundreds who have been interviewed for the books in this candidate series, the role of politics is relatively unimportant now.

There are still instances, of course, when congressmen will give a nomination as a favor to a son or daughter of an influential person or a political friend. However, according to everyone who commented on the matter, this is relatively rare. And besides, when you learn more about the nomination process, you will see that an occasional award of a nomination for political purposes actually has very little affect on your own chances of getting an appointment.

There are 435 representatives and 100 senators. Each has a quota of five cadets who can be at West Point at any given time. Thus, each year there is usually at least one upcoming vacancy because at least one of the five will probably be graduating. For each vacancy the congressman can make ten nominations.

Do not let all those numbers confuse you. Just remember that for each vacancy, the congressman is entitled to submit a list of ten nominees from his state or district.

There are three ways the congressman can list those ten nominees when he or she submits the list to West Point.

By far the most common method is to make what is called a competitive list. By this method the congressman gives all the names on the list equal ranking. By doing it this way the congressman is telling the West Point Admissions Office, "I have screened the candidates in my state/district and here are the ten who I think are the best. Now it is up to you to decide which candidates should be offered an appointment."

The second method is the principal-sequenced alternate method. By this method the congressman picks one nominee to get a principal nomination. This principal nominee, if fully qualified, must be offered an appointment to the Academy first, before any of the alternates on the list can be appointed. And if any of the alternates, which are ranked in sequence—first alternate, second alternate, third alternate, etc.—are appointed, they must be appointed according to their ranking—again, if they are fully qualified.

The third method, the principal-competitive alternate method, is a combination of the previous two. The congressman makes one nominee the principal nominee, but the nine alternates are competitive. After looking at the principal, the Academy can decide who, if any, should be appointed from the list of alternates.

West Point admissions officials will pick one nominee from the congressman's list—either the principal nominee or the most qualified nominee if it is a competitive list. That nominee will be offered an appointment. If he or she accepts the appointment, that person is the one who will count against the congressman's quota of five who can be at the Academy at any one time.

However, the Academy usually offers appointments to others who are on the congressman's list of ten. Those who accept are not charged against the congressman's quota. So, even though each congressman has a theoretical quota of five who can be at the Academy at any one time, it is not unusual for one congressman to actually have more than 10 and sometimes as high as 20 or more constituents at West Point at any one time.

And for you, the candidate, that is good news. It means that even though your three congressmen might only have three vacancies the year you apply, your chances of getting an appointment are greatly increased because of all the alternates who are also offered appointments. Three congressmen with a combined quota of three vacancies could easily end up with 10-15 of their nominees being offered appointments.

What counts is how the alternates meet the competition at a national level. For example, on Congressman A's list of 10 nominees there might be only one who is highly qualified and in that case, only that one might be offered an appointment.

But on Congressman B's list there might be five who are more highly qualified than the nine who were left on the list of Congressman A. Therefore, Congressman B might have five of his nominees offered appointments.

But before you can receive an appointment, you must get your name on one of those three lists of nominees.

And the first thing you must do is contact the three congressional offices—the offices of your two U.S. Senators and your U.S. Representative.

All congressmen maintain at least one office in your state or congressional district. Find the telephone number of those offices by checking your directory under "U.S. Government" or by asking help from your counselor. Then call each of the offices and ask for the name of the "staffer" who handles the service academy nomination process. Most of the time the staffer who does that is in a regional office.

If the staffer you need to speak with is in another regional office or in Washington, D.C., ask if there is a toll-free, 800-number that you can use to call.

When you get the staffer on the phone, tell that person you want to apply for a nomination to a service academy—you do not have to specify West Point. The staffer will ask you some basic questions such as your age, address, year of graduation, etc. In addition, there is a good chance you will be asked to write a letter asking to be considered as a candidate for a nomination—or a letter explaining why you want to go to a service academy

Why would a staffer ask for such a letter? Why not just send out the congressman's packet of application forms and instructions?

There are at least two reasons why a letter may be requested.

First, there is a common problem of young people calling up saying they want to apply for a nomination just on a moment's whim. Typically such a young person is thinking, "Hey, going to West Point sounds like a neat idea. Why not go for it!" Senators in heavily populated states will get well over a thousand young people who are serious about getting a nomination. Requiring a letter is one way of eliminating all the paperwork involved with those who are

106

really not serious. Those who are not serious are not likely to take the trouble to write the letter.

The second reason staffers may want a letter requires a little more explanation.

Staffers know there are parents out there who, mainly for economic reasons or to enhance their own prestige, want their sons and daughters to go to a service academy. Some push their sons and daughters openly—often it is a plea to get a free, one-hundred thousand dollar education—and save them that money.

But more often the pressure is subtle—so subtle in fact, that the young people are not aware that they are being pressured. They are manipulated in such a way that they have begun to think that going to a service academy is their own idea.

In either case, it is the sons and daughters who are going to suffer because the record of those types surviving at any service academy is disastrous. The academies are very tough—tough academically, tough physically and tough mentally. The record of who survives and who does not survive is very clear. Those who have very strong self-motivation are the ones who survive—in fact, they are almost certain to survive.

On the other hand, the record shows that those who go for reasons other than very strong self-motivation ARE ALMOST CERTAIN TO FAIL. Young people who have been pushed into going to an academy by their parents fall into the latter category. Those who go because it is something their parents want are almost certain to fail.

Staffers say they get many calls from parents wanting to know what a son or daughter has to do to get a nomination. And from the staffers' comments about such calls, the parent might as well be waving a red warning flag in front of the staffer's face. When a parent calls, the immediate question in the mind of the staffer is, "I wonder if this is a parent who is pushing a kid into applying for an academy?"

So, many staffers do what they can to flush out over-zealous parents—and to protect young people from the psychological trauma of eventual failure. When a parent calls about a nomination, some staffers will politely ask the parent to have the son or daughter call, saying—to be diplomatic—that there are several questions he or she would like to ask the candidate before sending out the congressman's information packet.

Of course, another way to make an end-run around an overzealous parent is to require a letter from the candidate. If the candidate is poorly motivated, he or she can procrastinate writing a letter and in this way thwart the parental pressure. At least that is what the staffer is hoping.*

After you have called the staffers and perhaps sent in letters that were required, you will receive three separate application packets—one from each congressman.

IT IS VERY IMPORTANT that you follow the instructions in each packet EXACTLY, because each congressman has his or her own philosophy and his or her own way of awarding nominations.

Almost nothing makes a staffer so angry as when a candidate takes the information from another congressman's packet and duplicates it. And as you will realize after reading the next chapter, YOU DO NOT WANT TO HAVE A STAFFER ANGRY AT YOU!

So take each packet and keep your materials for each congressman in three separate files. Also, make copies of everything that you submit, marking on each of them the submission date, and keep those copies in the three separate files. That way you have a record of everything. You will know what has been sent to whom, and when it was sent.

Almost every congressman (and also the West Point Admissions Office) will require that you solicit letters of recommendation. Here are some dos and don'ts that will help you get the best possible recommendations.

Do not just walk up to a person from whom you would like to have a letter and ask, "Mr. _____, I'm applying for West Point; will you write a letter of recommendation for me?"

---

*A field representative for another academy told the author that he always makes it a point to tell candidates, "Hey, if this is something you really don't want to do but you don't want to hurt your parents, just leave something out of the application that you send to the academy. The academy probably won't call or write you about it, and you won't hurt your parents because they will never know that you sabotaged the application."

Instead, tell the person you want the letter from that you are thinking of applying to West Point and you are wondering what that person thinks about the idea. This way you get a chance to feel out the person to see if he or she thinks it is a good idea. Perhaps that person will hedge a bit and wonder if you have the "right stuff" for such a challenge. Or, the person might be very enthusiastic and think your idea is wonderful.

Which person do you want writing a letter of recommendation for you—the person who is hedging or the person who is enthusiastic about you? The latter of course. That is the reason for feeling out each person first. Find out if the person is solidly behind you, THEN ask for the letter of recommendation. The competition is tough enough already. You certainly do not want any half-hearted letters of recommendation in your file.

When a person has agreed to write a letter for you, you should give that person three things:

(1) A self-addressed, stamped envelope for each letter that has to be submitted. Typically, each person will be writing letters to all three congressman and perhaps the West Point Admission Office, too.

(2) A written deadline that is at least TWO WEEKS before the actual deadline. Why? Because the person you ask may be very busy and might forget the deadline or forget to write the letter. Then there are those who are procrastinators—they keep putting it off. (According to congressional staffers high school principals are the worst procrastinators of all.) By giving an early deadline you can check to see if the letters have arrived and if they have not, you will have time to prod the letter-writers and still make the real deadline.

(3) A paper that lists all of your school and out-of-school activities, awards, elected offices, test scores, community work, part time jobs—and anything else a person writing a letter needs to know about you. Why? Because that person wants to write the best letter possible (you hope) and to do that he or she needs to know all the facts about you. It would be the rare teacher, counselor or principal who knows all of your achievements even though you may have been in the same school together for four

years. So do not take any chances. Give them plenty of ammunition so they can fire their best shots.

Then what?

There is much more advice that could be given, but it will perhaps mean more to you if it is given in the words of some of the 40-odd staffers who were interviewed by the author. Their comments are the subject of the next chapter.

ELEVEN
TIPS FROM CONGRESSIONAL STAFFERS

The role of the congressional staffer varies considerably.

At one extreme are the staffers who, by themselves, review all applications, interview all candidates and then make up the lists of nominees that they present to their congressmen—who usually rubber-stamp the list. Staffers like this are very powerful. They know it and they will let you know it.

At the other extreme are the staffers who only handle the paperwork while an outside panel or the congressman reviews the applications and makes up the lists of nominees. Staffers like this are strictly paper-shufflers and have no input at all on who does or does not receive a nomination.

Most staffers have a role somewhere between those two extremes. Many screen the applications and use their own judgement—often supported by objective criteria specified by the congressman—on who should be nominated. Also they may sit on panels and help interview candidates, or they may take the ratings of panelists and use them to make lists of nominees for the congressman.

And while most of the latter types will try to pass themselves off to candidates and parents as mere paper-shufflers, DO NOT BELIEVE IT. Chances are good that the staffers you contact will have AT LEAST SOME POWER TO DECIDE WHO DOES AND WHO DOES NOT GET A NOMINATION.

So be careful. When you are dealing with a staffer, it is prudent to assume that this is the person who is going to decide whether or not you get a nomination.

Now let us hear from the staffers themselves. Forty-two of them were interviewed. Many told of one or more visits to the academies. Most expressed strong feelings about the country's need for high-quality military officers. And most indicated that they were doing everything they could to recruit and nominate the best candidates from their district or state.

But they have frustrating problems with their candidates. One of these problems is the way some candidates procrastinate.

Said a staffer from Arkansas: "They [the candidates] put things off till the last minute and don't realize that I have responsibilities other than handling academy nominations. We have deadlines to meet, too. When a kid pushes me because he has procrastinated, it is going to affect his overall rating."

And a staffer from Washington State: "Some call you up the night before the deadline and say, 'I don't have my pictures yet,' or 'I can't take my SAT until next week.' Or they bring in their letters and transcript the day of the review and want me to put the file together. That doesn't reflect good organizational ability. That doesn't show dedication. We are going to be skeptical about such candidates. Will they follow through if they get to an academy? They didn't follow through with us when they were told in September what we would need by the first of December. How are kids like this ever going to make it at one of the academies?"

And a staffer from Iowa: "They should be more timely because I won't even consider anybody who doesn't get their paperwork in on time. How could they be successful cadets at an academy if they can't do that?"

Another frustrating problem for staffers is candidates who do not follow up and check on their files. They point out that numerous things can be missing from a file. For example, SAT scores could be missing because they were sent to Winslow, AR instead of Winslow, AZ—mistakes like that occur all the time.

Another common problem is that high schools, including those with excellent reputations, often leave essential information like class standing off transcripts that they send out.

"The problem [with not following up]," said a staffer from Arkansas, "is that few of these kids really understand how important it is to stay in contact with us. Often there is something missing from their files and before the cut-off date we used to write or call and tell them about it. Now, because of the volume of applications, we just can't do that. Now we just use what is here and some kids will get hurt simply because they don't follow up to see if anything is missing. Of course, in our instructions we tell them to do that. So if they fail to do it, they are not following instructions and in my book the ability to follow instructions has to be at the top of the list when it comes to considering candidates for an academy."

And a staffer from Texas: "What bothers me is that these youngsters put their trust in the people they ask for letters [of recommendation], then they fail in not double-checking with me...and I'm not perfect—something could get lost here or in the mail. But to be quite honest, they are supposed to be mature enough to handle four tough years at an academy...we can't coddle them. I've seen what happens at those academies. I know what these kids are fixing to get into. If they can't get their act together for a few pieces of paper, what are they going to do when they get up there and report to the academies for basic training—how are they going to handle that?"

Candidates who do follow up with staffers almost always leave a good impression.

Said a staffer from Iowa: "We do everything in our Washington, D.C. office, and since I never see any of the kids, it is the contact through the telephone and their letters that we use to help judge them. And one thing we know is that these kids hate to write letters. Therefore, it is really impressive when we get a nice letter or two from a kid checking on his file. Of course, we like them to call, too, but when a kid goes to all the trouble to write a letter, you feel that that kid is really motivated and wants to go [to an academy]."

And a staffer from California: "The bottom line is how much do they really want this thing? If they come to me for an application and for the interview and if that is all, they don't want it. I want them to bug me, to bother me. If they touch base with me, that shows that they want this thing. I remember one young man from a Catholic boys' school where 99 percent of the graduates go to college. Three kids from that school had applied but only one came

113

in to see me on a regular basis. West Point, his first choice, was not interested in him but one day he mentioned that he was also interested in Navy. Right away I got on the phone and called them. I asked if there was any chance for him to get a Naval Academy Foundation scholarship. Now, this year, he is a firstie [senior] and has a nomination to go on to graduate school and get his Master's. The point is, he came in and I worked for him...Sometimes the academies call me and say, 'What do you think about this guy or that guy?' I'll tell them, 'This guy, yes, because he comes in and follows up—that other guy hasn't shown up so I don't know.'"

The previous quote shows one way a staffer who is on your side can help you. But there are other ways. Said a staffer from Iowa:
"We had a kid this year who badly wanted to go to the Naval Academy but his grades were not high enough to make it. He came in for an interview—just to see what other options might be available. The kid looked like an outstanding candidate so later I just picked up the phone and called them and said, 'If you can't take this kid directly into the Academy, will you please consider him for the prep school?' He ended up there and I know that it will help him."

Some staffers are bothered by things that other staffers do not seem to mind. An example is when a candidate disobeys instructions and submits more letters of recommendation than were requested. Here are some typical comments:
A staffer from Ohio: "It is really dumb when they submit a whole pile of letters—one had sixteen sent— another had twenty and I was about to kill him! I have to write and acknowledge all of them! We ask for just three and we specify that they should be from persons who know them, who have been in contact with them, know their abilities, know their leadership potential, truly know them as a person. It is not going to impress me that honorable Joe Schmo who knew the kid's parents in the forties writes a letter—I'm not even going to put those kinds of letters in the file—I have to make four sets [for the panel who will interview the candidates] and I'm not going to duplicate all

of those. Then there are those from the neighbor and Aunt Tillie that tell what a fine person the boy is. I won't put those letters in. Our panel who reviews them doesn't care if your Aunt Tillie says you are a sweetheart and you mow her lawn. They are looking for leaders, not sweethearts."

And said an Arizona staffer: "...you know what I do when the applicant doesn't follow instructions and has a whole batch of letters sent? When I get to the Xerox machine to duplicate the letters for the committee, I take the first three letters, no matter who they are from, and I duplicate them. Those are the only letters that the committee sees and the candidate might be hurt if those aren't the best letters. I'm sorry, but that's the way it is. If the candidates can't follow the simple instructions that we give them, how can they expect to get by [at an academy]."

Some staffers also complained about candidates who try to puff their applications with extraneous material.

Said another Ohio staffer: "...we are not impressed with attendance awards or a twenty-page essay on why you will make a good cadet. We don't request that and we don't want it...we had one kid who put a whole book together—that and fifty cents would get him a cup of coffee."

Parents who want to help their sons and daughters with the nomination process are also a problem—not for staffers—their ability to handle all kinds of people diplomatically is a mandatory skill for their job. Unfortunately, the overzealous parent is a problem for those whom they most want to help—their own son or daughter.

Said a staffer from Arkansas: "I've been at this business for 14 years and if there is one thing I have learned, it is to be leery when parents get involved. When mamma and daddy are involved, we immediately get worried. We learned the hard way that those kids [who go because their parents want it] don't last at the academies. It is the ones who do it on their own who survive and graduate. My advice to candidates is to not let their parents run the show—we want to know what the applicant wants or desires— we don't want mamma and daddy wanting to put their kids in the academy."

115

Said a staffer from Nevada: "Leadership is what it is all about and they should be able to demonstrate leadership from the moment they start the application. I am not impressed by the child if his parents call me and say, 'What else does Johnny need for his files?' I always wonder what Johnny can do."

Said another staffer from Ohio: "We get a lot of calls from parents and I'm not saying that is wrong. But, if young people are serious about going to an academy, they should make the calls themselves. They should learn how to do this on their own and they should call again if they have questions. This shows maturity and I will remember a kid like that."

Still another staffer from Ohio was more adamant: "I get these calls all the time. 'My Freddie is interested in going to the Naval Academy, etc.' and I say, 'That is fine but let us hear from Freddie.' I guess the initial call is fine, but from then on it should be the kid who calls. And to the kid I would say, 'If you don't have the wherewithal to do things for yourself, you don't belong in an academy.'"

The author realizes that it is not always possible for a candidate to keep his or her parents out of the process. But give it your best effort.

When telephone calls need to be made, you make them.

If you need to visit the congressman's regional office, let a parent drive you if that is necessary, but go inside by yourself.

And by all means, when you go for an interview, do not let your parents accompany you past the door. An Arizona staffer told of one mother who became angry and created a scene because she could not accompany her son into an interview. "Can you believe that?" said the staffer. "How could we dare send a kid like that to an academy when mom is not going to be there to hold his hand?"

Most of the staffers' comments you have read have been negative in tone. But they were selected for that purpose because you should know the kinds of things that staffers do not like.

116

You should also know what kinds of things impress staffers. Thus, it is appropriate to conclude this chapter with a list of these things—some of which have already been mentioned or implied.

Staffers are impressed with candidates who—

—call them early—like during the spring of their junior year.

—are polite and use good manners when speaking over the telephone or when they present themselves in person.

—who are dressed neatly and well groomed when they appear before them.

—who have done their homework—who know what the West Point program is all about, who have talked with West Point cadets and graduates and who have either visited West Point or read about it.

—who get their paperwork in early.

—who follow up to see if anything is missing from their applications.

Perhaps most of all, they are impressed by candidates who write them letters. Therefore, if you really want a staffer to remember you, write when you apply for your application. Write follow up letters to let the staffer know what letters of recommendation to expect and, later, to make sure all of them arrived. Then write again before the deadline to make sure everything is complete in your file. Also, as a courtesy, if the staffer has done some favor for you or if you get a nomination, write a thank-you letter.

The staffers will appreciate the letters because they know how much you hated to write them. (Most of the staffers probably hate to write letters, too!) So, they will get the unwritten message in your letters which says: "Please pay special attention to me! I am not just one of your average candidates. I am much more serious and much more determined than the others—that is why I didn't just pick up the phone and call you like the others will do. I wrote those letters because I want you to know how badly I want to go to West Point!"

TWELVE

INTERVIEWS: ADVICE FROM THOSE WHO CONDUCT THEM

When you apply to West Point you will almost certainly be interviewed by a member of the Field Force, a representative of the Academy.

Often this interview is conducted in your home so the West Point representative can also evaluate your parents. The representative wants to know how strongly your parents are supporting your application. Cadets do better at the Academy when they have strong parental support.

The representative also will be looking for signs that your parents have pushed you into applying for West Point. Do not expect a high recommendation unless you can convince the representative that going to the Academy is YOUR idea and yours alone.

In addition to the interview with the West Point representative, you also may be interviewed by staffers or panelists appointed by one or more of the three congressmen to which you will apply for a nomination. (It is rare for congressmen themselves to interview candidates.)

In the case of the congressional interviews it is important that you go into them well prepared.

Your first concern should be with the kinds of questions that will be asked. Surprisingly, after interviewing more than 80 staffers and panelists, it appears that most candidates are asked about the same questions. Also there was agreement among those queried on the kinds of answers that are rated good and bad by the panelists.

Following is a list of the questions that you are most likely to be asked. After each question are comments about good and bad answers.

Why do you want to go to West Point? This question is almost certain to be asked. And many panelists said that even though the question is expected by most candidates, it is still the one that is most difficult for them to answer.

What panelists want to hear is how you personally feel about going to West Point. They want you to talk about your background, your interests and your goals. They want you to explain how West Point will fit in with the goals that you have set for yourself. "Personalize your answer," was a statement heard over and over from panelists.

Said an attorney from Pennsylvania: "Part of the problem is that their answers are so predictable. They'll say, 'It is something I have wanted since I was a child.' That doesn't tell me why—it just says that I want it. Or they will say, 'I have read about it somewhere and I've always wanted to do that.' That isn't any more helpful.

"Another predictable but useless reply is, 'I think it would be a challenge.' That doesn't tell me anything, either.

"I think they have to dig deeper for the answer to this question. They should relate their answer to their own personality—they should personalize it a little more—they have to talk about their goals and ambitions. They have to express their feelings to the extent that they are telling something about themselves. It is these personal kinds of answers that are impressive."

Said another attorney from Pennsylvania: "I like to hear things that indicate a strong motivation and commitment. I like to hear them talk about the Academy and tell what they like about it—what they observed if they went there for a visit...things that show a depth of knowledge—things that show they have made an effort to learn about it.

"I am also impressed when I hear things like, 'It has always been my dream to have a military career because...,' or 'I know myself well enough to know that I like a disciplined environment,' or 'One of my favorite things to do is to read about battles and wars,' or 'I have grown up hearing my father, a retired officer, and my uncle who spent 30 years in the Marine Corps, telling about their experiences. I liked those stories and I would like the opportunity to experience some of the kinds of things they experienced'— those are the statements that show motivation on the part of the kid—they show that the kid knows what he is getting into. They are personal and you know that they aren't rote, pat answers—that the kid is not just giving a canned response to the question."

119

Panelists do not want to hear such comments as: "I want to go because it is a place to get a great education." Great educations are available at lots of colleges and universities.

Nor do they want to hear: "I want to go because my parents cannot afford to send me to college and this is the way for me to get a free education." The panelists who object strongly to this kind of answer point out that West Point really is not free; a great amount of work is required to get through four years and, in addition, the graduate has to pay the government back by serving at least five years on active duty.

Other answers that irritate panelists are those like, "I want to go on after West Point and become a doctor," or, "I want to go on and become a helicopter pilot." The panelists point out that if those are the candidate's only goals, they can be more easily achieved by going to a civilian college or to a flight school.

What panelists are really trying to determine is whether or not you really want to go into the Army. That is the sole purpose of West Point's existence; it is there to prepare a select group of officers who will go into the Army and be there, ready, should the nation have to go to war.

Does that mean that you have to convince the panel that you intend to remain in the Army and make it a 20- or 30-year career?

Some panelists would, indeed, like to hear that kind of declaration. But a majority said they were skeptical of 17- and 18-year olds making such statements. Typical was a university professor from Pennsylvania: "He can say, 'I'm thinking about a military career, but I don't know for sure that is what I'll be doing [in the future].' That's okay, but anybody who tells me at eighteen that he knows he is going to be a professional soldier, that is malarkey. He has to be a lot more mature than the kids at the university where I'm teaching because they are never that sure about their future."

Said a West Point graduate from California: "Those who say they are enthusiastic about going into the Army for a 30-year career make me very suspicious. Those who say, 'I don't know; I haven't been in the service before...that I want to go to the Academy because that is what I think I want.' That is a reasonable answer.

"Another answer I hate to hear, but we hear it from a lot of them, is, 'I want to go to the Academy because it will give me a good education and I want the best education I can get.' I would much rather hear a kid say, 'I want the Academy because it is a good leadership school. I think I can be a leader and I want to have that opportunity.'"

What are you going to do if you don't get into West Point? The real wording of this question should be: "How serious are you about wanting an Army career."

If you are, indeed, serious about an Army career, the panel would expect that you have also applied for an Army ROTC scholarship. Or that you plan on attending a college with an Army ROTC unit so you can get the military experience and a year's college which will help you WHEN YOU APPLY FOR WEST POINT AGAIN NEXT YEAR.

If you do not have a contingency plan, the panel is likely to think that you have only a shallow desire to go to West Point. Consequently, do not expect high marks with an answer like, "Oh, I think I'll just go to Ponderosa College and study engineering if I don't get into West Point."

Suppose you went to West Point and later caught your best friend cheating. Could you turn in your friend? Some version of this question is asked to see how well you have researched the subject of the West Point Honor Code. The thinking of the panel is that a highly motivated candidate would know about that Honor Code and would already have thought about some of the consequences of living with it. So this question is just another one aimed to measure your motivation. (For a discussion of the West Point Honor Code see Chapter 20.)

What makes you think you can stand the stress at West Point? This question is asked so you will talk about yourself. The panel wants to hear about the difficult, stressful situations you have encountered in your lifetime. Perhaps those were on the football field with a tough coach who yelled at you all the time. If so, describe the coach's actions and how you handled the criticism.

But there are other possibilities you might discuss. For example, if your parents were divorced and you suffered in some way in the aftermath, do not be afraid to describe how you coped with the problem.

Basically the panel wants to see if you have had any experience coping with stress. They do not want to hear answers like, "Oh, I'm pretty tough; I can handle it," or "I just know I can do it."

The key to answering this question successfully is to talk freely about yourself and give examples that show you have some experience with stressful situations.

Who is your hero? This is a favorite question of some panelists so you should be ready for it. But with whomever you mention, you should also be ready to explain why you selected that person. Of course, your rationale will give the panel more insight into your beliefs and attitudes.

One word of caution. Before going into the interview, it would be prudent to check out the political bias of the congressman. A liberal, anti-military congressman may select panelists with that same philosophy. Consequently, they might not think so highly of a choice like Douglas MacArthur or George Patton. On the other hand, a conservative congressman might have the same kind of panel that would grimace at the mention of Jane Fonda (who was an ardent anti-war activist during the Vietnam era) or your favorite rock singer whom the panel is not likely to know or appreciate.

Do you have a girlfriend/boyfriend? Some panelists do not like this question and think it unfairly invades the candidate's privacy. However, several panelists mentioned it, so you should be prepared to discuss the matter.

Those who ask the question are trying to see how a girlfriend or boyfriend relationship might affect your future success at the Academy. With all the other pressure on the first year cadet, sometimes the pleading of a lovesick girlfriend or boyfriend is enough to weaken the resolve of the cadet to where he or she will drop out. If you do have a strong relationship, be prepared to explain how you are going to be able to essentially abandon it for the next four years.

What do you think of the comment the Israeli Prime Minister made yesterday about our weapons sale to Jordan? Many panels will ask a current events question like the one above. Some panelists believe that West Point candidates should be a cut above the average good student and be aware of world events. However, those panelists are probably in the minority.

According to most panelists who were interviewed, current events questions are asked primarily so the panel can see how candidates handle themselves with such a question. That is, they think most candidates WILL NOT know much about the question that was asked. But will the candidate fluster or try to bluff his way through an answer? Or will the candidate have the poise and confidence to look the panelists in the eye and say, "I'm sorry, but I can't answer that. I have been so busy the past two weeks I haven't even picked up a newspaper or a news magazine."

It might also help if candidates would explain that they are aware a knowledge of current events is required by plebes at the Academy. But then be prepared for this question: "If you are too busy now to keep up with current events, how are you ever going to do it at West Point when the pressure is much, much greater?"

What are your strongest and weakest points? This is a common question designed, not so the panel can pick at your weaknesses, but to get you to talk about yourself.

Show confidence when you talk about your strongest points. Many panelists say that young people are often too shy when talking about themselves. Try to remember that one of the things the panel is doing is evaluating your potential ability as an Army leader. And an Army leader cannot be shy. On the contrary such a leader must project a strong image. So do not hesitate with the panel. They asked you to talk about your strengths so this will probably be your best opportunity during the interview to sell yourself.

Be cautious when discussing your weak points. The panel does not want to hear about your sins or mistakes. Mainly they want to know what traits your are working to improve upon. For example, do you procrastinate like most people? If so, admit it, but also explain what you have done recently to try to overcome that weakness. Do you keep a messy room? If so, describe how you are going to try to change so you will be ready for the orderliness at West Point? Do you have a quick temper? This is a more serious weakness, so be ready to explain how you are learning to control it.

How are you preparing physically for West Point? West Point is a very physical place and most panelists know it. Therefore, you should be prepared to discuss a specific physical conditioning program that you plan to follow.

You are not likely to get good marks for an answer like, "Oh, I played football; I'm in good shape."

How have you handled failure? It is very difficult for some young people—particularly high achievers who are good candidates for West Point—to handle failure. To be sure, some high achievers have never experienced failure!

However, if a panelist asks that question, it is probably because he or she knows that failure at West Point is inevitable. Not major failure, of course, but failure in small things is purposely induced by the upperclassmen.

So think about this question before you go before a panel. If you have not experienced failure, you should present an attitude that says, "If I fail and I have done my best, then I can't do anything else about it. But the important thing about me is that if you keep knocking me down I will keep getting up. Temporary failures are not important to me. I am not the kind of person who gives up when things are going bad. I am not a quitter."

How are you, a big, aggressive, male athlete, going to handle it if your first squad leader is a female cadet and she decides to pick on you? Or, you are a female, probably with some feminist pride, so how are you going to handle a male squad leader who is biased against females and is determined to make you cry, or quit and go home? Such questions may be asked by panelists who want to know if you have thought about some of the sexist issues that often arise in our imperfect society. Perhaps you do not know how you might react, but you should at least think about the question so you can have an intelligent answer ready. Also, you should realize that the panelist who asks such a question probably has strong feelings about sexist issues.

So much for the typical questions. The next thing you should know about the interviews is how to prepare for them.

The most important thing you can do is to arrange a practice interview. This may sound silly to some candidates and, if fact, one West Point cadet said, when the practice interview was mentioned in a discussion, "Naw, that's no good. What kid is going to go out and arrange something like that?"

The fact is most candidates discover that they do far better in their second interview than they did in their first one. They give better answers to the questions. And they are more poised and confident.

Another fact is that you are reading this book because you want to get an edge on your competition. So try to remember what the West Point cadet said and realize that HE IS RIGHT. Most of your competitors will not take the trouble to arrange a practice interview. So do what they will not do and get ahead of them!

Some of the best persons to conduct a practice interview are military officers from any branch of the service. They can be located in almost any community or neighborhood and most would be very willing to give you a good workout—especially the retired officers who have plenty of free time. If you cannot locate one on your own, ask your West Point Field Force representative to help you. Not only will he be pleased to do it, but it is almost guaranteed that he will be impressed with your determination.

As soon as you know when your congressional interviews are to be held, begin making specific plans for them.

For example, plan what you are going to wear well ahead of time so your clothes can be ready. As for what you SHOULD wear, most panelists were in agreement.

Most panelists believe that young men should wear slacks, a dress shirt and tie. Many suggested that a sport coat should also be worn; however, most felt that a candidate should not go out and buy something just for an interview. Several said they would just as soon see a young man in a nice sweater as a coat.

Several panelists mentioned shoes—some with negative comments about old dirty "sneakers" and leather shoes that were scuffed and unshined. The best advice is to wear well shined leather shoes if you have them. But if you do not, at least wear the newest running or tennis shoes that you have.

There was mixed advice about female dress. A majority felt that the female candidates are most impressive when they wear a dress or a blouse and skirt. Some spoke negatively of slacks and pant suits even though slacks are a standard form of dress at the Academy.

Most who commented on the matter cautioned female candidates not to come dressed like they were going to a party. Go especially easy on the makeup and the high heels. Said a woman panelist from Nebraska, "I'll never forget one girl who came in teetering on three-inch high heels; the panel was not impressed."

While discussing clothing that candidates should wear, almost every panelist gave examples of bad taste that they could remember such as color mismatches of ties and socks. So get some help in coordinating colors if you are in doubt about your judgement.

Others mentioned poor grooming—things like dirty fingernails and unwashed or poorly combed hair.

Several panelists laughed about some candidates who come in jeans, T-shirt, without socks or in a sweat suit.

Said a retired Air Force Officer from Georgia: "Anybody can forgive a kid who is not well dressed because his old man is not a banker and he doesn't have the bucks. But there shouldn't be anything stopping a kid from wearing clothes that are clean and neat."

A retired general and graduate of West Point from Washington State perhaps summed up the matter the best. After discussing his belief that young men should appear in a coat and tie if they can, he said: "...[these kids at an interview] are looking at a very significant event in their lives...that little session [the interview] could change the next thirty-five years of their lives. A lot of the kids come in, first of all, not fully appreciating that, and certainly not showing much deference to the critical juncture where they find themselves."

The candidate should also plan ahead to make sure transportation will be available on the day of the interview.

Also take extra care to be on time—if you are given a specific appointment. And if transportation looks like it might be a problem, plan ahead. Ask for help from your counselor or your Field Force Representative.

And by all means, telephone the congressional staffer should an emergency arise and you will either be late for the interview or miss it altogether.

But now the planning is over. You are sitting in the congressman's outer office with many other candidates, waiting. And you are nervous. But you look around and see only one or two who look like you feel. But the others! They look so calm and confident! Seeing these others looking so confident may suddenly cause your self-image to fade. You may even begin doubting whether or not you should be competing in their league. And you may ask yourself: Would it not be better just to ease out of the room and forget about the whole thing?

Not if you really believe you have what it takes to be a leader. And surely not if you can believe that everyone waiting with you is just as nervous as you are!

A leader must have the ability to control his fears and make those around him believe that he is full of confidence. And if those who are waiting with you for an interview do, indeed, convince you that they are confident, give them an "A" for leadership potential. For they are as nervous as you are, only they are controlling it and projecting another image.

So, make up your mind that you, too, are going to take control and project a confident image. That is what the panelists will be looking for. Said a rough-talking, retired Air Force Colonel from Georgia: "...[the interview] is a test...part of the challenge [for the kid] is to keep from being flustered...you get a guy who goes all to pieces and wets his pants—you don't want him leading a platoon in combat and creating a panic..."

What else can you do while you are waiting? Rather than rehearsing possible answers to questions in your mind, you are probably better off trying to keep your mind uncluttered so you can give fresh, thoughtful, original answers to the questions when you get before the panel. Several panelists mentioned candidates who appeared to have all their answers memorized, then gave them with robot-like speeches.

Many panelists also complained about candidates who give brief answers to questions. "To get anything out of some of them, you almost have to drag it out," was a typical comment. While you are waiting, try to remember that the panel is waiting to hear what you are going to say. They want to do very little of the talking. So get your mind programmed. Convince yourself that when they start asking questions you are not just going to give an answer—you are going to DISCUSS the question with them.

A panel interviews a candidate. A West Point Liaison Officer serves as an advisor to this panel.

128

Remember, the panelists want to hear you talk about yourself. Do not make them work to pull answers out of you. Be open and outgoing with the panel.

Also program your mind so you are ready to DISCUSS YOURSELF. Every question they ask will be of a personal nature to some degree. PROJECT YOUR PERSON INTO THAT DISCUSSION!

Panelists also have complained that candidates often either do not listen to the questions that are asked or that they ignore them. "Either way, he makes a bad mistake," said a panel chairman. "The candidates who consistently get the highest ratings are those who answer the questions precisely..."

One further thing you can do while waiting is to ask the receptionist or staffer for a list of the names of the panel. You might not be able to memorize all of them, but you should at least know the name of the chairperson. Later, it will be impressive if you can call him (or her) by name after having heard it only once when you were introduced.

Now the time has finally come; it is your turn to go in and meet the panel. Usually the staffer will come out to the waiting area and escort you into the room with the panel.

Then you will be introduced, typically to the chairperson first, then to the other panelists.

If it seems appropriate and natural, shake hands with the chairperson and, perhaps, with the others as well. And if you do that, shake hands with a FIRM GRIP. Many men (and perhaps women, too) harbor very negative feelings about any person who gives them a limp handshake.

You will be given a chair in front of the panel and it is important that you sit erect. Of course, you will not be expected to sit as erect as you would a year later should you make it into West Point. But panelists often criticized the posture of candidates, especially those who slumped badly.

Panelists were also critical of those who cannot control their hands. Excessive wringing of the hands was mentioned several times, as was nervous movement. Probably the best advice is to put your hands in your lap or the arms of the chair and use them only for your natural gestures.

Another thing that bothered panelists was the use of current high school slang, and the excessive use of "you knows," "umms" and "uhs."

Candidates who expressed themselves well and who used good grammar were commended.

Panelists also commented favorably about candidates who exhibited good manners and who used respectful terms like "sir" and "ma'am."

Some panelists believe that candidates should maintain eye contact throughout the interview. The strongest statement came from a female panelist in Arizona who served on a panel the author observed. She said, "That is the single, most important thing that you can tell a kid who is going before a panel. Have him make eye contact and keep it. Now I don't mean that he is to look at my hairline or at my chin or at my nose. I want the candidate looking at my eyes! I watch for this with each candidate. The ones who are insecure and lack confidence don't do it—at least that is my impression. Those who have poise and confidence in themselves do. And which do I want to send to a service academy? No way am I going to vote for a kid who doesn't have confidence in himself because he'll never make it."

You can also demonstrate confidence by hesitating after one of the panelists asks you a question. The natural reaction, if you are tense, is to blurt out answers as fast as possible. Fight that tendency. Pause and think for a few seconds before you reply. Of course, that requires poise on your part. But outward poise is one of the best indicators of inner confidence.

At the end of the interview the candidate is usually asked if he or she has any questions of the panel. Typically, say the panelists, the candidates are surprised and often they think they should ask something. Often they ask a question like: "When am I going to know something?" which is a question that is better asked of the staffer before or after the interview.

Unless you have a specific question in mind, several panelists suggested that the candidate should use the time offered to say something like: "I really don't have a question, but there are a couple of things you didn't ask me which I think are important for you to consider. Would you mind if I just took a couple of minutes to go over them?"

Remember that panelists are human. In the course of one or two days of interviews they will sometimes forget to ask things that are important. So, during the interview, keep in mind the things you HAVE NOT been asked—especially those things, when brought out, that might make a difference in your evaluation. Then use the time at the end of the interview to point out those things.

Now the interview is over. The chairperson will probably stand up, and perhaps the other panelists, too. If it seems natural, shake hands again. But for sure, thank the panelists for giving you the opportunity to meet with them. Also, make it a point to thank the staffer, too.

In this chapter, the interview is over and the author can breathe a sigh of relief, hoping that he has put down for you every important bit of advice that came from all the panelists and staffers.

But you, the candidate, cannot relax. You still have the interviews to face. And you probably are trying to juggle all the important do's and don'ts in your mind: do use good English, don't wring your hands, don't slump in the chair, don't use high school slang or too many "you knows," do look the panelists in the eye, do use good manners, etc. etc. etc.

All of that together is enough to put anybody's mind into overload, especially when you have to go into a room with strangers for the first time.

And what to do about that? Perhaps the following story might help.

Just a few weeks before writing this chapter, the author received a telephone call from a candidate in Kentucky whose father is an old friend. The candidate had used the raw manuscript of *The Naval Academy Candidate Book* to guide his own candidacy. He called with the news that he had just received his appointment. That was wonderful news, of course, and, in the discussion that followed, the young man was asked what advice helped him the most.

"There is no doubt about that," the young man replied. "The recommendation you made to do a practice interview is the best advice in that manuscript. Be sure and put that in the book."

The author replied: "Should I say anything more about the practice interview—something that would persuade others to do it?"

"Yes, tell them that it helped tremendously, and I MEAN tremendously!"

That conversation relates directly to the problem of the candidate trying to keep all the do's and don'ts in mind as the first interview is impending. And the best advice for the candidate is: DO NOT LET THE FIRST INTERVIEW BE THE ONE THAT COUNTS.

Arrange one or more PRACTICE interviews. And use them to practice the do's and practice avoiding the don'ts!

THIRTEEN
ALTERNATE ROUTES
TO THE ACADEMY

The first time you apply to West Point you may not get a nomination. Or, you may get a nomination but not get an appointment.

In either case, if you are really determined to go to West Point, you should have an alternate plan of action.

The first part of that plan should include an analysis of why you did not make it. But do not just rely upon your opinion. Get some opinions of those who were involved with your application.

If you did not get a nomination, call one or more of the congressional staffers who have your file. Explain that you have no intention of giving up—that you want to apply again next year. Then ask the staffer if he or she would please look over your file and make recommendations on what you can do to make yourself a better candidate. Realize, of course, that the staffer probably cannot do this immediately—while you are on the telephone. So, with your request, also ask when it would be convenient for you to call back. This will give the staffer time to review your case and to think of advice that would be most helpful.

If you received a nomination but not an appointment, there are two persons you should contact. One is your Field Force representative. The other is an Admissions Counselor at West Point. Try to convince both persons of your determination to do whatever you have to do to get accepted for the next class. Then, as with the congressional staffers, give them time to review your application before you call them again.

While you are consulting with those who will be discussing your weaknesses or deficiencies, be very careful not to get defensive about yourself. Just listen to what they are telling you, and even if you think they are wrong, thank them for their efforts.

After the consultations, the next step is to evaluate what you have heard. Then you should develop a plan of action based upon your options.

One of the most common problems of unsuccessful candidates is an academic deficiency—demonstrated by a low grade point average or low test scores (SAT or ACT), or a combination of both. If this is your problem, you must show as soon as possible that you are capable of academic success at West Point.

How?

Get into a college as soon as you can. And take hard courses. If prepared for it in high school, take calculus. Take English. And take chemistry. And work as hard as you can. Do more than you are assigned. Get A's if you can and if you cannot, at least get B's.

Also, take the SAT and ACT as many times as you can— remember, it is your highest score that will be used to evaluate you.

In addition to your college classes you should also consider taking a specialized course designed to help you increase your SAT and ACT scores. Ask your high school or college counselor about local programs. Another option is to check your Yellow Pages under "Tutoring." However, before paying money and signing up for such a course, try to find out as much as you can about the class. At the very least you should visit a class and interview one or more who have been through it.

What kind of college should you attend?

A general recommendation would be to go to the best college you can afford and the best college that will admit you. Even better would be a college that has an ROTC (Reserve Officer Training Corps) unit that will accept you.

Ideally you should try to get into an Army ROTC program. However, if this is not possible, do not hesitate to get into a Navy or Air Force unit. It is the opportunity to prove yourself to military officers that you are seeking. The branch of service is of minor importance.

Perhaps your problem is not an academic deficiency. Perhaps you were not involved in many extracurricular activities while in high school. Perhaps those who evaluated your application felt that you were too "bookwormish" to make a good cadet at West Point. If so, what can you do?

First, go on to college and do what has already been recommended. But get active in things other than academics. If you are in Army ROTC, get active and try to become a leader in the Ranger Club or the Parachute Club—or whatever other clubs the unit sponsors that interests you. As one admissions officer at West Point said, "Get in and get dirty...and prove yourself."

If not in an ROTC unit, get involved in student government, the school newspaper, dramatics, intramural sports, clubs, or whatever else interests you. And strive for leadership positions.

Do not worry that you cannot be elected president of a club when only a freshman. Do what you can. Volunteer for committees and take as much responsibility as the organization will give you. There are always opportunities. For example, few organizations will deny an eager freshman the opportunity to lead a clean-up committee.

And remember what you are seeking. You are seeking leadership experience. Also you are seeking leadership CREDENTIALS that you can cite on your next West Point application.

What if you cannot afford to go to college?

If that is your problem, you can still try for an alternative route to West Point. You can join the Army and try to win one of the 85 slots in each entering class the Academy saves for active-duty enlistees.

You should realize that this option is much more risky than the college option. With the college option you can go on and get your degree, then apply to Army Officer Candidate School and perhaps get an officer's commission. Or, by participating in Army ROTC for four years, you can earn a commission at graduation. But if you join the Army, you might never get to be an officer. You might join for three or four years, not be admitted to West Point, and end up your enlistment without any college credit.

If you do decide to join the Army, here is some advice that has been handed down from others who have entered the Academy from that route.

135

First, you must excel at everything you do in order to earn good recommendations from your supervising officers. In basic training try to be the outstanding basic. In whatever technical training program you enter after that, strive to be at the top of your class both in academics and in soldierly qualities. Later, when you are given your active-duty assignment, try to be the best soldier you know how to be.

In addition, make sure you have a copy of the Army Regulation that explains the West Point application procedure. Cadets who went this route explained to the author that it is not uncommon for company personnel to know very little about the procedure. So do not depend upon someone else to tell you how to apply. Study the Army Regulation and be prepared to follow it on your own.

Cadets who came from the Army also recommended that you should let your supervising non-commissioned officers (NCO's) and officers know that your goal is to attend West Point. Those supervisors may give you responsibilities that will allow you to prove that you have leadership potential.

By joining the Army you do not necessarily give up all of your chances to improve your academic ability. Army enlisted personnel can subscribe to a number of college-level correspondence courses. Also, most Army posts have off-duty college classes available that you may be able to take.

Few go directly from the Army into West Point. Almost all spend a year at the United States Military Academy Preparatory School (USMAPS), which is at Fort Monmouth, New Jersey. The purpose of USMAPS is to bring potential cadets "up to speed" in math and English. Military training is also included, but it is not as rigorous as at West Point itself.

The author interviewed several cadets who had spent a year at USMAPS. They all agreed that it was the best thing they ever did—that they came into the Academy much better prepared academically and militarily than those who came there right out of high school.

Some candidates who fail to get an appointment to West Point are offered another route to the Academy. Often these are candidates who have promising leadership potential but who are somewhat deficient academically.

The most important thing you will learn at USMAPS is how to study.

Such promising candidates are offered an opportunity to attend either USMAPS or one of several private preparatory schools that have a cooperative arrangement with West Point. USMAPS is the best offer because the candidate enjoys free tuition as well as free room and meals and a small salary.

Unless the candidate can prove financial hardship, the expenses at the private prep schools must be paid by the candidate or the parents. In either case, at USMAPS or at a private school, if the candidate does well he or she is almost certain to receive an appointment to a West Point class the following year.

Candidates typically react in one of two ways when they are offered the prep school option. One candidate says, "Wow, that is a great opportunity. Where do I sign?"

The other candidate says, "What! You expect me to waste a year of my life in a prep school? You have to be kidding. I would rather forget about the whole thing and just go on to a college and take ROTC."

Before you react either way, you should think about some of the advantages of the prep-school option. First, it will give you a chance to strengthen your background in the three subjects that are most difficult for first-year cadets.

Second, and perhaps more important, the instructors—particularly in USMAPS—will see to it that you learn how to study. Not knowing how to study is the biggest problem of first-year cadets who enter West Point right out of high school.

Third, you will have one more year of maturity before you start the rigorous schedule of a plebe. That year of maturity will help you adapt to the many stresses of that first year. You will also be over the pain of homesickness, a malaise that creates problems for many who leave home for the first time.

A bonus of a year at USMAPS is that you will already have about 200 friends when you start as a plebe. Those will be your fellow students at USMAPS. Friends are valuable in any kind of stress situation. They are especially valuable when you are undergoing the pressure that the upperclassmen place upon the plebes.

One final bit of advice. Be realistic about your potential as a West Point cadet. For example don't expect to get in with SAT scores in the 400s.

However, do not let ANYBODY discourage you if you truly believe that you have the potential to make it. The author has heard numerous stories of high school counselors, Field Force Representatives and even Academy admissions officials discouraging young people who defied them all and made it through West Point.

So DO NOT GIVE UP without a fight if West Point is what you really want. And even though you might have to struggle to make it, just remember that almost everybody likes to root for the underdog. Keep trying, for even two or three years if you have to, and you might be surprised how many people may end up helping you.

Yes, the Academy wants cadets with academic ability and leadership potential. But they also want cadets with determination and guts.

So if West Point is for you, give it all you have—and do not give up until you have become too old to apply.

FOURTEEN
WHAT MINORITY
CANDIDATES SHOULD KNOW

Late one afternoon at West Point the author met with the Minority Recruiting Officer in charge of minority admissions. The following is an edited and shortened version of the dialogue that followed.

What minorities are you trying to recruit?
Primarily blacks, Hispanics and American Indians. But please don't use the word recruit. That term implies a hard sell—it implies that we're trying to drag them in here. Our

The Minority Recruiting Officer in charge of minority admissions discusses a candidate with the Director of Admissions.

job is more educational. We're trying to let minorities know the great opportunities that West Point offers. We believe that once they see what we have to offer, they will be strongly motivated to come here.

Do you see the difference? We're not trying to pull them in; we're trying to get the information out so they will feel that we've got something they want and need.

We're salespeople—we won't deny that. But we're selling education and opportunity and good jobs.

I can see the difference, but doesn't the Army have a great need for minority officers?

Yes, definitely—that's why we can sell job opportunities with so much enthusiasm. In the Army about 30 percent of the enlisted personnel belong to the three minorities that I have mentioned. But only about 10-12 percent of the officers belong to those minorities. There is a very definite need to equalize the ratios between enlisted and officer personnel.

Well, what would you like to tell minority candidates about West Point?

I just wish that I could get the real facts out to these kids. But I've got this enormous problem because of what they are hearing about the Army and West Point. As soon as West Point is even mentioned their dads and granddads start telling about the way the Army used to be—how it was segregated—how minorities such as blacks were always separated from the others—how there was no opportunity unless you wanted to be a cook or a police officer.

Even today that is the image?

Unfortunately, yes. I guess that's my biggest challenge—to get the word out—to get the message to these youngsters that, 'Hey, I want you to make a decision based upon the facts. Get all the facts. Get the complete picture. Don't just make a decision on what granddad said the Army was like in 1956.'

Well, how is the Army and West Point different now?

If there is any part of society where minorities have a fairer chance than in the Army or here at West Point, I'd like to know where it is. Just look at our Commandant right here at West Point, General Gorden. He was one of the first black graduates and now he is going on to become a two-star general. There are so many other things.

Go ahead and elaborate.

Let me give you a couple of examples. Let's take black students here and compare them to those in most civilian colleges. Here they are spread through each of the companies at random—they are pretty evenly distributed over the whole place. They are not a minority. They're just like everyone else.

But what do you see at most civilian colleges? There, the blacks tend to group themselves together—a mutual support kind of thing. And then they do in fact retain a minority status because as a group there are fewer of them. So then all the other aspects of being a minority come into play and inevitably there is polarization. We avoid that here. The only polarization we have is company against company—competition! And that is healthy. That is what this place is all about—people pulling together, not pulling apart.

Another example. Here we have strong safeguards to prevent any kind of racial harassment. We aren't perfect, of course. Occasionally there'll be a problem. Anyway, when the minority kids come in here the first year, we have a support system for them that we call the Plebe Contact Program. With this program we have officers who regularly contact the minority students and we ask them a series of questions—things like, How are the studies going? and What can we do to help you?

Through these questions we sometimes pick up problems, but with our system the kid is protected whenever he tells us something. For example, say I am interviewing a kid and he perceives there to be a problem with some upperclassmen or with his Tac Officer [the officer who supervises a company of cadets]. Well, if I hear that complaint from a kid, I have the authority to go directly to the Com [Commandant] and explain the problem WITHOUT USING THE CADET'S NAME. The latter is important because such matters can be cleared up without the cadet running the risk of retribution.

What else would you like minority candidates to know?
If I could just wipe away a couple of myths, it would help a lot. Take the myth that at West Point you aren't allowed to make a mistake. We see that all the time. Minority candidates are afraid to come here. They have heard about the pressure and the discipline and they question whether they are good enough to take all that without making a mistake and getting kicked out. We try to tell them, 'Hey, you've got us all wrong. We're all human beings. We make mistakes. Everybody makes mistakes. Sure, for some mistakes you will get penalized so you will concentrate harder on not making them again. But you're not going to get kicked out. The people here want to work with you, to teach you how to be a leader. We turn out leaders, not saints.'

And the second myth?
The second one is even worse. Every kid thinks you have to know somebody to get into this place. They hear about all the competition and they hear that it is a political process. Tell them that they definitely DO NOT have to know somebody in order to get in here. If they are truly interested, we will get them in—if we can get them qualified.

Then what should a minority candidate do?
The first thing to do is to call us here at Admissions. The number is 914-938-4041. When somebody answers, ask to speak to an Outreach Officer—we have seven of them on the staff—all of them are minority persons and their sole job is to help minority candidates. After that initial call, the Outreach Officer will take over and do everything possible to help the candidate get admitted.

Such as?
The paperwork, for example. Most kids are intimidated somewhat by all the forms that have to be filled out—things like the Precandidate Questionnaire and the Personal Statement. Well, most kids have a support system to help them—counselors, parents etc. A lot of minority kids don't

142

have that kind of support. Many are from poor high schools where the counselors don't always know what is going on. Some are from homes where there is little support.

So you take over?

If we need to, yes. We can do a lot over the telephone. We can walk the candidate through the Precandidate Questionnaire.

An Outreach Officer escorts a minority candidate on a tour of the practice fields.

But don't you also go out and help many of them in person?

Definitely. Each of our seven Outreach Officers has a geographic area to cover and we spend a lot of time out in the schools, working directly with the candidates. In fact, one of the biggest problems with our Outreach Officers is burnout. They come in here from their job in the Army and in a year or so the traveling has them beat down. It's a tough assignment.

What about nominations? How does a minority kid compete with all the others wanting congressmen to nominate them?

143

That's a good point. Tell them not to worry about the congressional nomination. We will counsel them and, sometimes, even make sure they have transportation to get to the interviews. But also we can often find nominations outside of the candidate's congressional district. Some of the sparsely populated Western States don't always fill their quotas and we can use those.

What other advice do you want to give?

Many things. We tell them to apply to West Point even if they think they are going to get a scholarship to Florida State. Why? Because it is important to have as many options as possible.

We also tell them that even though they have been offered a scholarship somewhere and also have been offered an appointment to West Point, do not turn down the West Point offer immediately—not until the deadline. That other option might not be as attractive after they go and look at it closely—then they still have the West Point option available if they haven't turned it down.

What should a candidate think about when considered such options?

The young people should try to decide what is best for them. But I ask this of any of them. Is getting a good job after graduation important to you? If so, think hard about the other institutions that are out there trying to sell their programs. What kind of job guarantees go with the program?

It is one thing to get a fine education. But it is another matter to get a job where you can use that education. We guarantee all of our graduates a job, and it will be a job where they will use what they have learned.

What else do you want to tell candidates?

We also try to get the word out to younger students to take the PSAT [Preliminary Scholastic Aptitude Test] when they are sophomores in high school. It is so important to get practice with those tests. The experience will help them greatly when they take the SAT the next year.

There is one other thing you should stress in your book. We tell the kids to call us early, like in the spring of their

Be ready to compete in sports that are new and unfamiliar to you.

junior year. This gives us more time to work with them and get them over the hurdles.

But, it is also important for them never to assume that it is too late. For example, it might be March or April of their senior year when they find out about us and get interested. Tell them to call us! It might not be too late to get them into the prep school.

Into the prep school so they can get up to speed for the following year?

145

Correct. Many of the minority kids need that year at the prep school. Are you going to cover that in your book?

Yes, in a separate chapter. I visited the prep school and have also interviewed numerous cadets who went there. All of them made very positive comments.

The most important thing is that they learn how to study. Many minority kids come from schools where they don't have to do that.

Any final thing you would like them to know?

Yes, one other thing comes to mind. All candidates have to take the PAE [Physical Aptitude Examination] and some of our kids, who are pretty athletic, think the test will be a breeze. Well, it is important for them to get a good score on the test and some of the things like the kneeling basketball throw and the shuttle run are much harder than they think. My advice is to practice for the PAE. Learn to throw that basketball on your knees. And practice the shuttle run. Of course, we'll tell them how to do it but they have to take it seriously.

But the main thing you want them to remember is to call your people at Admissions even if they are just mildly interested in West Point. Right?

That is correct. Tell them not to be shy about calling us. Our full-time job is just to help them. But they have to let us know that they're out there.

HOW TO SURVIVE

Be sure and visit West Point if you can. You will get straight information about what it is like from the experts—the cadets themselves.

FIFTEEN
WHY PRESSURE THE PLEBES?

The pressure starts on "R-Day," the day of arrival. It continues through the next six weeks of Beast Barracks. Then, when the academic year begins and the whole cadre returns, the plebes are outnumbered three to one and the pressure rises and continues through the next nine months.

In short, the almost eleven-month plebe "year" (minus vacations) is a long, difficult trek.

Why should it be? Why are the plebes given such a hard time?

There is a rationale for the Fourthclass Development System, which is the official name for the activities that create pressure on the plebes. However, that rationale is not what most incoming plebes believe it to be.

The incoming plebes typically believe that the plebe year is a rite of passage—that it is the equivalent of an eleven-month ceremony designed to weed out those who are unworthy of the high standards of West Point.

Upperclass cadets implement and administer the Fourthclass System with firm, but relatively hands-off supervision by a staff of officers. Thus, with the system essentially in the hands of about 3000 cadets, there is bound to be a variety of motives for bringing pressure upon the plebes—motives that do not coincide with what is official.

And the "rite of passage" reason for plebe pressure is one of those motives. "I went through it; now you're going to go through it." That is how some of the upperclass think and candidates would be naive not to expect some versions of that attitude from those who will supervise them.

Another motive that is unofficial but ever present in the upperclass cadre is the "stress injection theory." Put them under a lot of stress during the plebe year, goes the theory, then, later, when they are out in combat and under stress, that experience will pay off with the West Point officer standing tall in the face of every adversity.

149

The official rationale for the Fourthclass Development System does not mention the stress injection theory or combat. Instead, it focuses on how the plebe is to be developed.

Note the verb "develop," for it is the action word that drives the Fourthclass System.

The Fourthclass System is a system designed to take intelligent, highly motivated young men and women from every cultural niche in our country and to begin to develop them into the kind of officers needed to lead the Army.

And the basic conflict in the system—the conflict that creates the adversary relationship between plebes and upperclass—results because the plebes enter West Point with a variety of habits and attitudes that must be changed or eliminated.

Changes never come easily, especially when we are talking about changes in deeply imbedded habits and attitudes.

And making changes are doubly difficult when they have to be made ALL AT ONCE while the plebes are lonely, often homesick, and, for those who are unprepared mentally,

Get it programmed into your mind: you CANNOT avoid criticism.

150

while disillusioned and wondering why they got themselves into such a pressure cooker.

The key to survival, say the cadets, is to understand and ACCEPT the reasons for the changes the Fourthclass System is going to FORCE you to make.

So let us discuss those changes.

Most plebes come into West Point with a great reputation, earned on their home turf through sweat and hard work. Most were highly respected by their teachers and their peers—respect that they deserved for their academic and athletic performances, and for their leadership ability.

As a result of their years of exemplary behavior, the incoming plebes have only heard good things about themselves. They have heard the cheers on the athletic fields and in the award assemblies. They have heard the compliments from their teachers and from adult leaders with whom they have worked. "Great job!" "Wonderful!" Those and most of the other superlatives in the dictionary were sent their way at one time or another.

So, when they go to West Point they leave home with all those accolades ringing in their ears.

Then they meet the upperclass cadets who are responsible for their development. And the upperclass are just waiting to rattle the egos of these high school wondermen and wonderwomen.

The new plebes will hear no more accolades—unless perhaps they do something truly extraordinary. Instead, they will hear reprimands, negative comments, repeated warnings, and, from some of the more revengeful types (they did it to me and now I am going to do it to them), harsh, loud, raucous, abusive verbal criticism.

And, just hours after arriving, the young wondermen and wonderwomen find that they can never seem to do anything right. Despite what they believe are heroic efforts they cannot adequately shine their shoes, polish their brass or make their beds. Said one plebe about to become a Third Class Cadet as she reflected on the past eleven months:

"I thought that it would be different. I thought, sure, I'll catch it when I screw up and don't do things right. But I thought they would leave me alone if I did a good job and was trying as hard as I could. Wrong! They get on you no matter what. You can't escape the criticism. That was the hardest thing for me, knowing no matter how well I did, I was still going to get chewed on."

Why are the upperclass so critical?

There are many reasons and they all have to do with the changes they want the plebes to make—changes that will help in their development.

Some who come to West Point believe too much of what has been said about them. As a result they have inflated egos and think they are better than they really are. In a word they are arrogant.

That attitude has to be changed. An officer who is arrogant can be dangerous. For example, think of what happened to General George Custer when he charged toward the encampment of the Sioux and Cheyenne Nations. Custer's arrogance caused him to believe that his few undermanned companies armed only with single-shot rifles could defeat thousands of angry, defiant Indians. His men had to follow him, of course, and they paid the ultimate price for his arrogance.

High school all-stars have to learn what it is to start all over at the bottom and work their way up again.

The Army does not want other soldiers to pay that price while following the orders of an arrogant officer. They try to avoid that problem by making sure their officers have learned humility.

Persons with humility know their weaknesses as well as their strengths. The upperclass at West Point know this so they set out to push the new cadets farther than they have ever been pushed before. They want to create such a demanding environment that all the cadets will eventually go beyond their limits and fail.

Note the word fail. Many candidates have never let that word become a part of their vocabulary.

But you must get it programmed into your mind that you will fail at West Point. It will not be major failure—unless, of course, you completely give up. Rather, it will be repeated minor failures of small tasks given by the upperclass cadets.

The upperclass's ultimate goal, of course, is not for the plebes to suffer failure. Their goal is for the plebes to DEVELOP from their failures.

They want the plebes to find their weaknesses. They want them to know them and be aware of them.

They want the plebes to understand the temporary nature of failure—that failure is not an ending, but a beginning. They want them to know that failure is a point of departure, a place to begin again.

They want the plebes to develop an attitude about failure—a defiant kind of attitude that says, "You can knock me down but you cannot keep me down."

All of this will happen while you are in a fishbowl. As you discover your weaknesses, so will your roommates and classmates. But the communal sharing of this knowledge is very important because it insures that you WILL develop humility.

But that is just the beginning; there are other things that the upperclass cadets want to develop.

For example, they want to develop the mental abilities of the plebes. Most plebes have minds like a Corvette that has never been driven more than 30 miles an hour.

Therefore, most plebes do not have any idea what their minds are capable of doing.

The upperclass will see that they learn. Plebes will be forced to memorize far more than they think they can. In addition, they will be forced to do a lot of this mental work while other stresses are upon them.

And what are they trying to develop by this tactic?

Confidence, for one thing. They want the plebes to finish the year confident in the fine piece of mental apparatus they possess. And they want that fine apparatus running at the speed at which it is capable.

They also want the plebes to know how to concentrate—to know that no matter what is happening around them or how tired they are, they can focus on necessary mental tasks and get them done.

The upperclass also want to develop a group mentality in the plebes.

Many who come to West Point have a tendency to be self-centered, at least to some degree. This is nothing to be ashamed of. Persons who make it into West Point have to have done a lot of thinking about themselves; otherwise, they would never have marshalled the necessary drive to climb above their peers.

But those individualist tendencies have to be modified into a new type of thinking. Army officers must constantly be thinking, not of themselves, but of the welfare of the troops for whose lives they are responsible.

So the upperclass cadets will hammer the plebes throughout the year. "Think of your roommates!" "Think of your squad!" "Think of your platoon and your company!" Plebes will hear those commands like a broken record. And the plebes' punishments and rewards will be based upon how well they heed what they are being told.

The upperclass will also be working to rid plebes of habits that cannot be tolerated in the military service.

Most plebes will not, by training and habit, be neat and orderly. Yet, in order to survive in the close quarters of military life, where hundreds or even thousands of soldiers are concentrated in a small area, neatness and orderliness is not just something that will make things look nice; it is

Neatness is mandatory in the military because hundreds or even thousands are sometimes concentrated in a small area.

an absolute necessity. Without it there would be chaos, not to mention the potential health hazards.

That is why plebes will spend hours with brooms, mops, dust cloths and Windex. That is why a day will never go by when they do not pick lint from each other's uniforms. That is why they will shine and reshine their shoes, polish and repolish their brass, and make and remake their beds.

The upperclass cadets want them to develop lifelong habits that will enable them to live closely with others. They want to rid them forever of careless ways, of doing things halfway, of doing tasks just well enough to get by.

They also want the plebes to develop a sense of pride that will always be with them. Later, as they take that pride into the Army, it will be as infectious as a disease. Soldiers serving under an officer with pride cannot fail to catch some of it themselves.

Army officers serve in a unique society with its own special courtesies and customs. The upperclass have learned those courtesies and customs and they practice them among themselves, as well as with the officers with whom they are in contact.

The upperclass must also develop the plebes so they will emerge from the fourthclass year prepared to function in military society.

They want the plebes to know things like how to salute and how to address their superiors.

They also want them to learn essential social graces that go beyond the military realm—things like how to conduct introductions, proper dining manners and procedures, and the importance of writing thank-you notes to those who have befriended them. (The latter is, by far, the hardest to teach say the upperclass cadets and staff officers.)

Finally, it is the responsibility of the upperclass to develop in the plebes a deep, everlasting belief in the traditions of West Point, particularly in the motto: Duty, Honor, Country.

The plebes must be trained so they will perform their duties faithfully, without questioning why they must be done.

The upperclass must teach the plebes how to live by the West Point Honor Code, and they must try to instill in the plebes a sense of pride in living honorably.

And, the upperclass must also do what they can to develop in the plebes a love of country, which should be the ultimate motive behind an officer's desire to serve.

Can you now put what the upperclass do to the plebes into perspective?

Yes, some of them want to create misery for the plebes because that is what happened to them as plebes.

Yes, some of the upperclass cadets will yell and shout insults at the plebes even though their leaders have told them that such behavior will not be tolerated.

And yes, some will try to inject stress, thinking that the effort will pay off on some battlefield of the future.

But those aspects of the system, which are strictly unofficial, are relatively minor. Much more important is the difficult task of developing the Fourth Class Cadets in all the ways that have been discussed.

And the whole job of fourthclass development must be done in eleven months, mostly in the spare moments when the plebes are not in class or in intramural sports or studying.

While that eleven months seems like an eternity for the plebes, it is truly a breakneck schedule for the upperclass.

Just imagine how difficult it is to do a good job of developing nearly 1400 individuals—

—individuals who have been all-stars for most of their lives and know little about humility.

—individuals who, for the most part, have never had to use but a fraction of their mental ability.

—individuals who typically have been content with sloppy dress, messy rooms and perhaps careless grooming, and often with slipshod ways of performing tasks.

—individuals who may have scorned their parents' teachings about manners and courtesies and who probably have never written a thank-you note in their lives.

—individuals who have come from all cultures and environments, including schools where cheating and lying were the norm and honesty was scorned as stupid behavior.

The salute is just one of the military courtesies that you must learn.

If you can now see the magnitude of the job the upperclass have, and, in addition, if you can appreciate the relatively short time that they have to do it, perhaps you can adjust your own thinking about the plebe year.

157

It will be a long year. Nothing can change that. But it should help you to know that the upperclass are doing what they are doing, not because they hate plebes and, for the most part, not because they want the plebes to suffer like they did.

Most upperclass cadets are enthusiastic about implementing the Fourthclass System because THEY KNOW THAT IF THEY DO THEIR JOB RIGHT, THE PLEBES WILL END THE YEAR AS MUCH, MUCH BETTER PERSONS.

Can you accept that? It might be difficult, especially after the various horror stories you may have heard from those who think they know something about West Point. But try, because it is the truth, and because a solid belief in the value of the Fourthclass System will help you survive that first year.

Now, read on and find out what the cadets and officers say you must do to survive.

SIXTEEN
THE PLEBES TELL
HOW TO SURVIVE

Why are you still here while about 200 of your classmates are gone?

That question was asked repeatedly during a series of interviews with plebes who were within a week of finishing their first year at West Point. It was a lead-in question—a question designed to get them thinking about the kinds of survival advice they would give candidates.

What follows is a digest of the discussions that resulted during those interviews.

One of the first things the cadets agreed on was the importance of the candidate knowing what to expect during the first year.

Said one plebe: "A lot of those who left did not understand what they were getting into. I know that some of them thought the worst would be over after Beast Barracks. But the truth is that Beast Barracks is not all that bad—for me it was kind of fun. What was really difficult was AFTER Beast when the whole cadre came back. Then the plebes are outnumbered three to one and you have the pressure of academics. That's when the hard time begins. I knew that and expected that. I don't think many of those who left knew what was going to happen."

"It definitely pays to know as much as you can about this place before you come," said another plebe. "My advice is to talk to as many cadets as you can, and definitely come for a visit before you accept an appointment. That really helped me. I talked with a lot of cadets and I saw how the plebes were treated. I personally don't think the plebe year is so bad when you know what to expect."

Another plebe shook his head as he listened to the above comment. Later, he said, "I don't care how many people you talk to; you will never know how rough it is until you go through it. So my advice is to get your head prepared. Talk yourself into knowing it's going to be hard; then be prepared for the worst."

That comment prompted another question: What are the hardest things about plebe year?

"Getting yelled at!" exclaimed one plebe. "Everyone here was a stud in high school, used to hearing accolades. Here, you have to open yourself up to criticism."

"But don't take it personally," said another plebe. "Sure, it hurts when he [an upperclassman] yells at you. But he doesn't hate you...after getting smoked you can do two things. You can go to the room and cry and let the criticism eat away at you, or you can go to your room and laugh and say how stupid I was to do the things that he was criticizing. It also helps to look down the hall and see somebody else getting it."

"Yes, but it still hurts when you get yelled at for something you didn't do," said another plebe. "But you can't let it bother you. You have to realize that it is also happening to others. Also, you just have to go to your room, close the door and laugh about it."

Other plebes also commented on the importance of laughing about being criticized.

Said one: "You have to have a sense of humor to survive here. You get chewed out and you have to go in a room with others and compare stories. Then you laugh about it...I've never laughed so much in my life...that is how you get rid of your stress...just remember, when that door closes, they can't see you..."

Said another: "There are bad times and rough times, but you always look back with a smile at the rough times. I got ripped for days for some of the dumbest, stupidest things, and even talked about quitting. But this weekend [within a week of the end of plebe year] we were all laughing about it."

"You also have to be a good actor," said another. "You have to play your role. When they are yelling at you, you do not want to show emotion. They're pretending to be mad when they are yelling at you—you have to be just a little better actor. Don't look scared and don't smile, or you are in big trouble.

Said another: "You have to learn to look through people...let it go in one ear and out the other, and look right through somebody's eyes...it's all a part of being adaptable, of doing things you didn't expect to do."

Each of the discussions eventually led to the unfortunate plebe who becomes a "spaz." This term is used to describe a plebe who habitually "screws up" and thus incurs much more than the normal ration of criticism. Everyone agreed that the life of a spaz is much more difficult.

"You can often tell who has been a spaz," said one of the plebes as a discussion moved to the subject of upperclass cadets. "They are the worst of all. They have the mentality that says, 'I was treated like s____t; now I'm going to give it back tenfold.'"

Another plebe agreed but said: "You can't always just be passive and take it—you have to think of those types the way you would think of a football player just across the line. You have to think of it as competition. For example, my greatest moment this whole year was when I won out over an upperclassman that we hated—he was a former spaz. One day he called me to his room because I messed up. He kept hazing me and I gave him everything. He was trying to get me to break but I kept my cool and was stronger than he was. And I realized that he was going to lose it and that I was going to break him. Finally he realized that I was in control and he didn't know what to do. He went crazy, threw his hat against the wall and broke it, kicked the door and told me to get out of his face. After that I smirked all the way back to my room." [This was doubly rewarding because the smirk, a knowing smile, is an expression that is especially antagonistic to upperclassmen.]

In the same discussion another cadet said: "There are definitely good ones [upperclass cadets] and bad ones but they tell you to profit from both with the "bag method" of learning leadership.

"What they mean is that you can learn how to be a leader by keeping your own bag. When you see what you think are good examples of leadership, you put them in the bag. When you see bad examples of leadership, you put them in the bag, too. However, you use those examples of bad leadership a lot more because they teach you what not to do.

"You see all kinds of leadership here and by keeping all the different examples in a bag, you slowly mold yourself toward the types of leadership you think are good, and away from the types that are bad. This year I had one squad leader who is a man I will respect to the day I die. All his methods are in my bag and I can't wait to try them out. But I also had another squad leader I don't want to see for the rest of my life. I have his methods in my bag, too, but they are all examples of what I don't want to do."

But what about the really bad days—the days when you get so depressed you want to quit? That question always triggered a lot of serious discussion. Here are some of the comments.

Said one: "You get down—everybody does—that's a part of the system so you'll learn to pull yourself up again. But the important thing is not to get down on yourself. You have to keep saying to yourself, 'I'm not as bad as they say I am.' You have to believe that. Also, I did something else that I'm not exactly proud of but it worked. When I started

One key to survival is to get out and get involved.

162

getting down on myself, I would think of the geekiest looking upperclassman in the company and I would constantly tell myself, 'If he made it, I can make it.'"

Said another cadet: "It's real easy to get down on yourself when you're tired—and you're always tired. Things that were easy at home aren't always easy here because of the constant tiredness. It's hard to stay awake in class. It's hard to concentrate on the books. All these things pile up and it is easy to begin doubting yourself. You're wondering, 'Do I really have what it takes?' Then you start doubting yourself. Everyone does. But that's when you have to fight back. You have to believe in yourself."

"You also have to get enough sleep," said a plebe in reply to the above comment. "My roommate started staying up after hours studying and he got so burned out he almost didn't make it. I realize now, after seeing what happened to him, that you are the most vulnerable to stress when you're tired. I've since learned a technique that helps me get rid of my own stress. Just before going to bed I sit for two or three minutes in a chair and just think back over the day. I laugh to myself about the dumb things and think about the next day and what I'm going to do. It's a winding down process that gradually relieves the stress for me—then I sleep like a log and I know what I'm going to do just as soon as I wake up."

Several of the plebes mentioned the value of calls home when they were down.

Said one: "It really helped to have someone who would listen. It helped to get it all out and to have someone reminding you that you can do it. You can't complain here—nobody wants to hear griping. My parents were wonderful, though I feel guilty now that I'm through it for all the dumping on them that I did. And my letters during Beast—they're laughable now!"

Said another: "My dad had been through it and he kept telling me, 'Take it an hour at a time and then a day at a time. Don't think ahead because it will frighten you. Just concentrate on getting through each hour and each day.' That helped me a lot."

West Point is not all work. The cadets also manage to have their share of fun.

To that comment another cadet said: "That is true, but you also have to be futuristic. You have to think that a weekend is coming, that you'll see your family at the next football game, that you'll eventually be recognized and the guys that are giving you the hardest time will shake your hand and call you by your first name. You have to know that the longer you are in the system, the better it is going to become."

"Don't let your parents meddle, either," added another plebe. You call home, down, maybe talking about quitting, and they get all worried. Then they call the Tac [Tactical Officer who supervises a company of cadets] and he roars down to the upperclassman and you get labeled. The word spreads like wildfire in the company because the CQ [cadet charge of quarters] can hear the phone conversation in the Tac's office. The time to call the Tac is in an emergency—he can facilitate emergency leave if you need it."

Several of the plebes commented about the beneficial effects of belonging to West Point clubs.

164

Said one: "There is a real advantage to belonging to clubs. For one thing, it is a good way to get to know upperclassmen. Those who aren't in your company will help you because they know what's going on—those in your company don't talk as much with you. The second advantage of clubs is that they take trips and anything that gets you out of here as a plebe is good. I belonged to a music club this year and we went to a symphony and a rock concert. Language clubs are also good because they have a lot of interesting trips. You have to get out of here or go insane and club activities are the best way."

Most of the discussions concluded with another perspective on survival. Many plebes felt strongly that thinking about the positive aspects of being at West Point were as much or more important as surmounting all of the negative factors that they had been discussing. This chapter concludes with some of their positive comments.

Said one plebe: "I started thinking about coming here when I was in the ninth grade. Now, after just one year, I love this place too much to quit. I like working with people and the great bonds that you build here. Where else can you build such strong friendships—friendships that will last a lifetime?"

Said another: "You have to keep everything in perspective—you have to think of the positive things as well as the negative. For me the positive things far outweigh the negative. I'm getting the best education I can get anywhere and I'm getting paid for it. And I don't have all the worries that my friends have at their colleges. Here, everything is done for me. I don't have to worry about anything. I sign a piece of paper and my laundry is done. When I'm ready to eat, my meals are ready. I don't have to worry about clothes...I have a computer...I have lots of friends that I can depend on...here I can bear down and focus on what needs to be done, without worrying about anything else. Best of all, I have a guaranteed job when I graduate—none of my friends going to civilian colleges can say that."

Said another: "You really realize the value of this place when you go home for Christmas and get around your friends. You can tell that you have grown as a person—you can tell that you are different just after a few months. This gives you another perspective and it reinforces your feeling that what you are doing is right even though it is difficult... you have to grow here—we've done more [growing] this year than other people will experience in four years of college."

SEVENTEEN
SURVIVAL ADVICE FROM FIRST CLASS CADETS

Advice from First Class Cadets is valuable for two reasons.

First, they have the best perspective on West Point because they have been there for three or four years (depending upon when they were interviewed).

Second, they have the responsibility for implementing the Fourthclass System. Thus, they can give advice based on their current experiences with plebes as well as their own experiences during plebe year.

From all the interviews with First Class Cadets, three were selected for this chapter because they represent a wide range of views and experiences.

The first comments are from an Augusta, Georgia firstclassman who was raised as an "Army brat" and who enlisted in the Army when he failed to get into West Point right out of high school. He served in the Army two years, then went to the USMA Prep School. He said:

"Candidates for this place should get as much advice as they can before they come here. For example, find out exactly what you do at a meal. Get all the details on how you use your fork and knife—have somebody demonstrate everything step-by-step. Also, try to visit here and see what it is like. There is nothing like a visit—I had heard a lot when I was in prep school, but the experience of coming up here was much better.

"As for your frame of mind when you come in here, you have to know you're not going to enjoy it, at least for several weeks or months. Expect it not to be fun and then it won't seem so bad.

"And make sure you are coming for yourself. During Beast it was my job to talk to those who wanted to go home. Often they had come for their parents or family or because of local town pressure. If they don't come for themselves, they are probably not going to make it.

"Another problem, I think, is those who have never had any discipline at home. It is also hard on those who have never been criticized. They try their hardest to avoid criticism but no matter how hard they try, they will be yelled at. They have to expect that.

"It is really hard on the egos of some of them. They have to think, 'Hey, I made it through today and nobody patted me on the back. Then I'll just pat myself on the back. Of course, that's hard for the high school prima donnas—they're not used to hearing criticism. Also, I think they realize after they have been here awhile, that they could go elsewhere and do well and they would get patted on the back.

"I should also say that most of those who did come crying to me wanting to go home ended up staying. And I know that the few who quit later said that they were glad that they stayed as long as they did. What they learned by toughing it out was not to worry about their limits. The Fourthclass System guarantees that they will constantly raise their sights on what they are capable of doing. That is one of the best things about it. In my own case, for example, West Point has taught me that I'll never set a limit on myself again.

"Every plebe will have bad days, but you have to learn to make the best of them. For example, I saw plebes in Beast who couldn't finish the morning run. Then they started getting down on themselves. They start saying to themselves, 'I can't believe I fell out of the run—I'm never going to make it here.' That's the wrong way to think. What they should say to themselves is, 'I didn't make it halfway today but tomorrow I'm going to make it more than halfway.' In other words, they need to set realistic goals for themselves; then when they achieve them, they will feel good about themselves. The days aren't nearly as bad when you are realistic about yourself.

"Of course, almost everybody thinks about quitting at one time or another, especially after a bad day. But what I recommend is physical exercise to get a release from the tension. Go for a run, or workout at something you enjoy. It's amazing how differently you look at a problem after you have worked up a good sweat.

"Speaking of sweat reminds me that you should make sure everybody knows that this place is physically demanding—that you are going to sweat and get dirty. I say this because we had this girl in Beast who came because of the academics. She didn't realize that she was going to march with a forty-pound pack and rifle or that she was going to get sweaty and dirty crawling in the dirt on her belly. This is no place just for scholars. The Army is a physical place.

"What are some of the hardest things? One thing comes to mind immediately. It is very difficult for those who get injured during Beast and have to go to the hospital. It's hard because they have a difficult time adjusting when they come back into the system.

"Another difficult problem occurs after three weeks of Beast. At that time each squad gets a new squad leader. So just when the new cadets have gotten used to their first squad leader they have to start all over with a different one. This causes a lot of anxiety and stress, but if they know that it is going to happen, they can get themselves mentally ready for it. That's why I mentioned earlier that they [the candidates] should get lots of information from somebody who has gone through it. Every little bit of knowledge helps.

"One tip I would pass on is to rely on those in your squad who have come from the Prep School—usually there is at least one of them in each squad. They can help you learn things like shining your shoes, making your bed, etc. This is a responsibility that they will expect. They are told at the Prep School that leadership is expected from them.

"Another thing they should keep in mind is that everything keeps getting easier. For example, when I first had to read the newspaper, I could read for 15 minutes and not know anything. Later, as I got used to it, I could scan it in two minutes and be ready for any questions they would throw at me.

"Also they should know that Beast is not the hardest part of the year. The hardest periods are Reorgy Week and the Gloom Period.

"Reorgy [reorganization] Week is the week after Beast when you are outnumbered by the upperclassmen and they have nothing else to do but see how well you have been developed. In my opinion this is the hardest week of the whole year.

"The Gloom Period is the first couple of weeks after Christmas when everything is gray—the sky, the buildings and the uniforms. It is a depressing time for everyone, but for the plebes it is worse because they have just come from home where everybody has been making over them, and then, suddenly, the upperclassmen are on them trying to get them shaped up again.

"What was my own secret in surviving the plebe year?

"Looking back I think, because I was older and had been in the Army and the Prep School, I felt a responsibility to help others who did not know as much as I did. I think by helping others it took my mind off my own problems. It definitely helps to get outside yourself."

The second account is from an Ann Arbor, Michigan firstclassman who is one of the regimental commanders. The interview was conducted two weeks before graduation when the cadet was looking forward to a two-month vacation, which was to include a four-week tour of France. After that, he was scheduled to go to the Infantry School at Fort Benning, Georgia, then to Fort Ord, California as a light infantry platoon leader. He said:

"I would like to start out trying to explain the Fourthclass System because I think it is important for anybody coming in here to understand it.

"First of all, the official mission of the Fourthclass System and what cadets perceive it to be is often quite different. The official mission is to teach the fourthclassmen what it is like to be a subordinate in a hierarchal system, which is what the Army is. The mission is to teach them discipline, self control and how to perform in a structured environment. But the official mission also has a dual purpose; it is also supposed to teach the upperclassmen about realistic Army-style leadership—how to lead subordinates at the entry level in such a way that the leaders earn the respect of the subordinates.

"Unfortunately, I would say that most upperclassmen see it as a system to put plebes under stress—for two reasons.

"First, is what we call the 'stress injection theory'—that if you give it [stress] to them now, then later, when they are confronted with similar stressful situations like combat, then they will find it more easy to adapt.

"Second, you can weed out plebes who aren't suitable for West Point by putting them under stress and seeing how much they can take. Those who can't hack it will resign.

"The first theory is somewhat accepted by the Army, but we believe we can put them under stress without harassing or abusing them, and without treating them in an undignified manner.

"We also feel that it is inappropriate for cadet leaders to be weeding people out. The admission standards are high enough already. What we should try to do is meet those standards—and if they resign, it is because they have overcome our best efforts to keep them here.

"My problem this year, as a cadet leader responsible for implementing the Fourthclass System, was that my views tended to coincide with the institutional mission, but were not the views of many in my support groups. Despite my best efforts, they [his subordinates] engaged in activities that were abusive of plebes at times.

"For example, we had an incident during reorganization week—the week when everyone was moving back to West Point, and when many of the upperclassmen get their first look at the plebes. This week is the traditional time to annoy the plebes and one squad leader in one of my companies had a plebe cite knowledge to him in the latrine for about an hour and a half. Believe me, that is not one of the worst things that can happen, but it was a clear violation of the guidelines. Under the circumstances it was not an activity that would develop the cadet and make him a better cadet, and he was needlessly taking the plebe's valuable time.

"I found out about that about a month after it occurred—not through the cadet chain of command—and I wanted this individual [the squad leader] suitably punished. But the platoon leader, and company and battalion commanders felt the squad leader had done nothing bad enough for him to be punished. They felt that he was basically a good cadet and that what he did was not that bad. So, because I did not have the support of the cadet commanders in the chain of command, I let the squad leader off.

"In general I think that cadets tend to talk in a disrespectful manner to the plebes because they [the plebes] are not accepted into the Corps yet, and when you get right down to it, it is a rite of passage that the plebes have to go through. That is not what it should be, but what it is right now. It is one year of hazing—we are officially trying to eliminate that word—without physical abuse. It is not like a fraternity-style hell week. It is mental pressure, and, when combined with the physical demands, it creates an intensely stressful year—at the end of which, having proved yourself, you are ceremoniously accepted into the Corps as a full-fledged individual—this is, in fact, what the Fourthclass System is now.

"Physical hazing, which used to be common at West Point, is almost never seen. I, personally, have seen it twice in four years. In both cases a plebe was required to hold out his arms with palms up, and after one of the instances, the upperclassman was punished.

"The upperclassman still speak harshly to plebes who are undeserving of that kind of treatment. Also, they still belittle them and there are a fair amount of insults given. But we are making slow, discernable progress, and I have seen it in the four years I have been here. However, I would like to emphasize that progress is very slow, and if we wish to continue giving cadets the authority to implement the Fourthclass System, progress will continue to be slow.

"It is a tradeoff. If the officers supervising the system were more heavy handed, things would change quickly. But then the cadets wouldn't have as much responsibility. So how fast do we want to move and how much authority do we give the cadets? After all, if the cadets don't practice using authority here, they won't learn it.

"From my perspective I would advise the incoming candidates that they should take a lot of the bad treatment with a grain of salt. Remember, all of the upperclassmen leading you are inexperienced leaders and many of them are administering it [the Fourthclass System] in incorrect ways. If you realize that, some of the less good things that happen to you will be easier to bear. For instance, you don't

172

want to get worked up because you can't cut dessert into equal pieces—or you don't want to think that you're stupid because you didn't know three articles on the front page of the New York Times. You should never believe that you are a worthless individual. You shouldn't let them reduce your self esteem.

"Keep a mental catalog of those things done as bad examples and good examples, and keep those in mind when you become a yearling [thirdclassman] and practice good leadership. It's what we call the "duffel bag" theory of leadership. You'll see all kinds of leadership examples to put in the bag. But the leadership that coerces you or fails utterly to motivate you will be more prevalent during plebe year than any other.

"Also, they need to realize there is more to West Point than surviving the plebe year. Too often the attitude is, now that I am a yearling or cow [third-or secondclassman] and not fighting for my life every day, I can just coast along. My advice is don't just concentrate on surviving here; concentrate on doing well during all four years. I would encourage them to focus on what interests them and to become involved in as many things as they can—sports, physical conditioning, leadership in the cadet chain of command—anything that will allow them to get more out of the West Point experience.

"One common misconception of those who come here is that they will have it made when they get into the Army— that the West Point graduate has an advantage in the Army over officers who come from ROTC, for example. That might have been true several years ago, but that advantage is fast disappearing. The promotion rates of ROTC officers has a tendency to be right on line with West Point graduates and the percentage of general officers as West Pointers has continued to decline. The point is, when you come here, do not think you will automatically graduate as a better officer than someone who has gone through another program. You have to work at learning leadership here. You have to want to be a good leader.

"I found that too many cadets have a blind trust that it is just going to happen because they are here. Too many think leadership is just giving an order and seeing that it

173

When you are a new cadet and plebe, it helps to believe that the upperclassmen are really trying to develop you into a better person.

is carried out. Here, in the cadet chain of command, you learn that your subordinates don't always agree—many of my orders and directives were not executed like I wanted them to be. You learn that in any organization you have to make compromises even if you have seniority. You have to listen to junior leaders or they will think they have no credibility.

"But you also may have to do some hard things. For example, I had one clear case of Fourthclass System abuse

174

and I dealt with it harshly. But, I am going to be a platoon leader next year and I don't want to go into that job cold turkey—I have to be ready to make harsh decisions when they are needed.

"But new cadets are different from army troops. They are intelligent, extremely subordinate and scared. But they should be treated like any entry level troops. We should get them to do things because they want to—if we can. The goal is not just to coerce them and see how badly they can screw up—a lieutenant doing that with regular troops won't last long. Upperclassmen here don't always think that way, partly because they don't know what real Army leadership is like, and because the upperclassmen who abuse the system are their buddies and they don't want to do anything about it.

"My last bit of advice would be to concentrate on academic survival rather than just plebe survival. Take time to study every night—there's nothing more important than the books regardless of what an upperclassman will tell you. The yearling down the hall can't kick you out for not shining your shoes but the math department can. You'll get more out of concentrating on the books—if you must make a choice.

"And if you do get into academic difficulty, don't completely ignore your fourthclass knowledge, but do let your leaders know that you have a problem. For example, if you are asked to do something that interferes with some critical homework, say to the upperclassman, 'Sir, can I make a statement.' Then, tell the upperclassman that you are in trouble. Say, 'Sir, I'm failing math class.' Doing this, you will learn that the upperclassman aren't totally negative. Most of them are great when it comes to helping someone with their academics. Just don't be afraid to ask for help.

"I would like to sum up what our overall philosophy is regarding the Fourthclass System. In one phrase we say that we want it to be 'demanding but not demeaning.'

"Why demanding? We are in the business of developing leaders and well-rounded individuals. You can't develop people when you don't put great demands on them. We feel if we are undemanding, we are not going to get the most out of them—and they don't get the most out of themselves.

"Nobody comes here wanting it to be easy. They shouldn't and it would be a mistake and the nation would be cheated. We do put people under harsh academic demands and physical demands, and, in general, we get a better batch of graduates. Of course, some of this is applicable to any of the prestigious academic institutions—they put great academic demands on their students and because of it, they get a better product."

The next firstclassman was, at the time of the interview, Deputy Brigade Commander—the number two cadet officer at West Point. It was just before graduation, when he was looking forward to his Officers' Basic Training at Fort Sill [in Artillery] and then to his assignment in the First Armored Division in Germany. He said:

"The biggest thing for me [then] and any fourthclassman [in the future] is adapting to two different components: individual and group survival.

"The first part—individual survival—is a highly personal thing; it is something you have to do on your own. And to do it, you have to know who you are and what you are and you have to come to terms with that.

"But you also have to know, or learn, that you can't make it on your own; you must have the support of your classmates.

"I think the latter is a bigger problem for fourthclassmen to cope with. The problem is that everybody who comes in here is in some way very talented, very gifted, and they are used to having their own way as leaders. What happens, if they try to keep that independence, is that they find themselves as an individual facing an experience on their own—something that can't be done without help. You WILL learn that you need group support.

"That is the lesson that takes the longest. To learn it quicker, be prepared to learn as much about yourself as possible. What you learn will disappoint you to some degree, but DON'T HOLD YOURSELF BACK FROM OTHER PEOPLE. Ask for help and offer to give help.

"During the fourthclass period, especially at the very beginning, they will feel that the upperclassmen have singled them out in particular and that they have discovered every

176

weakness they have ever had, and found everything they have done wrong. When you find out that EVERYBODY feels the same way, it makes it easier to accept.

"What I'm saying comes from experience. I had a problem adapting to the group because of my independence. When I was a fourthclassman, I had a member of the cadre call me in and tell me he thought I was selfish. He talked to me for about an hour. When he was done, I went back to my room and thought about it and realized it was true. Of course, you might not find out that way; you will probably have to find it out for yourself.

"Advice for survival? One thing that helped me was to think of all the people before me who had already gone through the same thing. My attitude was, if they could do it, so can I.

"I came in here with wild-eyed idealism, expecting the absolute best. Now I am more realistic. I don't expect perfection—you don't get perfection in anything. My advice is to just accept what comes—and realize that it is a real test. Also, you will never get what you expect; everybody's experience is going to be unique.

"Another thing I would advise is to bear down on the studies. They [plebes] should realize that every effort will be made to make sure that they succeed academically. Help is always there—it is the personal interest of the professors. What they will have to decide is that they are going to use that help.

"This past year I talked with a lot of those who left. Many of them came here because they got a nomination; then they got accepted and felt they couldn't turn down such a good opportunity. There were others who came because brother went here or father thought it was a good idea. My advice is to come for yourself. If you are not here for that reason, it is very rare for some other kind of motivation to be enough to keep you here.

"Also they should realize that everybody gets down and thinks about quitting. That's normal. But when you are down and trying to make that decision, you have to get support outside of yourself. Do you know enough to make a decision or are you just quitting because your feelings are hurt? Are you surprised because it is not what you expected?

Talk to friends and the family. Usually friends are the best. I'll admit that they did a lot of talking to me when I was in Beast.

"The worst part is the yelling. Nobody can prepare you for it. But know that it is going to happen to everybody, although some may not get much and some will get a lot. It was a new experience for me and I found it distasteful. I had never been yelled at—somehow I expected it would be different if you tried to do things right. I got through it mostly by ignoring it. There's nothing else you can do. By yelling, somebody is trying to send you a message, not necessarily in their words; they're trying to get your attention.

"To withstand that, you have to know yourself and you have to have self-confidence. You have to believe that you are a worthwhile person. You have to believe that they can say nothing that will discourage you. Really, everybody wants to see the new cadets succeed and make it—but it is not easy—if it was easy it would be worthless.

"I will also make a comment that might be thought sexist, but it needs to be said. I think women have more of a tendency to take criticism personally and because of that, they tend to get down on themselves. I don't think many of them have ever been tested in adverse situations—they've pretty much had life their own way up to this point. They have to realize that nobody is going to pat them on the head and tell them they are doing well. I think women are used to a lot more expression of approval and they aren't going to get that here. Here, nobody is going to cut you any slack.

"Also, this place can be hard on males who come in with sexist feelings. It will be hard on some of them to have females yelling at them. My advice is, if you are coming in with old fashion views, you had better get ready to change them. Our philosophy is: men and women are different but soldiers are not. If they are good at what they do, it makes no difference whether they are men or women. In that way West Point is a great equalizer; you are judged on what you do, not on who you are.

"As a rule, plebes are more sensitive to women exerting authority because they don't expect it—while they are expecting it from men. But in any case, the women are a minority and the things they do are going to be emphasized...and some will create legends. From my viewpoint there are good women here and good men here, and there are equal proportions of mediocre ones of both sexes.

"Regardless of sex, there are some plebes who will catch more than others—they are called "spazes." I ran into this problem a lot last summer—some of the firstclassmen thought they were doing everybody a favor by riding a new plebe so hard he would resign. That is a stupid attitude, but you should come in here knowing that you will encounter it from some. However, I do think that the feeling of plebes that somebody is out to get rid of them is overexaggerated.

"Interestingly, some of the guys who were terrible plebes turned out to be some of the best upperclassmen. Conversely, some of the best plebes didn't turn out as well as expected.

"My personal opinion is that those who have had a hard time at the beginning become the most resilient cadets— they end up better than somebody who did fairly well and hadn't been challenged.

"Basically, I think everyone should keep this motto in mind: It is not what you were or what you could be but what you are today.

"Also, it has been my observation that the upperclassmen who are the hardest on plebes were the worst plebes themselves. I think they fully expect that that is the way they are supposed to act. That was their experience so they don't know any better. And they're really good at it because they received a lot and they know how to give it. Nobody comes in here knowing how to yell in somebody's face. You have to learn that. Nobody comes in here thinking that is expected—they know how to do it after seeing it done. Also, they figure they have gone through their test so everybody else has to pass the test.

"It is everybody's job to help develop the fourthclassmen. However, I object to the people who consider it an adversary process where you have to scream and yell at them. Upperclassmen of this type are not the only problem, however. There are those who don't want to do anything. There are some who are selfish and don't feel they

179

Part of the difficulty of surviving the plebe year is the variety of leadership styles to which you must adapt. But this is good, say the upperclassmen, because you get the opportunity to select the leadership style that best suits you.

should waste their time messing with the fourthclassmen. That's wrong, too. Anybody who cares about the fourthclassmen wants to help them. Really, there is nothing worse than just standing there by yourself. Attention is good even if bad. [Author's comment: most plebes would not agree.]

"What I tried to teach was positive leadership and I always tried to be an example. For instance, I went to the fourthclassmen's rooms and if they were shining shoes, I would talk to them for ten or fifteen minutes, giving them hints, and telling them how it was for me. I wanted to encourage them, not beat them down. And I believe there are as many people like me as there are screamers and yellers. But probably the vast majority are somewhere in the middle. They don't want to bother plebes unless they do something wrong right in front of them. Most people feel sorry for them [the plebes] to some extent. They know they have to make it on their own and that if they do, it is going to make them into better persons.

"Sure, I had people who were hard on plebes, who insulted them. But the best thing that can happen is for a firstclassman to take them aside and say, 'You don't have to do that.' I have done that to upperclassmen many times. And people have done it to me, too. There were times I have said things in anger or in a moment of callousness, and I've been told about it. But that is what leadership training is all about. We're supposed to be made aware of our mistakes and be forced to learn from them.

"I'm leaving now and I'm really pleased with some of the changes that we have been able to make—changes that will make leadership training more positive and more in keeping with what the Army is like.

"For example, when I came here, all plebes had to 'ping' everywhere they went—they had to walk at this crazy, awkward gait—which was demeaning, and they had to swing their arms in an exaggerated way. I always felt that it was required because it made the plebes look silly—pinging came in several years ago after the plebes were no longer required to double-time [run] everywhere. Now that I'm leaving, I'm happy to say that we won't see that again. Now the plebes are going to walk like normal people—faster, of course, and along certain routes, but at least they won't look silly. I'm really happy about this change.

"Another change I'm happy to see is the change in mess hall behavior. Starting this semester, the plebes can dine at ease—they don't have to sit rigidly as before.

"As a final thought I would ask you [the author] to put something in that book from me. Would you please tell them [the candidates] that there are an awfully lot of upperclassmen who want to be sure the fourthclassmen make it. Tell them that most of us, when we are giving them a hard time, are doing it because we want them to grow and develop. We know we have become better persons because of our West Point experiences and we want them to have the same opportunities. If they will keep that in mind going through plebe year, it will help them a lot."

EIGHTEEN
HOW TO GET ALONG WITH CLASSMATES AND ROOMMATES

If you go to a civilian college, you can be a loner. Or, you can pick your friends and associate with whomever you desire.

Not at West Point. During plebe year you will be placed in a room with two others, and whether you like it or not, you will have to share your life with those persons. You have no choice in the matter. Your roommates are a necessary factor in your survival.

Also, at a civilian college you are free to remain as anonymous as you would like to be. You can remain a private person. Your faults can be concealed and, for the most part, your actions, so long as they are acceptable in the liberal society of most campuses, are your own business and none of the business of others.

Not at West Point. At West Point you will spend all four years in a fishbowl. You will most likely stay in the same company for the entire period, and many of its one-hundred members will know almost everything there is to know about you. They will know your strengths and your faults, your likes and your dislikes, your conquests and your failures, your romances won and lost. During those four years it is almost impossible to retain any degree of privacy. The results of your words and deeds spread quickly in the close living quarters of a barracks. And if your words and deeds do not meet the conservative standards of those in your company, you can expect to be reproached.

What does this mean to you as a candidate?

It means that you should go to West Point prepared to do everything you can to get along with your classmates and roommates. The purpose of this chapter is to give you the knowledge you need to make that preparation.

The natural desire of any plebe is to be as inconspicuous as possible—to be a "ghost" in the words of the cadets. However, that desire conflicts with the obligations of plebes to move about the halls delivering laundry and mail, and to accomplish the other chores that fall upon them in the company. By exposing themselves in the halls they become fair game for any upperclassman who sees the need for a little plebe development. In the minds of the plebes such exposure is hazardous and the natural tendency is for them to keep it to a minimum.

But do not become one of those faint-hearted ghosts who shun the barracks and plebe responsibilities say the cadets. "I can sympathize with a classmate who wants to ghost out," said a plebe. "Who wants to deliver an upperclassman's laundry just so you can get smoked and flamed? But everybody in the company eventually learns who the ghosts are. The upperclassmen will eventually get on them harder. And they don't earn respect from their classmates. Some ghosts see it as a no-win situation. But I don't agree. It's better in the long run to take the hassle and be respected by your classmates."

The plebes who are "Corps Squad" (intercollegiate) athletes have a special problem. They eat at tables where they are free from the hassling other plebes endure, and they are excused from certain duties. It is easy for such plebes to extend their immunity from upperclass pressure using athletic excuses to stretch their time out of the company area and to become a ghost.

Do not do that if you end up being one of those athletes. That was the advice of cadets and officers who commented on this problem. Said one of the professors, a four-year football letterman, when asked what he would do differently if he were a plebe again and could use his 20-20 hindsight, "There is no question in my mind that the biggest mistake I made was not doing as much in the company as I could have done. I used athletics to ghost out of a lot of the duties and to avoid the hazing. You don't win points with your classmates for that, and if I had it to do over again, I would make an extra effort to pull my weight."

Getting along with roommates is a much more difficult challenge said the cadets. There are several reasons why.

It is essential that roommates cooperate with each other in a host of tasks that have to be accomplished. (For many

Roommates have to share the work, their possessions and themselves. But the reward is friendships that last a lifetime.

years the slogan has been, "cooperate and graduate.") Strict standards of cleanliness and neatness are rigidly enforced. All the necessary cleaning and shining cannot be done in the severely limited time allotted to such work without the best efforts of all three roommates.

But roommate cooperation goes beyond the cleaning and the polishing. Roommates have to look out for each other as well. They have to anticipate their mutual problems, many of which probably seem mundane. For example, it is extremely important for the roommates to look over each other's uniform, particularly for lint. If a plebe (or any cadet) shows up at a formation with pieces of lint on his shoulder or back, that is damning evidence against the roommates who let the plebe down by failing to inspect properly before the plebe left the room.

If a plebe is late getting to the room before noon formation, roommates have to anticipate all the things that the plebe might need for a quick change of clothes. Do the roommate's shoes need more shining? Is the roommate's brass polished well enough? Have all parts of the roommate's uniform been given their first inspection for lint? Those are the kinds of anticipatory questions that must be asked as a prelude to action. Otherwise the late plebe is headed for trouble.

And so are the roommates!

The West Point cadets do not take kindly to roommates who do not look after each other. For example, during an inspection, if one of three roommates has shoes not properly shined, it is not the sinner who is punished. It is the other two roommates who have "dicked" on their roommate who will incur the wrath of the inspectors.

The cadets use the term "dicking" for any kind of behavior where cadets make themselves look good at the expense of others. In the case of the plebe with shoes not adequately shined, the two roommates have to take the blame because they didn't see to it that the third roommate shined his shoes properly. They dicked the roommate because they made themselves look good at his (or her) expense.

Punishments for such offenses are sometimes hard to take, say the cadets, especially when the individuals who are punished are independent types who have always taken pride in their own accomplishments.

For example, how are you going to feel after you have hustled and made yourself ready for a formation, yet have to wait in the room for a roommate who, comparatively speaking, has been dawdling along. You do not dare leave such a roommate and go to the formation without him. That would really incur the wrath of the upperclassmen. But, if you have to wait on the roommate, it is certain that you will be late for the formation and in just as much trouble.

Are you ready for that—you who are the exalted kings and queens of your high schools—you who are never late and who would do almost anything to avoid such transgressions? The cadets say that you probably are not. They were not, and many poignant stories of their roommate educations were heard.

The worst problem, which you can hope you will not have, is the slothful roommate who refuses to adapt to the team effort. There are always some of this type who feel that cleaning floors and windows is beneath them. Others object to what they believe are ridiculously strict standards. No matter how badly the roommates are criticized or punished, there are always some who steadfastly believe that their sink is clean enough, their shoes and brass polished enough.

A father, who himself was a graduate, told of an extreme case that affected his son. "He [the son] went to the Academy with extreme enthusiasm and high hopes," said the father. "And he was doing wonderfully. He loved Beast Barracks and the whole Fourthclass System. He was on his way to being an outstanding plebe. But there was a problem with one of his roommates. He [the roommate] would never do his share of the work. He felt that it was beneath his dignity. Of course, my son and the other roommate caught all the flack. Well, this went on for almost the whole first semester, the two roommates trying to cover for the other and tough it out until the semester was over and they would change roommates. [It is a policy to switch roommates every semester.] But, unfortunately, there was a crisis just before Christmas and my son's good roommate got in a fight with the kid who had been the problem. The fight only lasted for a few seconds, but later my son was given severe punishment—along with the other two—for not stopping the fight. Ironically, the kid who was the problem was flunking his classes at the time and he left before his punishment could be carried out. The other two walked theirs off, but the experience really soured my son on the whole West Point experience for the next couple of years. Thankfully, by the time he was a firstclassman, he had put the experience behind him."

During the interview with the Deputy Brigade Commander who was quoted in the previous chapter, the above experience was related and he was asked what advice he would give a candidate who might be unlucky enough to get such a roommate. The Deputy Brigade Commander replied:

"I think you have to confront a guy like that and keep confronting him until he changes. And if that doesn't work, take it outside. [The father who related the story said the two roommates were afraid to report their problem to their superiors.] I don't agree that you can't do that. I would have talked to my squad leader about it; I wouldn't have let the problem keep building. I would have asked for a new roommate and I would have gone back to the room and told the roommate [the problem roommate] what I had done. I would have explained that the problem was getting out of hand and if it continued, there would be a confrontation which would be bad for us all. Personally, I wouldn't mind carrying somebody who is trying, who is making an effort, but I don't think any upperclassman is going to object to a complaint when the problem is severe. After all, the upperclassmen doing the room inspections already know about the problem—they know what is going on."

Following that reply, the firstclassman went on to tell of a problem he had with one of his roommates. He passed on his own advice on how to survive with roommates and classmates. His comments follow:

"It just so happens that my most difficult problem during plebe year was a roommate problem. There were three of us, which is normal, but two of us turned out to like each other and we became friends, while the third one was not particularly cared for by either of us. We had some of the same problems you described. Things were not getting done in the room and there was constant disagreement. However, in our case, there was also an honor problem, and we ended up having to turn him in and testify against him. He was not found [a term meaning that he was not found guilty of the honor offense], but after the semester he was moved to another company. I know he was guilty and it bothers me now that he is graduating with the rest of us, especially since my other roommate and good friend has physical problems and can't graduate until next December—hopefully. That whole experience was disillusioning to me, also, and I can understand how that other cadet felt.

"But I would give anyone coming in here some basic advice about dealing with roommates. First, you are going

187

to have at least ten different roommates during the four year period [two during each semester of plebe year and, normally, one each subsequent semester] and the key to surviving is to make up your mind that you are going to get along with each other. There is really no other choice, unless there is a drastic problem. Your roommates will end up being the most important people in your life and you will almost always end up being best friends.

"Why? Because you have to look out for each other all the time and you have to share so much. And with everything else that goes on here, you don't need stress or strife where you live. I had a certain attitude every semester when I got a new roommate. I'd go into the relationship knowing that I am going to get along with him and that we will become good friends because that is the way it has to be and at the beginning I have to make every effort to be sure that it is true.

"There is one word of caution I would pass on. You can request that a good friend be assigned as your next roommate but I don't recommend that. I think a relationship between close friends can be too distracting. I know I did my best academic work when I had roommates who were good academically. Their study habits helped me develop good study habits. I know if I had my closest friends as roommates, I would not have spent as much time studying.

"What does a good roommate do? First, you have to share, not just your things, but you have to share yourself, also. You have to be willing to talk to them about anything. You have to remember that when any two people have to live in such close proximity, it is always the little things that bother you or irritate you.

"But the best way to handle those problems is to be straight up front about it. It takes some diplomacy. Sometimes you joke about the problem; sometimes you have to be serious about it. But don't let things build up—that is when you really get problems. If you wait two months while you hate his music, he uses your towel, leaves the sink dirty and clogged with hair, and constantly borrows your razor and runs the battery down—then you are going to have a big fight, eventually. You can't let things like that build up for two months. You have to solve such problems quickly.

188

"I personally always went into a new situation saying that whatever I leave out you can have—if you need it, go ahead and use it. But everybody needs some privacy and also I think you should always show respect for the other person's property. When you do need to use something of your roommate's, it is better to say something like, 'I'm going to use your razor, all right?' Or, 'Do you mind if I borrow some toothpaste?' This is just courtesy and with that, sharing never becomes a big sticking point.

"And you have to work out problems. The typical one is the roommate who thinks he has to have the music on to study while the other roommate can't concentrate with the music on. But that is easy to resolve. Use headphones. Say, 'Hey, I need it quiet, so can you use a Walkman or whatever.'

"A lot of times you and your roommate are going to have different friends. It's going to happen that his friends want to come in and have pizza parties. In such a case you have to say something or be diplomatic and leave.

"Or maybe the guy has a girlfriend who comes by all the time and disrupts your studying or eats all your food. You just have to find a way to go along or solve the problem in some other way.

"Everybody likes to do different things at different times, but since everybody has to get up at the same time and use the one sink, there is a potential conflict. But you have to work it out. You stagger the times, either you or he using it five or ten minutes earlier.

"And you're bound to have problems. I guarantee that you will get somebody that you don't care for, or somebody you liked before but can't room with because you discovered that he is a neatness freak or that he likes heavy metal at 120 decibels—suddenly you find out when you can't get anything done.

"The key is, don't let it build up. Make sure the problem stays small. And remember, if you do let something go trying to be a nice guy, it has a way of becoming serious very fast. But by dealing with the problems quickly and not letting them build up, I have never had a serious problem with a roommate [since the first semester].

"Another key is to share the duties and cover for each other. There will always be times, such as when you are a plebe and have to count off minutes before meals for the upperclassmen. If your roommate hasn't showed up in time to do that some noon, don't wait; step out there and do it for him. And you should be able to expect the same from him—and don't worry if you have to do it more often. It will drive you crazy if you try to keep track of who does what for whom.

"On the other hand there has to be some equity and if one of the roommates isn't doing his fair share, there are going to be problems.

"But the most important thing to remember is to share. Check each other off [check all aspects of the uniform and rifle] before going to formation. Help each other with classes—maybe one is good in math and the other is great in military science. And look out for each other. If one is getting out of shape, say, 'Let's go running together.' Or, 'I see you had problems with pushups; let's do fifty before going to bed.' And share the good things. Say to him, 'I just got a boodle [food and goodies] package. Want some cookies?'

"Don't let problems build up. Go into a relationship determined to look out for your roommate and to share with him. Those are the keys. That's what will let you leave the relationship as very good friends."

NINETEEN
ACADEMIC SURVIVAL TIPS

A staff person who has worked with hundreds of cadets in academic trouble was commenting on some of their problems.

"The sad thing," she said, "is that they can take all of the criticism from the upperclassman and their Tac Officer. They seem to adapt to that without too much trouble. But when they get low grades on their first exams and papers they can't accept that. Many of them have never had a "C" before and when they get "D's" and "F's," it is very traumatic.

Notice she said WHEN they get "D's" and "F's," as if it is the normal course of events.

It is the normal course of events for many of the plebes. Those who were not held accountable for their assignments in high school and who were bright enough to get high grades just by listening in class are the ones who have problems. They have problems because they did not have to learn how to study.

Plebes will learn to study at West Point or they will go home. Those are clear, black and white choices and there are no alternatives. Write the last part of that statement down in your mind. There are no alternatives.

This chapter is for those who want to be ready for the academic crunch when they get to West Point. Mostly it is a collection of do's and don't's picked up from cadets, graduates and former cadets who are now back on the faculty.

WHEN YOU ARE IN CLASS

Sit in the front row and as close to the professor as you can. This will help keep you alert—many days you will be tired and struggling to stay awake. Also, your physical presence in such a prominent position will subtly motivate you to be better prepared. By taking such a position you are less likely to "blow off" an assignment say the cadets.

191

Take good notes, especially in classes where the primary material to be learned is presented by the lecture method.

To make your notes more effective as a study-aid, the following method is recommended by the person in charge of the cadet How To Study Program.

Using a ruler, divide each page of your notebook into two sections, with two-thirds of the space on the right and one-third on the left.

Write your notes in class on the right side of the page. And while you are writing the notes, pay close attention to the lecturer's manner and tone of voice. Most have some way of signaling the things that they think are most important. Be alert and underline those things in your notes.

After class, go through the notes and find the main concepts and key words and write them on the left side of the page. In addition, highlight those things the professor indicated as important. If you do a good job of this analysis, the left side of your notes should be transformed into the "study" side of the page. It should have the high priority facts, concepts and vocabulary—the material that will most likely be asked for on future tests.

STUDY TIME:

In the evenings prior to next-day classes (Sunday through Thursday) there are hours set aside for mandatory study. The specific times may change, depending upon the current administration's philosophy. However, there are generally three or four hours set aside prior to taps, which, currently, is at midnight.

During this mandatory study time, no other activities can be scheduled. More important for the plebes, this time cannot be interrupted by upperclass cadets for plebe development.

Most cadets who were interviewed admitted that they initially made very poor use of this allotted study time. What follows is a series of recommendations based upon their 20-20 hindsight and upon their own modified study behaviors.

The first thing you should do is make a time budget. You may be familiar with a money budget, which is a schedule for how available money is to be spent and for

If you have never made a time budget, get help! Remember that there are many who will be eager to help you if you are determined to help yourself.

what. Its purpose is to protect whomever the budget is made for. If the budget is followed, there should always be enough money available for each item in the budget whenever it is needed.

A time budget is not much different. For example, suppose as a plebe that you will have three and one-half hours of study time available for the evening. That is the bottom line for your budget. You cannot (or should not—more later) spend more than that.

The first step in making the time budget is to analyze your homework assignments. This is a critical step, and one that most plebes do poorly.

The analysis requires you to look realistically at what you have to do. But it also requires something much more difficult. It requires you to decide on what you ARE NOT going to do.

Not going to do?

Absolutely. According to the cadets (and several professors who had been cadets), you are never going to have enough time to do everything that you want to do.

Therefore, your time analysis is an act of prioritization—a process of setting priorities. What you must do is decide which homework has the highest priority for your grade standing. Are you beginning to have trouble in math? Are you afraid that you are going to fall behind in math and get into academic hot water? If so, math has to take a high priority. You have to give your math homework whatever time is needed.

And what about work for chemistry, English, psychology and history? Which have priority in terms of your grade standing and which have assignments that must be done this evening?

Those are the questions that should be asked.

Then decisions must be made and time allotted for each subject. Mentally, the process goes something like this:

I must spend two hours on the math because it has the highest priority. There will be a chemistry quiz tomorrow and I'm behind on studying my notes—I have to allow at least one hour for that. That leaves thirty minutes, which I had better spend on the English essay that is due day after tomorrow. And the psychology and history? I'll just have to gamble that I won't be called on to recite—and if I am, I'll just have to take the hit.

Then what?

Formalize the time budget. Put down on paper the starting and ending times for each study period. Then set your alarm clock so you will not get busy and run overtime. (Cadets say wristwatch alarms are very useful, especially if you are studying in the library or in an empty classroom.)

Also, it is important to schedule a break between each study period, or in the middle of a long one. This should be looked upon as a reward for your diligent work.

On the break, get up and walk around. Eat or drink something. Visit with your roommate or a friend. In general, do anything that will refresh your mind and seem like a reward.

Cadets say they mentally ridiculed the time budget idea when it was first proposed to them. It sounded good, they said, but it seemed too formal, too much like a recommendation coming out of a book.

But they had nothing but praise for the idea after they had begun to use it—which, for several, was after they were flunking and they were required to submit time budgets as a part of their probation.

"You don't overlook something staring you in the face," was a typical comment.

"If it's in front of you and the clock is ticking, you pay a lot more attention to what you're doing," was another.

What about listening to music while studying? That option is usually available sometime after Christmas when the plebes are allowed to have a stereo.

The majority of cadets and midshipmen who were interviewed at all three service academies said that they could do better, more efficient studying without the music. Many of them admitted that they believed otherwise when they were in high school and that they had changed their minds after encountering much more demanding assignments.

However, there was a minority who still believed they could study better with music. The drowning out of noise in the barracks was the most common benefit that was cited.

Besides the time budget, the cadets also emphasized that certain study techniques have helped them.

For example, it is not a good idea just to open a textbook to the first page of the assignment and start reading. You are like a rat trying to get through a maze when you do that. You do not have any idea where you are going. All you know is that you are going somewhere. And you have to do a lot of unproductive backtracking.

Leaf through the pages of your assignment before you start reading. Get an overview of what it is you have to learn. (That is like looking at the top of the maze to see where you have to go to get through it.) Mentally catalog what you know and do not know about the content of the assignment. Then, to test yourself, check off in your mind all of the things you are going to learn.

Some textbooks have a summary of what you are going to learn at the beginning of each chapter. Ignore those, say the cadets. Just reading those summaries is not enough. It is the tour through the pages of the assignment that is important. Also it is important to have firmly in mind what it is you are going to learn. Seeing it page by page while evaluating what you know and do not know is far more important than just reading a summary.

The next step depends upon the difficulty of the subject. If it is a hard assignment like fifteen pages in a chemistry text, it is far better first to read the pages fairly rapidly. Read to get a general understanding of the concepts. Also you should identify and highlight the most difficult material—the parts of the assignment that will require slow, repetitive reading the next time through.

And the first time through the assignment, forget about trying to memorize the new vocabulary. Just learn to pronounce the words—that is the most important first step. It is very difficult to remember any word that you cannot pronounce.

The next step is to reread the assignment slowly. And when you come to the difficult material that you highlighted, read that material two or three times, or whatever is necessary for you to understand it.

Math assignments require a special technique. You may recall from Chapter Four that the math department does not teach like you were taught in high school. At West Point math assignments are not explained before you have to do homework problems. You have to read the textbook assignment and figure out how to do the problems yourself—then be prepared to demonstrate on the chalkboard what you have learned the next day.

Most plebes do not take enough time studying the textbook before they start on the problems. Typically, they skim the author's explanation and charge right ahead, wanting to get the problems solved as fast as they can.

That is a big mistake said both math professors and cadets. Spend twice as much time as you first think is necessary studying the author's explanation. And most important, study the way the author solves the sample problem or problems. MAKE SURE YOU UNDERSTAND EACH STEP.

That is very critical, because as you move through the text, the author tends to eliminate steps in his examples—steps that were shown earlier. If you do not understand each

West Point cadets know how to stand before a group and speak because they get lots of practice.

step in the problems as you go through each assignment, you are headed for certain trouble. Eventually, you will not understand how the author is solving the sample problems and you will have no choice but to go back, perhaps many pages, and try to figure it all out. This is a disaster, especially if you are already struggling in the class.

Some cadets are enthusiastic believers in making an outline of each reading assignment. The process forces the reader to pull out and write down the main ideas in the text. It also forces the reader to identify and explain each new fact and term. Advocates of the process also stress that the outline is far easier to study than the text, especially in the last minutes before a test.

WEEKENDS

For most people weekends are mini-vacations. They are for travel, for play, for hobbies and games, or just plain sleep and rest.

You probably became conditioned to weekend mini-vacations while you were in high school. You slept in on at least one of those days, right? And, did you not feel that the two days out of school were vacation time you were owed by the school itself, or at least something that you had earned after five straight days of getting up early and attending classes?

Most cadets said they felt that way. They said they felt like they were being cheated if they did not get their weekends to do as they pleased.

If you feel that way, get ready for some bad news.

You are not going to get many free weekends at West Point.

And the sooner you get your mind programmed to accept that, the sooner you can own an insurance policy for academic survival.

Cadets who have pulled themselves out of academic fires are the most vocal in praising the value of weekend study.

One value of studying weekends is that it allows time for catch-up studies. If you are behind in reading, the weekend is the time to catch up. If you need to work on math problems that you did not understand last week, do it on a weekend when you can get help from another cadet.

But the greatest value of weekends, say the cadets, is that they allow you TO GET AHEAD.

"Surely you are kidding," the author said when he first heard that idea propounded. "I'm an old high school teacher and I have NEVER seen students do work before it was assigned."

Well, the author is convinced now that some miracles do happen at the service academies. He became convinced after seeing the enthusiasm of cadets who do it.

Every professor in every class hands out a syllabus on the first day. That syllabus has every assignment for the semester and that is what the cadets use on weekends to get a head start on the next week's homework.

"It gives you a tremendous sense of relief to wake up Monday morning knowing that you have already done a lot of the hard stuff for the week." That was a typical comment.

Your weekdays are intense...

Another typical comment: "The best thing about it is that it gives you a large block of time, which you need to do papers and essays. Also, it's a great feeling not to have the worry of a paper hanging over your head. You don't feel guilty all the time."

A former cadet (of another academy), now a professor and counselor of cadets in academic trouble had this to say: "My plebe year was a nightmare—the worst year of my life. I almost flunked some classes and I barely managed to get a two-point. But the second year I started working ahead on the weekends. Sure, I also took some time off—you have to do that. But I also outlined every one of my assignments for the week ahead. Then it was a piece of cake. I was on the Dean's List both semesters the second year and on the Supe's [Superintendent's] List for the next two years. Part of it can be attributed to escaping the fourthclass hassle, but most of the credit was due to the fact that I used the weekends to get ahead."

There is also a practical reason for getting your papers and essays done ahead of time. All cadets have computers and practically all written assignments have to be done by word processing. However, the diskettes that store the writing have to be taken to a central area where there is a printer. That, it turns out, is a bottleneck.

When most cadets wait till the last minute to write their papers, they also tend to end up wanting to use a printer when others have the same need. (The problem is exacerbated when the printer you are counting on has broken down—a not uncommon happening.) Of course, by getting your writing projects finished ahead of time you can print them at your convenience.

Just one word of caution. Do not get so enthusiastic about working weekends that you forget to reward yourself with some time off. You cannot work all weekend without getting burned out. So, plan on some time off to do whatever you enjoy and can get away with in your company.

SCRAPS OF TIME

The last bit of advice comes from the retired head of the math department. It was revealed in a long interview and it is best explained in an abridged version of the person's own words:

But you should use the weekends for catching up and having fun.

"When I was a cadet, we were all brought together in the old theatre—we would all fit into the room at that time. We were there to hear a lecture by the famous historian, Douglas Southall Freeman, best known for his biography of Robert E. Lee.

"It was a great experience because he just rambled on about the little things he had learned in his lifetime—things that he had picked up that made his own life and work more efficient and enjoyable.

"I don't remember many of the details, except for one thing. He said that one of the things that helped him the most was when he began using his scraps of time.

"Scraps of time are the little blocks of unscheduled, free time that you have each day. One scrap of time might be five minutes before a class. Other scraps of time might be fifteen minutes before supper or thirty-five minutes before intramurals.

"The important idea that Southall Freeman left was that we should USE those scraps of time—that they should not be wasted.

"Well, later I came back as a math professor and I was reminded again what a hectic life the cadets lead. Of course, they have to learn time management or they won't survive, but when they came in for AI [additional instruction] and complained of not having enough time, I began to promote the scraps of time idea. I tried to convince them that they could do a lot of necessary things in the short blocks of time that normally go to waste.

"That experience convinced me that the idea needed a larger audience, so when I became the head of the department, I gave a lecture on the subject to the plebes. And purposely I ended the lecture early, saying, 'Now is your chance to apply what you have heard. I am letting you out early; now see what you can do with this scrap of time.'"

The "scraps of time" concept can be very helpful if you will use it. But you have to keep looking for things to do. If you are in your room and have only five minutes, do a five-minute task. Work on your shoes or brass. Clean the mirror. Straighten your roommate's top blanket. Dust the shelves and window ledge.

And when you have a period to kill between classes, do not waste the time walking back to your room and then back to class—especially if you are tempted to go back to your room and sleep. Instead, plan ahead so you will have study materials with you—materials that you can take into a vacant classroom and use to work on an assignment.

Here is a final tip, repeated from an earlier chapter. Whenever you get behind, you will be tempted to use a small reading lamp and study after taps. Cadets do it all the time even though it is against regulations. But resist that temptation because the loss of sleep will get you down and burn you out—to use two of the cadets' phrases.

If you get caught in a bind, use your weekends to catch up, or put off something else to the weekend and make good use of your assigned study time.

You need your sleep to stay healthy mentally and physically. Staying up after taps is about as foolish as using the walls of a building for firewood. Eventually the roof is going to cave in on you.

TWENTY
LIVING WITH
THE HONOR CODE

A cadet will not lie, cheat, or steal, nor tolerate those who do.

What you see above is the Code that every new cadet must live by at West Point. This is the Code that binds all the cadets to a common purpose, which is to live honorably at West Point and, later, as officers in the U.S. Army.

Thus, if you decide to go to West Point, you also have to be prepared to live with the Honor Code and the system that implements it.

And the system is not supervised by a committee of "black hoods" that snoops around looking for ways to bounce cadets out for honor violations. The system is administered solely by cadets who have been elected by their peers. So to live with the Honor Code, you have to be prepared to be a judge of your classmates' behavior and to have your behavior judged by them.

The cadet who is the administrator of the Honor System at West Point is a firstclassman with the title: Chairman of the Cadet Honor Committee. This Chairman explains how the system works:

"The program at West Point is run by the Cadet Honor Committee, which is made up of 80 cadets.

"Seventy-two of those cadets are Company Honor Representatives who are elected within their own companies. [Two representatives from each of 36 companies] Then there are four Regimental Honor Representatives and the Brigade Executive Staff. The latter includes the Chairman—my position—two Vice-Chairmen, one for education and one for investigations, and the Secretary.

"I want to stress that these higher positions are not appointive. We are elected by the honor reps from the companies and regiments. Unlike the other administrators, for example, the regimental and brigade commanders who

203

are picked by the officers at West Point, we are completely independent. This is very important. It guarantees that the Honor System stays in the hands of the cadets—and that makes it something the cadets can believe in.

"When the new cadets arrive, we spend a lot of time teaching them about the Code and the System. Last summer there were eight cadets who supervised the honor education for the new cadets during Beast Barracks. We believe those first hours of instruction are very important because they set the tone for the cadet's career.

"Later, during the academic year, the plebes have an additional six classes. In the other three years the cadets get three to five hours of instruction each year.

"This sounds like a lot of time but we feel that the better the cadets understand the System, the easier it will be to live with it.

"Many new cadets worry about the System. They are afraid that they will violate the Code unintentionally and get kicked out for it. Therefore, it is important for them to know how potential violations are handled—and how many checks we have in the System to be sure that it is administered fairly.

"Let's start with an incident and carry it through. Suppose a cadet sees something that he suspects is an honor violation. It is that cadet's duty to approach the suspected offender and try to clarify what he has seen.

"This first step in handling a potential violation is called the 'approach for clarification.' In the approach for clarification, two things can happen. One, the approaching cadet [the one who thinks a violation has occurred] can clear up the question and be satisfied that nothing really happened. Two, the cadet can decide that an honor violation has possibly occurred. Then the cadet says, 'I think you did violate the Code, and either you go to the representative or I will.'

"There are two reps in each company, one a second-classman and the other a firstie. What they do when they are notified of a potential offense is work together and do a company level investigation. They gather facts and written testimony from everyone involved, then make a recommendation to forward or drop. Then they give their evidence to the Regimental Honor Representative.

"The Vice-Chairman for Investigations will then review the case and decide to drop it, or further investigate the matter with an investigative team. These investigators will be company honor reps, but from a different company. What they do is conduct a complete investigation from an objective point of view, and then recommend that the case be dropped or forwarded. Then the case is again sent to the Vice-Chairman for Investigations. The regimental rep also attaches his own recommendation to the case.

"Note that the company honor reps are required to turn the case over to the regimental rep even if they think it should be dropped. The same goes for the regimental rep who must send it on to the Vice-Chairman for Investigation. Thus, the only cadet who can drop a case is the Vice-Chairman. This is important because it keeps honor interpreted the same throughout the Corps.

"Usually when the company reps recommend that a case be dropped, that is what happens. It is rare when a Vice-Chairman will overrule an investigative team.

"If the Vice-Chairman decides that an investigative hearing should be held, the documents are forwarded to the Commandant. This is the first officer who becomes formally involved with a case. The Commandant, then, has the authority to refer a case to a hearing. He also has the authority to drop a case; however, he cannot overrule the Honor Committee if the case is dropped.

"When a case goes to a full hearing, a committee of nine cadets, including four honor reps and five cadets at-large, will hear all the evidence. In the hearing this committee will hear all of the testimony from witnesses who have specific information to contribute regarding the allegation.

"A military lawyer, called the 'hearing officer', also sits in on the hearing just to make sure that due process is followed. But after the hearing, the nine cadets go into a room by themselves and discuss the case. Then they vote, and it takes a two-thirds vote to convict. Six out of the nine have to decide that an honor violation has, indeed, occurred.

"We think that it is important that a majority of the hearing committee be made up of cadets who are not honor reps. That way the cadets in the Corps will not think that their fate is solely in the hands of a "black hood gang" [the honor reps]. This, I believe, is what gives the cadets faith in the system.

"After the hearing, if the accused cadet is found [found guilty of an honor violation], the case goes to the Superintendent. He reviews the paperwork, and looks closely at the convicted cadet's record. He also interviews the cadet and judges the cadet's attitude about the offense. Then he makes a decision. He can retain the cadet. He can recommend separation. Or, he can suspend the cadet for a period of time.

"If the Superintendent recommends separation, the case goes on to the Secretary of the Army who makes the final decision—almost always in support of the Superintendent.

"If the Superintendent recommends suspension, it is probably because he feels that the individual is a cadet worth salvaging—that the cadet just made a dumb mistake and needs a few months away from West Point to mature and grow up. If a cadet is suspended, that cadet will usually come back in as a member of the next class—not back to his old class.

"What factors cause the Superintendent to separate some cadets and not others?

"One factor is the time under the Code—is the offender a plebe or a firstclassman? The fourthclassman would have a lot better chance of being retained because he may not quite grasp the importance of what he has done. Remember, the plebes are still immature—they're 17 or 18 years old—and retaining them is often better for the Academy than separating them. On the other hand, firstclassmen should know better and they shouldn't expect anything but separation.

"Another factor is stress or duress or unusual factors. In other words, did the cadet's parents die, etc.

"A big factor is the attitude of the cadet regarding the violation. The cadet who stands up and says, 'Yes, I committed it,' when the violation might not have been found otherwise—that takes courage and it is a statement of that cadet's character. Personally, if a cadet would say, 'I violated'

206

when nobody else would have known about it—I think he made a harder choice and is more honorable than a lot of other cadets.

"I can give two examples to illustrate the difference. Both are cases that were decided this past year.

"One case was a firstclassman at a golf course in a nearby town, playing with two friends, both cadets. As they were playing this one hole, he sliced the ball down over a hill. You couldn't see from the fairway, but there was a road down there and the ball smashed through the window of a car.

"This cadet went down by himself—the others couldn't see him—and encountered a concerned couple who explained how this cadet was going to have to pay their 400 deductible and how he was going to be liable, etc. When the couple asked for the cadet's name and address, the cadet's first reaction was to lie, and he gave the man a false name and address.

"Then he climbed the hill and joined his friends, who did not know what had happened. But the cadet, now almost in a state of shock, said: 'You can't believe what I just did.' Then he told them, and they talked it over briefly. The cadet then went back and gave his real name. And he turned himself in for an honor violation. There was a hearing and he was found, but the Superintendent retained him—which was extraordinary since he was a firstclassman. But after all, he did behave honorably. He could have not said anything to his friends and no one else would have known.

"Now I'll give you a case where the cadet was not retained. There was this thirdclassman who got a physics test back so the instructor could go over the answers—then he was to turn it back and discuss his answers with the instructor if he felt that any of them were graded unfairly.

"Well, this thirdclassman, in a space that he had left blank when he took the test, wrote in an answer that was worth about 23 of the possible 25 points allowed for that question. Then he went up after class and said, 'Look, sir, I had this worked and you cut me for it; it deserves the points.'

"What the instructor did, when he graded the test, was put a minus 25 very big with some lines that radiated out from the 25. But the cadet's answer was written over the top of some of the lines, so there was no chance that the instructor missed those points. We sent this case to an honor hearing, the thirdclassman was found and he was separated for cheating.

"I should also point out that there are no other punishments—it is either retention, separation or suspension for a definite period. We don't want to confuse the breaking of regulations with honor offenses. We don't want a guy "walking the area" next to an honor offender. You can play games with the regulations—that's a part of cadet life. But you don't play games with honor.

"What advice would I give candidates regarding the Honor Code?

"I would tell them just what we tell the new cadets. It is a good system, and you will enjoy living with the kind of people who believe in it."

TWENTY-ONE

FIVE WOMEN GRADUATES: WHAT FEMALE CANDIDATES NEED TO KNOW

Women were first admitted to West Point in 1976. Since that time they have made up about ten percent of each entering class.

Because women are in the minority, and because of the traditional "macho" attitude of many West Point males, female survival presents a unique challenge.*

Numerous women cadets were interviewed and their general comments about survival have been woven through the previous chapters. However, the real experts on female survival are those who have made it through all four years and graduated. They know what it takes to survive as a plebe, but they also have the larger perspectives of the upperclassman and the U.S. Army officer.

For that reason interviews with five women graduates were selected for this chapter. One of them entered with the first women and is now back on the West Point staff. The other four are recent graduates who are out working in their Army professions.

The first graduate, a Pennsylvania native, was in the 1976 class that had the first women. She is currently a captain, soon to be a major, and back on the staff teaching mathematics. Her Army profession is engineering and after her next tour, which will be at Fort Leavenworth for advanced leadership training, she will return to the Corps of Engineers. In addition to all that, she enjoys a husband (also teaching at West Point) and two children and is expecting her third. She said:

"Come here as informed as you can be—that would be the first thing I would tell any woman candidate. Talk to cadets, listen to their war stories. There'll be some

---

*But certainly not an insurmountable challenge. The First Captain (top cadet) of the Corps of Cadets for 1989-90 was female, the first in West Point history.

exaggeration but you will get the general idea of what is going to happen. And if it is at all possible, visit and see things for yourself. It just happened that there were two people from my hometown already here and they told me everything that would happen on R-Day. That helped because I was able to anticipate things a bit.

"Also come physically fit. Running is extremely important because it is a mark of acceptance for women. I wasn't such a hot runner and I should have worked on it more.

"Be yourself. Don't conform to what you think people expect you to be like. Remember that you are a woman. Just don't go too far in one direction or the other; don't try to be one of the guys and don't be too feminine. Also, don't use your femininity to get things.

"When I came in, it was too easy for us to try to become one of the guys. We forgot that we were women and we let our appearance go. Women here now take care of themselves a lot better than we did. They act professional, but they are still obviously women—that is important. When we first came in, we were so afraid of being women that we tried to be like the guys—we didn't want to stand out at all—we wanted to blend in as much as possible. Women now are not afraid to cut their hair in a more flattering way. We didn't learn that until we were halfway through the first year. Remember also that people will notice if you are not being yourself—if you are playing games. So be yourself.

"Another thing is to accept the fact that you are always going to be a minority person and that you have to live with the consequences. For example, you have to be prepared to accept that some cadets will be biased against you because of your sex. Because of that, you are not going to be accepted by some people. A lot of high school girls have always been popular and always liked; then they come here and find that no matter what they do, they are going to be disliked simply because they are a minority. That is hard on them—it was hard on me. Accept the fact before you come that you may never win some of them over—then come and be level headed about it—don't let it bother you emotionally.

"I was luckier than most because there was a guy from

From the very beginning you must accept the fact that you are a minority person. Your biggest challenge is to earn the respect of the male majority.

my high school in my company. He knew me and that helped me get accepted easier. But that is a rare kind of luck.

"Minority groups need a support system and I recommend that women participate in whatever group is available. For example, the Corbin Seminar is one such group. It used to be thought of as a woman's bitch group. But now the group is doing some very valuable work, getting women ready to handle dual careers [when husband and wife are both Army], teaching women about the Army branches open to them, etc. I am a mother and we [my husband and I] have dual careers. I spoke at two meetings and there were a lot of men in attendance, too. I think such groups are personally and professionally helpful.

"West Point is a lot of work, but don't take everything so seriously that you don't have any fun. Some get into a mold thinking they have to prove something because they are women and they miss out on a lot of activities—they think they have to be working all the time. Definitely use your weekends to catch up or to get ahead with your studies. But don't take the whole weekend! Don't hibernate in your room at the expense of getting out and regaining your sanity. Go to Ike Hall [where there is a recreation center] or to a movie. But do something!

"I was that type [who stayed in too much], and now I wish I had had more fun. Join clubs and get a break from the routine. Get out and do some things with your friends. In four years you are going to graduate and have a lot of responsibility—but this is also your college experience and you don't want to feel like you have missed something.

"Then there are a couple of little things. Before you come, cut your hair in the style that YOU want to wear. Just make sure that it is shorter than the regs say—regs that you'll get in the mail. If you let the barbers do it the first day, it won't look nearly as good. And if you leave it at regulation length, there is always someone to argue that it is too long. It is hot and humid here in the summer and you may think you have it right to your collar. But collars are different and because of the humidity, it may stick out. So it's better to have it shorter than the limit and then you don't have to worry about it.

"Another thing—they are going to issue you a lot of uniforms very quickly. And, because you are frightened of everything, you will have a tendency to accept your things too quickly. Don't do it. Try everything on to make sure they fit before you accept them. Otherwise you are going to go back and buy the same things again. I remember, I was running for two weeks in Converse shoes that were several sizes too big. Don't worry about your grays—they fit those carefully. But be careful with the other things.

"I suppose everybody will be warning you about the dating. I'll just say, don't frat [date upperclassmen while you are a plebe]; you'll lose the respect of your classmates even if you don't get caught. They will know—you can't hide anything. Later, [when no longer a plebe] you'll meet upperclassmen in activities and I would encourage you to date them and have a bit of a college experience. But don't get the reputation that you run around. Watch your conduct because rumors fly quickly and they are not always accurate.

"Also realize that some guys are harassed for dating women cadets—it's the same ones doing it who don't accept women in the first place. It's amazing to me how men can have so much respect toward mothers, sisters and women civilians and yet treat woman cadets in such a degrading way. It's true that the outward, verbal hazing of women has decreased since we came. But the covert harassment has not decreased—in my opinion. It is still here even if it isn't spoken. You just have to accept it and not let it bother you.

"Stay in the middle of the road. Don't be too macho or too feminine. Don't be a radical out with a banner and don't sit back saying, 'Step all over me.' Be level headed, middle of the road and professional—that is how you will gain respect.

"The best thing about West Point for me? There were two things.

"Primarily, it was the people who you end up being friends with. That friendship and support can never be replaced. The friends you make are true friends forever.

"The other best thing was the opportunities I had, which were so much different from what I would have had at an ordinary college.

"At the ordinary college you can hide out and do nothing but go to class for four years. You can't do that here. There are athletics [she was on the gymnastics team], intramurals—you're always participating on some kind of team. There is summer training—ranger school, airborne school, etc. Then there are the leadership experiences—at Camp Buckner and later in training the new cadets. Also you get the chance to try out your leadership training in the real Army during one summer. You can't get those kinds of experiences in any other way—and I wouldn't trade them for anything."

The second account is from a first lieutenant, soon to be a captain. She is a transportation officer, married to

213

another Army officer and, at the time of the interview, was expecting her first child. She said:

"One thing I would recommend is to enjoy the month before you come. I made the mistake of being too tense, too uptight, especially with my family and friends. You're going to need to draw on your high school friends and family for support. So relax and enjoy them before you go.

"But definitely work out before you go so you are in shape to run. You don't have to be in really tip top shape—the program isn't so strenuous that an average athlete can't do it. It's challenging but not intimidating.

"Talk to cadets before you come and find out all you can. Also, if possible borrow a copy of *Bugle Notes*—not to memorize everything, but just to read and get a feeling for the history and tradition of West Point—and to learn some of the vocabulary.

"Also, know why you want to go, and go only for yourself, not for anybody else. I was appointed to all three academies but decided on West Point because of its history and tradition—that was ironic because there were guys who thought I shouldn't be there.

"Another thing is to understand the fine point between quitting and leaving. My parents would never let me say that I was thinking of quitting. They felt anyone who got appointed is not the kind to be a quitter. But they said, 'If you give it a fair trial and it isn't right for you, you can leave.' In my mind I knew if I left, it wouldn't be because I failed or because of something I didn't agree with or something that was unfair. That would be quitting. I guess you can see the difference when I say that you quit for bad reasons and leave for good reasons.

"I cried the whole way up there from Ohio, and stayed up the whole night before I reported. I was a nervous wreck and I'm not a nervous person. I was just scared, not knowing what to expect. I was not prepared. I'm not from a military family and didn't know what things like a web belt was, and I didn't know what to wear when they told me to put on low quarters.

"My point is, you should visit West Point if you can and talk to as many as you can about it.

214

"I also have some recommendations for when you get there.

"From day one you should support your classmates. In my squad there were 11 guys and I was the only girl. But I never wished—not for one second—for another girl. I didn't feel I needed it. I felt on the same level as the other 11 guys. We were all in it together and we all supported each other. And to this day, I still talk to a lot of them. They are like brothers. They would come to me with letters from their girlfriends, asking my advice on what they should do about their problems. We really became close.

"You should also try to get along with your different roommates. Conflict doesn't solve anything. And if there are problems, work them out. You shouldn't go complaining, saying, 'Move me!' The Army way is to get along. After all, you will never get to pick your boss or any of your fellow workers in the Army. You work with whomever you have to—and you get along by being courteous to each other— you get things done by sacrificing some of your own wishes and compromising on others. So you should practice that by getting along with your roommates.

"I worried a lot about the physical aspects. I weighed 98 pounds and was five-six. But I wasn't strong and had to build up to the pushups and pull-ups—the running was no problem because I had been a sprinter.

"The main focus should be on academics. I had a 4.0 in high school and when my first grade was a "C", it was devastating. I never failed any physical tests but certainly failed academic tests. So my advice is to take the hard courses in high school; don't take the kickback classes. Don't cheat yourself in high school by taking Home Economics I, II and III. Take trigonometry and precalculus.

"Also, I was not used to asking for help. But you will almost surely have to do it when you get there. Ask your classmates and instructors for help any time you are having trouble. Those who continue to have problems are the kind who won't reach out. It is very difficult to fail if you ask for help.

"The hardest thing for me was to get my shoes shined properly. It seems dumb now but at the time it really had an impact on my life.

215

"They just wouldn't take a shine. I had demerits after one inspection and another one was coming—but so were my parents. I was so afraid my parents would come all the way from Ohio and I would be walking on the area and couldn't see them. I tried, oh, how hard I tried. But they wouldn't shine. Then I totally broke down. I cried and cried and couldn't stop. Then, at midnight, before the inspection, I went downstairs to the phone and called home. I told them, 'Don't come up; I'm going to get into trouble with my shoes.' Then I sat down and cried downstairs at the phone. And I was saying to myself that it [West Point] wasn't worth it.

"Then I went up to my room and while I was gone my roommate, who had been in the Army, shined my shoes and they looked good [she passed the next day's inspection].

"I learned two things from that. One, that you are really in it together. It really made me feel good that at midnight this girl put out that extra effort for me.

"The second thing I learned is to share your problems with your parents. My mother got off the phone that night and felt absolutely helpless—she would have shined my shoes and sent them Federal Express if she could have done it. But I hadn't been sharing my problems because I felt I didn't need them [my parents] for anything because I was getting paid and was supposed to be independent. I called them back but they worried needlessly [in the interim].

"And, yes, it would be helpful to learn how to shine shoes. My problem was that I didn't have a good base on them—we were supposed to build that up during Beast Barracks—and I hadn't.

"I think one reason I got along with the guys was that I was all business. I didn't laugh at the upperclassmen's jokes even if I thought they were funny. I saved the laughing until I got to the room. It personally bothered me when I saw other girls laughing—I always felt they were trying to be cute. I didn't have a mean, butch kind of attitude. I just tried to tend to business and be professional.

"I think that helped me a lot because when I was a sophomore, I ran for class secretary. I had to get out and campaign, and I know the word was out about me. I got elected, and I was the first woman ever to hold a class office. Later, when I was a firstclassman I was appointed XO [executive officer] of my regiment. But being elected by my classmates was more satisfying than being appointed by the officers.

"The best thing, by far, about my West Point experience was the friendships I made. After graduation, I cried all the way home, sad because I knew we would never be there together again. It was the people who made West Point great for me."

The third graduate was originally from Minnesota and is currently a battalion S-4 (supply and maintenance) officer in Newport News, Virginia. She is single and is enjoying the Army much more than she thought she would. She said:

"I think it is very important for women to go there in good physical condition. Running, I think, is especially important. They put you into one of three groups named after the West Point colors, which are black, gray and gold. I was the only woman in the black group [the best] and that really put me in a good light—it helped me earn respect.

"But before you come, if you have the time, make sure you take calculus and physics. I didn't have either and it really put me at a disadvantage. I went to a lot of AI [additional instruction] and I still struggled near the bottom in math. I just didn't have the background.

"I also strongly recommend a West Point visit and that you talk with as many cadets as possible. I didn't know anything. They told me to come with a pair of military shoes and I died my topsiders black and showed up with them! Don't be embarrassed like that. Find out what to do—find out what a minute-caller does!

"They also tell you to bring plenty of underwear. Well, bring double what they say. What happens is that it can take a couple of weeks before they send out the laundry—then, when mine went out, they lost all of it—and there was no place [then] to buy more. My mother had to send some by Federal Express.

"Also, try to keep your sense of humor about the whole thing. It is easy to get down when you are getting yelled at. It seems like everybody in the world is down on you and that you can never do anything right. It's easy to get a warped perspective. You have to take a step back and look at everything in its real perspective. So the laundry got lost—so what. With some perspective you can realize that things like that are pretty amusing. So don't let things get you down!

"The hardest thing for me was learning to budget my time. There was so much to do—I was Corps Squad cross-country and indoor-outdoor track—then on the marathon team. So, while I was practicing long hours, I had fourthclass duties and then hours of homework to do in a short time—all while I was exhausted!

"The thing I learned that helped me the most was to make a list of the things that needed to be done. Then, when I made that list, I got real pleasure out of crossing things off.

"The yelling was also hard on me even though I had an older brother who did that all the time growing up. But I got used to just letting it go in one ear and out the other.

"But don't cry in front of the upperclassmen no matter how much you feel like it—keep everything inside until you get to your room. Once a girl does that, they say, 'Oh she's weak.' Then they get on her ever more.

"But guys do it too, sometimes. There was this one guy in my company who was told to report to the meanest upperclassman in the company. The guy in my company was scared to death, but when he reported, the upperclassman told him to close the door. Then he explained that his parents were good friends with the parents of this plebe and he just wanted the plebe to know that he [the upperclassman] was going to look out for him that year. The guy came back to us and broke down crying—crying because the upperclassman had been so nice. I tell this story not to make fun of the plebe but to show how everybody gets so tense and worried that crying can be an outlet for anyone—male or female.

"I also want to say something about keeping your femininity. Don't lose it. There were some of the women who tried to become like men—and that is not the goal. You can be a good leader and a professional without being totally masculine. I had one friend who was there—she was pretty and she was very feminine just in the way she presented herself. But she began to change. She got more and more masculine. She cut her hair as short as the men, she started smoking, and she began hanging out with the guys. Then the inevitable happened. As a firstie, the plebes began calling her 'sir.'

"Don't let that happen to you. If you start feeling unfeminine, do little things—paint your toenails—put feminine things on your desk—present yourself in a feminine way. Later on you can wear feminine civilian clothes and wear a little makeup. Guys don't like women who try to be masculine.

"I didn't have any problem getting along with all those guys. I ended up being the only woman in my company and the guys all looked out after me like they were all my brothers. At graduation they all bought me a rose!

"The main thing is to show them you can keep up physically and academically and that you are willing to work as hard as they are. As a plebe, if you pull your load and pull your duties, they will respect you for that. But if you fall out on runs or they think you are trying to use your femininity to get out of things—even if you are trying—you are not going to earn their respect.

"But don't frat! My first roommate did and she got kicked out for misconduct. My advice is not to worry too much about dating that first year—your life is almost totally occupied with surviving. Then, later, be careful. Women can easily get a bad reputation by going out with several different guys. It can really be hard on women who date around—rumors always get going.

"My best experience at West Point? Meeting all the people, definitely. You meet so many high-quality people there, and you make friends you will have for the rest of your life. Also, I've found out since I've come into the Army that you have an instant bond with anybody who graduated from there. This has helped me in the Army—it's kind of a mutual 'I trust you, you can trust me,' kind of situation."

The fourth account is that of a first lieutenant, originally from Rhode Island, and presently a transportation officer at Fort Devens, Massachusetts. While a cadet she had the unusual experience of quitting after her second year, then reapplying and being allowed to join the class one year behind her original class. During her year away she spent a lot of time in Germany, working and skiing, and getting

*her feelings about West Point sorted out. Now she is married
(to a WP graduate) and has a new baby. Here is her advice
to female candidates:*

"I have a lot of comments and in preparing for this interview I organized most of them into a list of "do's" and "don'ts." But before I get into those I want to make a couple of general comments.

"The first one is to make sure that you know why you are going to West Point. There could be a lot of reasons and any reason is as good as another if you are comfortable with it. I've seen lots who were pressured by parents and they were very unhappy. If that is one of your reasons and you are comfortable with it, fine. But don't go if you are not comfortable with it.

"The second thing is to realize that it is normal to be very emotional about leaving home and going there. For example, I cried for the entire four-hour drive from Rhode Island. I was scared of leaving home, I was scared of West Point, and I felt all alone. But you should expect that and realize that it is a natural feeling. My roommate said she cried for ten hours. Later, I was rarely homesick but there where a lot of other women who were. It should be emphasized that homesickness is natural.

"The third thing is to program yourself to stick it out after you get there. It is tempting to quit after three weeks— or whenever you get the first opportunity. That is a big mistake. You should stick it out and see what the academic year is like.

"Now for my 'do's' and 'don'ts.'

"DO come physically fit.

"I found it difficult to work out when my friends were partying at graduation, but I ran track and because I wanted to stay in shape, I put my books in a book bag and jogged home. When I got there [West Point], I didn't have any problems with the running.

"The attitude of the upperclassmen is much better toward new cadets who are in shape. And your classmates don't like to double back and pick up people who are dragging. Both as a new cadet and as an upperclassman I saw women who were out of shape, crying and acting in ways I didn't think appropriate. Everyone was angry with

Develop your upper-body strength BEFORE you get to West Point!

them and it made their life a lot harder—it's just another lick against you if you are a woman.

"I do want to stress that upperclassmen don't expect you to be a superwoman. They just expect you to keep up an eight or eight and one-half minute mile pace—not a blistering pace.

"I don't think I got as much flack as the other women because I was in good shape. My two-mile time was 12:30 and that beat some of the guys. Of course, some were a bit hostile, but that didn't bother me. Besides, it earned the respect of most of them.

"DO be feminine.

"This was one of my biggest problems. I thought I had to be one of the guys and I felt guilty about being feminine. I was afraid to dress up in civilian clothes—later, when it was permitted—because it is such a masculine school. It is very important not to lose your femininity. But don't flaunt it either. Don't try to be too alluring. Don't load up with makeup, wear tight clothes or a lot of perfume.

"I remember back to my first year. The worst time was in March of that year. I was really lonely and angry because I didn't like being unfeminine. I felt that the Academy didn't want me to be feminine and that I was somewhere between

Sometimes it is hard to feel feminine, especially when you are wet and dirty.

being a woman and man. The guys called us "female cadets" and I didn't know how to handle that. I was young and emotional and it was difficult to handle those emotions. The guys themselves were just called "cadets." Why couldn't we be called "cadets" also? It was hard knowing that I was feminine but not being able to display that.

"Looking back, I don't know why I thought like that—it was stupid. I guess I felt that to be accepted I had to be as much like the guys as I could and it had built up in me. My parents came down one weekend and I cried a lot. I felt it wasn't right for me even though I loved West Point and wanted to graduate. I just didn't like being set in this unfeminine position.

"When I came back [after being out one year], I felt things were different, but I know now that it was my attitude. That year out give me a solid feeling of who I was and when I came back, I was no longer the impressionable, naive girl. I had matured and I felt comfortable with who I was. That helped others to view me in a better way and they treated me better. I did much better, too—I did exceptionally well in academics—and I had a much more positive attitude. Before, I had tried to be too much like a guy, honestly, and I think that was a mistake. I was unhappy with that and I finally realized that I am going to be who I am and that was much easier for me.

"DON'T cry in front of upperclassmen.

"If you do, it will put you in a very awkward situation where some upperclassmen will feel that you are using the tears as a manipulative tool. That won't be your reason—you'll be doing it out of frustration, probably, but it won't help you.

"This advice is based upon one of my own bad experiences. I had gone on the bayonet assault course—it was near the end of the summer [Beast Barracks] when they teach you rifle drill with bayonets. As a part of this exercise they give you a pugil stick [a padded stick] to use one-on-one in fights. We had done this before and I had been paired with another woman.

"But that day I got the living daylights beat out of me by a male and I wasn't expecting that. It showed me that

You must be mentally prepared to engage in rough-and-tumble physical challenges.

combat was tough, but it also devastated me and the only way I could react was to cry. I really created a big hullabaloo. A woman squad leader wanted to help and the platoon sergeant wanted me to stop. But everything just snowballed. I just cried and cried and couldn't stop. It was terrible.

"The same thing almost happened during Reorgy Week [the week before classes start] when I got surrounded by about ten upperclassmen. I had done something wrong and the guy in front got on me; then the guy in back made me turn around and the other guy got mad when I did it. This went on for about twenty minutes and I really got flustered—but I held it back long enough to get to one of my classmates' room. Then I really cried. Later, after recognition [at the end of plebe year], one of the guys who was on me— who bragged to others that he had made every plebe cry— came up and said how much he respected me because I was

224

able to control myself in front of him. That made me feel good—it was a small victory and you need those.

"My advice is to try and keep everything in perspective. They're going to get on you because you forgot to square a corner properly or for pens sticking out of your pocket. Just remember, you aren't the worst creature on earth because of that. Try to remember that these are small things and not that important.

"You shouldn't cry and you shouldn't smile, either. That was another one of my problems—I smiled too much and that got me in some trouble. Of course, even the upperclassmen can joke about it. One noon while eating I was told to wipe the smirk off my face—they call a smile a smirk. But then I was told to put it on the table, call it to attention, then march it off the table. I thought, this is stupid. I'm 18 years old and I'm to march a smirk off the table? But you do it and laugh about it later—the upperclassmen were laughing about it, too. So they aren't all grim times. There are many fun times and the upperclassmen laugh because they remember when they were plebes.

"DON'T ever give up.

"It is easy to drop out of a road march or a run because you are tired. But once you drop out, it is easier to do it the next time, and I personally feel that you will be resented for it. I know I was a lot more critical of other women [as an upperclassman] than my male counterparts. But it was because they reflected poorly on all the women. Guys would see that and generalize and give us a bad name.

"You should get ready for that attitude among the women. You will find that women are more critical of other women than the guys, but it is because we don't want women coming in and hurting our reputation.

"Do carry your own load. I'm speaking of things like carrying your rucksack on a road march. I firmly believe, even if you are tired, that you shouldn't expect men to do it for you. Thirteen miles is a long way, that's true. But you are going to be an officer and you should be ready to meet the standard. If you were in the Army, you wouldn't give up your rucksack to your platoon sergeant—that wouldn't be setting a very good example.

225

"I know there are some women who will be physically unable to do it—not carry all the weight. And maybe some would recommend giving up some of it to complete the march. But it is my personal opinion that it is a bad thing to do.

"DO NOT—and put this in capitals—FRATERNIZE, PERIOD.

"It is forbidden for plebes to date upperclassmen [they can date other plebes] and a lot of women feel tempted. Maybe it's because the upperclassmen are off limits and that makes them more appealing and more exciting. Also upperclassman probably feel that the plebes are like forbidden fruit, and that makes them more tempting.

"The penalty for frating [dating an upperclassman] depends upon the circumstances. If it is dating with no sexual misconduct, it could mean confinement to post or area and maybe a sixty-hour slug [walking tour]. If there is sexual misconduct, both could very likely be kicked out.

"I think it is probably natural for plebe women to be attracted to upperclassmen. They [the plebe women] are brand new, fresh and innocent, and upperclassmen are very attractive. It's much the same kind of thing I saw in high school where the tenth grader wants to date seniors.

"But besides the institutional risks, both can end up with bad reputations. However, the male's mistake will tend to be forgotten by classmates, while the woman, because of her minority status, will stand out more. Also, the woman runs the risk of losing her respect among her classmates and that could be a serious problem.

"None of this means that the girl shouldn't date. But during plebe year, at the limited opportunities, just be careful and date only another plebe. The next year there is nothing wrong with dating upperclassmen.

"But be careful. The men talk a lot and some of the talk is malicious.

"DO watch your diet when you get there.

"West Point has a very high calorie, high carbohydrate diet that men can handle because they are so physically active. But women's bodies can't handle that kind of food in the quantities served. It makes them large, not necessarily with fat, but it can put on a lot of muscle.

"The men have a term for the women who get larger. They call them 'thunder thighs'—the term really does depict some of the women.

"There is usually not too much of a problem during Beast Barracks, and perhaps the first year—because of all the energy that is being burned off. The real problem usually comes during yearling year [sophomore year] when there isn't as much pressure.

"The male cadets are always poking fun at overweight women and that just makes it all the more difficult for them. One of their [male cadets] favorite things [when I was there] was to make jokes about the two overweight female cadets who go to a pizza parlor and order a big pizza and diet cokes. Of course, that was a very true joke because some did that.

"DO get to know your male classmates.

"It is easy to sit in your room and hide out or be a ghost. But fight that tendency. Get out of your room and go to other rooms and meet the guys. Get to know them and be friends with them. That really helps you get through the Academy. Misery loves company and the more friends you have, the more you can share it with. I can't stress that enough!

"Actually I think the women tended to get out more than the men and were actually more friendly than the men. I know I felt, because there were only three of us in the company [with nearly a hundred men] that I had to get out because I wanted them to accept me. I think the experience will be a lot harder on a woman if she stays in her room—it's easier for the men to dislike her.

"DO get involved in extracurricular activities.

"You have to break the monotony and you need to meet other cadets and experience things other than school, drill and sitting in your room. There are enough clubs and activities for any person's interests. Take advantage of those.

"DO seek out woman friendships.

"It is important to have women friends because there are difficult, emotional times and men don't appreciate what women are going through. Also men can't appreciate that women feel lonelier because they are in a minority. It is important to share those feelings with other women. My women friends were very valuable and they helped me be a happier person.

Visit West Point if you can and talk to women cadets. They will show you what it is really like.

"DO visit the Academy before you come—if it is possible.

"I went up there in April of my senior year and at that time I was undecided whether I should go to West Point or take ROTC at a university. I lived in the barracks, went to classes with cadets, ate in the mess hall and spent an entire weekend. That was very good for me—in fact it clinched it. I had been wishy-washy before, but after seeing West Point, I saw that it was something very different and I knew it was something that I really wanted. Those who don't go are much more likely to be shocked when they haven't seen the emotional stress of someone being yelled at.

"DO get out with other parents if you have the opportunity.

"Some of the cadets have parents who live close by and they come to West Point on several weekends. The first year there isn't much they can do, but they can have picnics and walk around together. My advice is to tag along whenever you get the chance. It is easy to sit in the room and feel miserable. So don't do it. Get out if you are invited with your roommate's parents. It will do you a lot of good."

The fifth graduate is a new second lieutenant who was going through airborne training at Fort Bragg when she was interviewed. She said:

"First of all you have to realize that you will spend the entire four years in one company. And when you enter that company you will be with 32-33 plebes, but there will only be four girls at the most—many companies have only one or two. So you have to get used to living in a fishbowl—all those guys will be watching you closely for all four years.

"So the biggest challenge is to get along with the guys in your class, and the best way to do that is to earn their respect. But to do that, you have to walk a fine line between being feminine and being professional.

"The secret of getting along with them? Well, there are several things that you don't do.

"You don't do what one of my roommates did—you don't get the guys to carry things for you just because they are heavy. This roommate had the guys do that, and she had a lot of problems because the guys wondered what she was doing there if she couldn't carry a rucksack or duffel bag.

"Another thing you don't do is go the opposite way. There were some girls, for example, who put down other girls to the guys, and who laughed with the guys about female jokes. Those girls were trying to get in with the guys by being one of them. That does not work. The guys see through that and they make fun of those girls behind their backs. Definitely do not try to be one of the guys because you will never get their respect.

"One of the biggest problems for women is the diet at the Academy. The food is loaded with calories, and even the diet tables for the weight management program, in which 90 percent of the participants are female, has a diet that is too high in calories for many women.

"I know from experience about this problem—I dropped out of the Academy for a year because I had become overweight. I still think their standards are too harsh for females, but that is the way it is and you have to meet them.

"The biggest problem with being overweight or in the weight management program is that it gives the guys a chance to label you. Some of them are really bad—they'll take the slightest thing out of whack with the girls and use it against them.

"I know some say that women don't have to worry about their diet during plebe year—that the overweight problems come later. But that isn't true. With that diet, which is very hard to resist, plebes can gain weight, too. My advice is to be careful from the time you get there.

"I also disagree with those who say that the plebe year is the hardest part of the experience. I think that Camp Buckner [a reservation near West Point], where cadets get infantry and armor training the second summer, is much harder on the women.

"Why? Because the goal of Camp Buckner is to simulate combat conditions and it is under those conditions when the guys are the most negative. That is when a lot of them decide that girls don't belong there.

"It's a general attitude. They start making anti-female statements, and some even say it to your face that you don't belong there. Actually, most of the time the prejudice is more subtle and not all of them [the men] are like that. But there is enough of it [the prejudice] to make you miserable if you let it bother you.

"The key is to do your job and not listen to what they are saying. But it is hard because these are your classmates and you want their approval and respect.

"Of course, some of the women bring criticism on themselves because they are not prepared to do all the physical things. More girls than guys fall out of the runs, and it is obvious that some don't like the rough part of foot soldiering. I didn't like it myself. I liked armor much better and I think armored warfare, more than infantry, is the force of the future.

"My final advice is to do little things that will help you remember that you are feminine. Sometimes, when I thought I could get away with it, I wore makeup at breakfast. Also, one year I had nails very long—longer than regulation, but with no nail polish. I got a lot of satisfaction out of doing those things. I would advise women coming in to do things like that—to do little personal things that will make them feel that they are feminine."

TWENTY-TWO
ADVICE FOR PARENTS

This is a chapter for the parents of West Point candidates.

It is a collection of advice on the typical problems a candidate's parents are likely to experience, starting with the admissions process and continuing through the cadet's first year at the Academy. (After your cadet survives the first year, there is not much more you will need to learn.)

All of the advice comes from parents who have been there—parents whose sons and daughters have at least survived the first or "Plebe" year at the Academy. In addition, much of the advice is from parents who are, or have been, presidents of West Point Parents' Clubs. Their advice has extra value because, in addition to experiences with their own sons and daughters, they have helped numerous other parents cope with a variety of problems.

GETTING IN

Getting admitted to West Point is a two-step process. One step is the application to the Academy itself, a process more involved than applying to Stanford or Georgia Tech.

The other step is the application for a congressional or Vice-Presidential nomination—a process unique to the service academies.

The procedures for accomplishing both steps are explained in Chapters 9-14. However, in both processes there are some things that parents should and should not do according to the parents who were interviewed for this chapter.

One of the problems parents should be aware of is the bad information that candidates can receive when they initiate the admissions process. This is a troublesome problem because the information often comes from those whom one would expect to be authoritative—persons like school counselors, teachers and administrators. An Idaho mother and parents' club president commented on this problem:

"These kids can get a lot of erroneous information about West Point, and it can come from people who seem to know what they are talking about. I'm speaking of people like their school counselors and their vice-principal who can easily discourage kids with an off-handed comment like, 'Oh, you can't get into West Point unless you are in the top ten percent of your class or unless you have a 3.5 gpa [grade point average].' I advise parents not to listen to things like that. Don't let someone like that discourage your kid. Mine was told that, yet he ignored what they said and got in with less than a 3.5 and I know now that there are many others who have done the same."

Another problem that should concern parents is the complexity of the process. The candidate has to fill out forms and write letters and essays. Also, senators and congressmen have their own unique procedure for applying for a nomination—procedures involving letters, documents, deadlines and, perhaps, appointments for interviews. Most parents believed that high school seniors need help with the logistics of the process. Following is a typical comment, which came from a Minnesota mother and parents' club president who has been through the process three times—twice for sons at West Point and once for a son at the Naval Academy:

"I really believe that most kids need help from their parents during the admissions process. That senior year in high school is really overwhelming—the typical candidate is heavily involved in athletics; they're taking advanced courses and have a heavy study schedule; they're in clubs and community organizations; they're taking the SAT and ACT; and, in addition, they don't have experience managing paperwork and keeping track of deadlines.

"I think that parents should help them to become organized. A mother can do things like help them with a master schedule so they know when everything is due. She can also help with the filing so that there is a separate folder for each senator and congressman. The kid should write all the letters, of course, but there is nothing wrong with helping them get the letters typed. Copying is another chore—the

233

kid should keep a copy on file of everything that has been submitted, but making those copies takes time that most kids don't have.

"I remember when my first one started applying. We had no idea how much was involved and we learned that a kid can have problems if you don't help them with their appointments and deadlines. There are deadlines for everything and if they miss one of them, that can be the end of it right there. The kid's tendency is to try to keep everything in his head. That is a bad mistake. Appointments and deadlines should be written on a master schedule and everything else should be adjusted to them. And sometimes their appointments interfere with classes or their sports schedule, so it is up to mom and dad to talk to the school so the kid doesn't get in trouble for missing classes or practices."

Another problem parents should be aware of is that many candidates are reluctant to follow up on the application process. The typical candidate thinks that once a high school teacher or administrator has been asked for a letter of recommendation, then that is all they have to do. They do not realize that those who are asked to submit letters often procrastinate past deadlines or fail even to write the letters.

Numerous congressional staffers spoke about this problem (they said high school principals were the worst offenders) and they strongly recommend that candidates follow up to make sure their files are complete. Of course, following up is not something high school seniors are used to doing, so it is important for parents to encourage the process.

Several parents commented on other types of follow up that are important in the admissions process. An example is a comment from an Iowa father and parents' club president:

"Parents should constantly encourage the son or daughter to apply early and then follow up with both the Academy and the congressmen. By applying early they have time to overcome problems if they come up. Also, they have the opportunity to make what I call a communications trail. As the year progresses the candidate can update his files with his latest grades, an announcement that he has been elected to the student council, that he was voted captain of the football team, that he received an award for selling the most magazines, etc. This is important because, one, everybody [the Academy and congressmen] is looking for candidates with good credentials and, two, they are looking for candidates who really want to go to West Point. When the candidate follows up, this lets them know that he is serious—that he really wants it.

"I can cite our personal case to show the value of follow up. When our son applied, he was rejected by the medical review board out in Colorado Springs—the board that reviews candidate physicals for all the academies. His problem was that he had a history of two head injuries. One was a mild fracture when he was a child and the other occurred in junior high when he was hit above the eye with a baseball. The impact of the baseball made a slight indentation, which was corrected at that time by surgery. Well, with that on his record he was automatically rejected—I guess because they thought he was some kind of a risk.

"But our son did not accept that decision. He found out how to contact that board and he asked for a special review of his case. We also got medical statements from his doctors and some evidence to support the review, including an electroencephalogram. And all during the process he would pick up the phone and talk to the people in Colorado Springs, politely asking when his case was due for review, telling what new evidence he was submitting, etc. He also followed up the phone calls with letters saying that he appreciated the discussions and that he wanted them to know how much the opportunity meant to him.

"Later, when he was found medically qualified and notified of his appointment, I believe it was the happiest day in his life. I also believe that his persistence was a big factor in his success. I'm afraid too many candidates and their parents would tend to accept the review board's decision as being the end of the line. In my opinion, parents definitely should be advised to encourage the candidate to challenge anything they believe to be unfair."

This is a good place, however, to warn parents against getting too involved in the admissions process.

Everybody who has anything to do with evaluating candidates, including congressional staffers, liaison officers, panelists and Academy officials, is looking for candidates who are victims of too much parental encouragement. They know from experience that candidates who want to attend West Point for any reason other than their own deep, personal desire are very poor risks. They know that when the going gets tough, the cadets who are there because of parents, grandparents, teachers, coaches or whomever, are the ones who are going to quit.

Therefore, as a parent, try to stay in the background as much as possible. Help the candidate in the ways that have already been mentioned. But when it comes to actual contacts with those who are involved in the admissions process, let your candidate do the actual writing or telephoning. Of course, it may be tempting at times to use your experience to solve a problem, but such efforts can backfire and actually hurt your candidate. Just remember that everyone evaluating candidates wants to have a good record—they want a high percentage of those they select to remain at West Point and graduate. Whenever they see a parent getting too involved, this is like a red flag warning them that the candidate's parents may be more highly motivated than the candidate. If your son or daughter really wants to go to West Point, do not let them think that of you.

One final bit of advice on the admissions process— encourage your candidate to make application to places other than West Point. If the young person is truly interested in an Army career, he or she should apply for an Army ROTC scholarship. Those with broader career interests should also apply for the Air Force and Naval Academies. In addition, each candidate should have at least one acceptance at a civilian college to fall back upon if the military options do not work out.

BEFORE THEY GO

Most candidates are aware of the physical challenges of cadet life at West Point. They prepare with workouts designed to increase both their strength and endurance.

However, those who supervise incoming cadets say that about 20 percent of them are inadequately prepared physically and that this handicap is responsible for the high percentage of resignations from within that group.

What should a parent do about this? Nothing, of course, if your candidate is truly in top shape. But if you suspect that the opposite might be the case, encourage the candidate to do his or her own fitness test using the standards (numbers, times and distances) given in Chapter 7.

There are two reasons for doing that. One is that it is common for high school athletes to overrate their physical condition—they think because they were good football or basketball players that the physical challenges at West Point will be a breeze. They may find out differently if they do their own physical fitness test. Then, if they don't meet the standards and have adequate time before they leave, they can get themselves in shape and avoid potential trouble.

The second reason pertains strictly to female candidates.

Right from the first day every female has a handicap because of her sex. This is because of the belief by some classmates and upperclassmen that women have no business being at West Point or in the Army.

West Point officials have made heroic efforts to discourage such beliefs, but, according to all the women who were interviewed, the prejudice is still there and every female candidate should be prepared to deal with it.

The surest way for women candidates to earn the respect of the male majority is to be in excellent physical shape when they arrive. Nothing impresses males more than a gutty female who has the stamina to hang in there with them when the going is tough. On the other hand nothing exposes women to more ridicule (often expressed silently or in very subtle ways) than when they have to drop out of a road march or give their pack to someone else to carry.

So if your candidate is a female, do whatever you can to help her get into excellent physical condition. The payoff will be huge, both for her psychological health as well as for her physical well being.

One word of caution. Some of the candidates take the physical challenge too seriously and spend all their time after graduation worrying about getting in shape. Numerous cadets and parents cautioned that the weeks after graduation should also be used for fun and relaxation. To do otherwise, they say, is to invite a good case of the blues when, during Beast Barracks, the "new cadets" (that is what they are called until after the end of Beast) think back at all the fun their friends had that they missed. During Beast the new cadets have plenty of legitimate things to feel sorry for themselves about without the additional feeling that West Point caused them to give up a fun period in their life—a period that they will never have a chance to experience again.

THE "R-DAY" TRAUMA

Most parents had comments about "R-Day" (Reception Day), which is the early July day that candidates report to West Point. They report in the morning and, after a short ceremony, are told to take a minute and say goodbye to whoever may have accompanied them. Then they head off to get their haircuts, inoculations, uniforms and their first taste of military indoctrination.

If you go along on R-Day, be prepared to keep your emotions in check. The new cadets are going to feel bad enough without worrying about your feelings.

Parents reported mixed opinions about whether or not the candidates should be escorted to West Point on R-Day.

The majority believed that if it is economically feasible, as many members of the family as possible should accompany the candidate on R-Day. They said that this is an expression of support that will sustain the cadet in the weeks ahead when the rough experiences of Beast Barracks are compounded by loneliness and homesickness. Also, they said that the lectures and tours that are arranged by West Point for that day helped them better understand the institution.

An example of the majority view is this comment from an Iowa mother and former parents' club president:

"We felt that it was very important for our son to know that his family was behind him so we made a family vacation out of it. We rented a motor home and took the younger kids, grandma and grandpa, and the girl he was going with at the time. It was a very good family experience for us, and while the parting was traumatic for us all, I think it was important for him to be sent off with love."

An example of the minority view is the following comment from a California parent who is also an official in a parents' club:

"He wanted to go by himself and I agreed because I think that if they want it bad enough, it is something that they should do on their own. Of course, it was very hard for me to see him go, and it is very hard on most parents. Luckily, when we got to the terminal, he met some others who were going back and that made it easier. If I had it to do over again, a few weeks before R-Day I would find out the names of others who are going from the region and try to get them together. The kids my son went with have since become very close because they have been riding the red-eye specials together for the last three years."

Numerous parents spoke of the trauma they experienced on R-Day. But many said they would advise parents to try not to let their emotions show too much because the cadets are going to have it hard enough without worrying about the pain their parents are suffering. Said a mother from South Carolina who is the co-president of a parents' club:

"We have a parent in our club who says to this day, 'I just don't think I can stand it—it is just killing me not being able to see that boy.' My point is that it is very difficult for some parents. I went through the whole first year with my husband feeling that way. It was gut wrenching for him; I mean really gut wrenching because they had been so close. It literally almost made him sick.

"Psychologically it is like giving up your child and I don't think some parents know how badly it is going to affect them until it happens. It is especially bad when a mother or father doesn't really believe in the kid's decision. I would say to parents that they should sit down during the application process and really talk everything over; then make sure the kid visits the Academy and talks to as many knowledgeable people as he can so he knows what he is doing. But once that decision is made and he says, 'Yes, mother and dad, this is what I want;' then it is important to support that decision even if it kills you inside!

"If that is what your child has chosen to do with his life, that is his destiny. From then on I think it is wrong when parents fight it. I think they have to dig down deep and find whatever it takes to support that child, and they should put their own wants and needs away somewhere. Most important—and I want to stress this—they should not complain to the child and tell them how much they miss them. All that does is make the child feel guilty for being up there and they don't need that.

"One more bit of advice I would give is to expect the absolute worst. Expect all the bad things you can think of—sadness, isolation, depression. If you expect the worst, it isn't going to be so bad when you start feeling that way. If you think it is going to be hard on you, maybe it will be easier."

SUPPORT FROM HOME

Even the most highly motivated cadets will have problems and periods of depression during the first year at West Point.

The main problem is the abrupt transition from hearing nothing but accolades in high school to hearing nothing but derision from the upperclassmen.

240

Before they left home, they were touted as outstanding young men and women. After their arrival at West Point, they are instantly dropped to a status that would challenge the Untouchables.

Before they left home their exemplary behavior had earned them freedom and respect. At West Point that freedom is suddenly taken away and no matter how hard they try, they seem not to be able to earn an ounce of respect.

All of them got to West Point believing that they would get chewed out if they goofed up and made a mistake. But all of them have to learn the painful lesson that they will get chewed out even when they do not make a mistake.

While they are going through all of this, it is natural that they will feel lonely and depressed. So this is the time when parents are really needed—the time when parents need to mobilize the support brigade and do the kinds of things that will help their cadets' morale. It is the time when the cadets need to know that at least SOMEBODY loves them.

Here are the kinds of things parents who have been through it say you can do.

Said a father and parents' club president from Florida: "Those kids badly need to hear from home and we tried not to let a day go by when we didn't put something in the mail. They weren't long letters much of the time. They were just notes with little things—what the cat did or what trouble the dog got into. Sometimes we just sent silly things..."

A mother from Rhode Island: "It is most important that they receive a barrage of letters. They don't have to be 12-page epistles. Just notes of what's going on, maybe with a daily comic strip, or a funny card or even a postcard—just so there is something in that mail box for them each day—even if it is a crayon drawing from the two-year old next door, it is important!"

A mother and past parents' club president from Ohio: "Letters are so very important but you have to be careful what you say. You need to write and keep them informed but don't make it sound like those at home are having too much fun. Already they are thinking about their buddies and things they are missing out on. You don't want to write and tell them all the things they are missing—that we did this and that and had so much fun. Nor do you want to tell

241

them how much you miss them. You do that and they will begin to think, 'Hey, I should be there instead of here.'

"Another thing that is important for them is to know that things are the way they were when they left. If they have a car, they need to know that it is still in the garage and not being abused. They like to know that their room is unchanged and that you haven't rented it out or given it to a younger brother. They like to have that security and when they come home, they will spot anything that is different. For example when our son came home that first Thanksgiving, he had just stepped into the kitchen when he said, 'Mom! You've got new salt and pepper shakers!'

"Also, if there is a girl friend and you have a good open relationship with her, try to discourage her from writing and saying, 'Oh, I miss you so much,' or 'Gee, I wish you were here so we could do this or that.' They are lonely enough without the girlfriend making it worse."

Letters from home are important, but so are letters from other people. Several creative parents told of how they were able to generate such letters. One mother put a request on the church bulletin board along with the cadet's address. Another mother gave stamped, addressed envelopes to her son's coaches and close friends. Still another mother persuaded all of her cadet's uncles, aunts and cousins to write at least once during the first semester.

After you have expended heroic efforts getting mail to your cadet, you and the other letter writers should not be disappointed when the letters are not answered. Why? Because the cadets are too busy. Almost every waking moment in their day is taken up with some activity—and many fall behind and have to use their weekends to catch up. Also, when the cadets do get a few spare moments, they should spend that time getting what they need the most: SLEEP! First-year cadets are always tired—so tired that they often have to stand up and walk around in class just to keep from falling asleep! So when you cajole uncles, aunts, cousins and friends to write your cadet, also explain why they are not likely to get their letters answered.

Another way to support your cadet is with packages of good things to eat and drink—packages that the cadets call "boodle boxes."

Many parents gave detailed information on every aspect of sending boodle boxes. Here is a sampling of their comments.

Said the mother who has had two at West Point and one at Navy: "Lots of parents wonder why they need to send all that food to those kids. They don't realize that it isn't like an ordinary college with a 7-11 just down the street."

A mother from Rhode Island: "You must send boodle boxes—the other kids will be getting them and yours will feel left out if you don't. And when you send them, if you send one candy bar, send ten so everyone in the squad will have one. They all share so your cadet will be paid back.

"What kinds of things did I send? I found that granola bars are really appreciated. If you send candy, don't send chocolate because it melts. Send peanut bars—they have lots of energy. I also found that peanut butter and crackers went over well as did any kind of baked good. Powdered drink mixes they love! My daughter never drank Tang at home but she drank a lot of it that first year. If you do send a drink mix, send a plastic glass the first time along with a spoon to measure and stir and a can opener. Another thing that's good is the little boxes of raisins—even if your cadet doesn't like them, the rest of the squad will eat them. The guideline is: send things with a high caloric value that are quick to eat.

"Also, it will be helpful to send the first boodle in a plastic container like a bread box so they can keep it for all the stuff that comes in later packages. They can keep plastic in their rooms but cardboard boxes are a problem because of the mice. Another tip: if you send cookies or brownies, pack them in plain, unbuttered, unsalted popcorn. This will cushion them; then they can eat the popcorn later.

How should you send boodle packages, by mail or UPS? That question was asked of many parents and practically all of them said that UPS was better and faster. "You can deal with UPS if something doesn't get there and you can get results," said one parent. "You won't have much luck dealing with the post office if something is lost."

Another advantage of sending things by UPS is that the package is delivered to the cadet's room whereas the cadet has to venture out and run the risk of meeting upperclassmen while picking up a mail package.

Several parents also warned against sending a birthday cake the first year without consulting the cadet first. In some companies the new cadets or plebes do not dare draw attention to themselves—to some upperclassman the "birthday boy or girl" is free game for whatever harassment they can dream up.

Said a mother from Rhode Island, "The mother may think she is doing a terrific thing when she sends a cake or flowers to a young lady, and she has no idea what the poor girl suffers because of it."

Every year parents receive information on local companies that will deliver treats to the cadets—things like fresh baked chocolate-chip cookies and birthday cakes. The parents who used those companies said that they do a good job and they recommended them to other parents.

Another way to support cadets is to get them a telephone credit card and encourage them to call home as often as they desire. True, the cadets can run up quite sizeable phone bills, but every parent who was interviewed felt that the money was well spent. Some parents (obviously those who could afford it) felt that the cadet should also be allowed to use the credit card to call friends. Parents justified that additional cost by citing the morale value of such calls and the fact that they were saving much more than the cost of the phone calls by not paying college tuition and living expenses.

Typically, there is a problem when the cadet calls home. It seems that every person in the house wants to listen and talk; then after the call, the family begins a debate that goes something like this:

"Did he say he was flunking math?"

"No, he said he had flunked a chemistry test and he was afraid he was going to flunk math."

"Well, I don't think that is what he told me. Also, did you feel that he was a bit depressed?"

"I don't think so; he was just tired. He also said he was coming down with a cold."

"A cold? He told me he was feeling good. But I really worry about him flunking math.

"I told you! He isn't flunking math yet!"

"Etc. Etc."

Does that sound like something that could happen in your family? If so, here is a suggestion from a California father that will solve the problem. He said:

"Sometimes I am gone when he calls and sometimes my wife is gone. But we found an easy solution to that problem. I went down to Radio Shack and bought an adapter that screws into the phone and into our tape recorder. Then I bought some of their cheap tapes and when he calls, whoever answers simply turns on the recorder. That has been a wonderful thing for us because we have a record of the changes that have occurred in his life since he has been at the Academy. Also it allows others to hear from him. His aunt listens to the tapes when she comes over and when one of his good friends comes over and says, 'Do you have Bill's latest tape?' we can give it to him to put in his Walkman. Also, we can listen to them over and over. I definitely recommend that parents do that. It leaves you with a wonderful record of the four years at the Academy."

An indirect way you can support your cadet is to urge him or her to take advantage of the West Point Mentor Program.

Mentors* are West Point officers living on the post who are married and who have volunteered to let cadets use their home as a place to relax and experience some of the pleasures of family life when the cadets have free time.

Many parents gave the mentors rave reviews and they were cited for doing many wonderful things. For example, some were praised for taking cadets to New York to catch planes home for Christmas when the public transportation system went haywire. Others were cited for visiting cadets in the hospital and keeping the parents informed with regular phone calls. Then there was a parent who told of his son who had made up his mind to resign after Christmas of his first year, but who was convinced to stay by his mentor. (The son, now a graduate, was asked about this incident and he confirmed that the mentor's efforts had, indeed, greatly influenced him.)

A minority of the parents were not that enthusiastic about the mentor program. Mostly they cited poor rapport

*"Mentor" is a new term; the old term is "sponsor" and when this book was published, most cadets and parents were still using the latter term.

between the cadet and mentor, and mentors who were only mildly interested in the program.

So what can parents do when cadets do not have a *simpatico* mentor?

The first thing to do is discuss the mentor program before your cadet leaves for the Academy and urge him or her to request a mentor when the opportunity arises. The typical new cadet is not aware of the mentor program or its value.

The second thing you can do is to urge your cadet to get a new mentor if the first one does not work out satisfactorily. There are three ways to do that, one official and two unofficial.

The official way to get a new mentor is to go to the Company Tactical Officer and ask for another one. If there is another mentor available, the switchover is relatively simple and straight forward.

One of the unofficial ways is for the cadet to ask a friend or roommate who has a good mentor if he or she can tag along. However, before your cadet does that, it is good for the roommate or friend to clear it with the mentor first.

The other unofficial procedure is to pick up a mentor at one of the Sunday church services. With each service there is a social period where, according to several parents, the church members look for cadets whom they can bring to their homes and for whom they can help ease the pangs of loneliness. Of the two unofficial methods for getting a good mentor, the latter is highly recommended for the cadets who will be attending church services.

PARENT VISITS

One of the best ways to support cadets is to visit them.

After the first two weeks of Beast, new cadets are allowed to sit with their parents at a Sunday church service and to visit with them during the social hour that precedes or follows the service.

The parents who commented on these visits had mixed feelings about them. Some believed that such visits helped their cadets while others felt that the visit was too short to be worthwhile or that seeing the family for such a brief time was tantalizing and only increased the cadet's anxiety.

An Academy official who is a graduate and whose son is a recent graduate discouraged frequent visits of this type. His main concern was parents who try to remain overly involved in the cadet's life. "Hovering parents," he said, "cause the plebes to have great turmoil."

The first good opportunity to visit cadets is during the Labor Day Weekend. Parents strongly believe that a visit at this time can be very beneficial to the cadet. They also gave several specific recommendations, including this very important one: get your motel reservations the same day your cadet accepts the appointment! (A listing of motels can be found in *The West Point Parent's Almanac* that you will receive on or near R-Day.)*

*The Hotel Thayer is on post and it is a wonderful old hotel. However, cadets are not allowed above the ground floor. This is not a problem during the Labor Day Weekend because cadets cannot leave the post. However, during visits when cadets have off-post privileges, such as Plebe Parent's Weekend in the Spring, the cadet will want to go to the parent's room and relax, and this is not possible if you are staying at the Thayer.

Always have a prearranged meeting place because there is always a crowd on the weekends that parents visit.

Other recommendations:

A father from Illinois: "Definitely fly into Newark if you can because you can rent a car and get right on the freeway and head north without the hassle of going through the Bronx or crossing any of the bridges.

A mother and parents' club president from Kansas: "When you come from the midwest, New York can be a shock. Get ready to be roughed up by the rude crowds and don't look for people to be courteous the way they are at home."

A father and parents' club president from Rhode Island: "If you have a meeting place worked out, always have a contingency plan. We told our son to meet us at a certain flagpole but then we were delayed because of a storm. He wasn't at the flagpole and we didn't know where to look. I recommend Eisenhower Hall because there is always a cadet on duty who will page cadets there."

A father and parents' club president from Florida: "Be prepared for a shock if you go up there Labor Day Weekend. Our son had lost fifteen pounds and that stupid cover on his head was too big and sitting down on his ears. We have a snapshot of me standing by him and I don't even recognize him. There is no need to worry, though. They monitor the cadets' weight and they will gain it back. But there is a real need for them to have things like peanut butter and jelly to take back to their room."

A father from Michigan: "You have to go there on Labor Day Weekend realizing that your cadet may get put on restriction or may have duty sometime during the three days. It is a good idea to have him [or her] call before you leave home."

Because the cadets cannot leave the post on Labor Day Weekend, one of the best things parents can do is to plan daily picnics. Here is a variety of recommendations:

A mother from Rhode Island: "As soon as you arrive, stake out a good picnic spot and leave your food there. Nobody will bother it—we left our food at seven in the morning and didn't get back until one in the afternoon.

"Also, don't picnic on the level of the parade field— the kids are not allowed to walk there and they can get in trouble if the parents do. The best place is down by the

248

river—turn right just past the Thayer Hotel and go down and scout out the area when you first get there. That area is traditionally off-limits for upperclassman—if they are there, they are careful not to bother or make eye-contact with the plebes. Other places to picnic are up by the football stadium. I think the river is better, however, because it is cooler and it is relaxing just to sit and watch the water.

"Other things. Take an extra towel to put over your cadet's lap—they are in trouble if they spill something on their uniform. Also take bug spray and a blanket and pillow—and don't be upset if the kid goes right to sleep and doesn't visit with you. Also, take a small portable gas grill if you want to cook anything at the picnic. And take brothers and sisters along if you can, even if they didn't get along at home. Your cadet will be pleased to see them.

A New York mother and parents club president: "I think

The cadets love tailgate parties.

249

But always take extra food for your cadet's friends.

an even better place for a picnic is Constitution Island, which is in the middle of the Hudson about three-quarters of a mile from the Point. The only problem is that you can't go out their ahead of time—you have to be escorted by a cadet."

A Pennsylvania mother: "Just warn them [the parents] that it is going to be crowded down by the river and that they had better stake out a place early. I also agree with the mother who said to be sure and take the other kids if possible—it really brings the family together."

Another mother from Rhode Island: "Always take enough food for four or five more because your cadet may bring along some others who don't have parents there. And be sure and have food that your cadet likes even if it isn't picnic food. One parent's kid loved tapioca pudding and she brought that. My son craves McDonald's food. [McDonald's is just outside the gate.] I would stand in line there and leave him inside the gate waiting for me. That first time I think I bought sixty dollars worth of McDonald's food!

"One thing to remember—if you go up there for that Labor Day Weekend—don't go with any preconceived notions of what you are going to do [other than a picnic].

250

Let the cadet decide what to do. Some are more adventurous than others and they will approach their mother and give her a kiss or give their father a hug—but they're told they can't display affection in public so they may not do this. Just be ready to react to their wants and needs—and realize that you may spend a lot of time just watching them sleep.

"One final suggestion. Bring a portable radio and cassette player with headset along with a box of their favorite tapes. They haven't had a chance to hear any music for several weeks and they crave it almost as much as junk food."

A mother from Kansas had other suggestions for things to bring: "This is the time to build their morale. Bring surprise letters that they can take back to their room and read. Bring things from home, like a leaf of mint from the back yard or pictures of the dog. Then, when you are ready to leave, hand them an envelope with two or three tickets for Sunday brunch at the Hotel Thayer. Later, when your cadet has the opportunity, he or she can take one or two friends and they can enjoy a wonderful meal."

A mother from Rhode Island cautioned parents not to be inquisitive when they visit their cadet. She said: "I think one of the biggest mistakes parents make is when they begin pumping the kid for information. I know, it's natural to be curious—you want to know what they are going through and how they are doing. But just try to remember what you feel like after a hard day, when everything is very difficult and things have gone wrong. Do you want to come home and begin talking about it? My advice is to relax and simply enjoy your cadet, and if he wants to bring up something and talk about it, let him do it. And remember, the system they're in makes them feel like they are not doing well—so don't ask how they are doing or if they like it. If they are truthful, they will have to say negative things. So just let them lead the discussions."

The main problem with the Labor Day Weekend is that the cadets cannot leave the post. So for the three days (if your cadet has that much time off) all of your socializing has to be done in public, and, except for the picnic grounds, in places where your cadet cannot really relax. However, there is a wonderful solution to this problem—if you can afford it. An Ohio mother explains:

"We found the ideal solution for that weekend [Labor Day Weekend]. We rented a mobile home—there are plenty of places to park on post—and he was able to come inside, get out of his clothes, sleep, and totally relax. It was a neat hideout for him because it was a place where he didn't have to constantly be looking over his shoulder, worrying about who was watching him. I highly recommend doing that if you can."

But what if you live in Mountain Home, Idaho, have four children at home, and simply cannot afford to travel all the way back to West Point on Labor Day Weekend—or any other time?

That is unfortunate, but there is still a way you can help your cadet. A mother and past parents' club president from New York explains:

"The thing for those western parents to do is to look in their copy of the *West Point Parent's Almanac* and find the Parent's Club Roster. Look over the clubs that are in the Northeast and select one to call or write. Explain to the club president that you cannot be back for the Labor Day Weekend and ask if there might be a club member who could adopt your son or daughter for that weekend. Now I realize that a parent might hesitate to do this, but believe me, we would be honored to do this—that is what we are here for.

"Parents need to realize that there are club members like me whose cadets have graduated, but who remain in the club just to keep up with the Point. It is an empty feeling not to have a reason to go there and enjoy the tailgate parties and all the other activities. Why right now I could name you five families off the top of my head who would be thrilled to adopt a cadet—and the advantage of using us is that we have a tremendous wealth of experience—we have been through so many things and we would be happy to share with somebody coming up through the ranks. I'm positive the other clubs in this region would feel the same. We all have a love for the Academy and we will feel that connection for as long as we live. And what if twenty-five parents called me all wanting help? That would be great. I would get them in touch with any of 154 families and I know they would be thrilled to have a reason to go up there—for them it would be like having an adopted child at West Point."

PLEBE PARENT WEEKEND

Each spring in March or April—depending upon when Easter falls—the upperclassmen leave for spring break and the Academy is turned over to the plebes. The last five days of that week are set aside for Plebe Parent Weekend, which is a very popular event—about 90 percent of the plebes' families visit. All the parents who were interviewed had attended and they strongly urged other parents not to miss it. Said a mother from Minnesota:

"We would do it again even if we had to take a second mortgage on our house—it is so important for your cadet. We took seven other children when we went—the airline had a promotion where kids under 16 could fly free—and we rented two cars. The kids still talk about that weekend—they had so much fun—I could write a book about the whole weekend—I'm so glad we didn't miss it."

A father and retired Colonel from Rhode Island: "I strongly recommend it—there are no upperclassmen around, you get to tour everything, eat in the mess hall—it gives the parents a very good sense of what West Point is. Also it gives the cadets a chance to show the parents everything—their rooms—we even toured the kitchens as insiders."

A mother and parents' club president from Pennsylvania: "I think it is very important, especially on the Friday when the barracks are open and when the Tac Officer meets each parent. You get to know how the Tac feels about your cadet and he [or she] gets a feel for what the cadet has at home. And of all the tours, I would say don't miss the tour of the Superintendent's home—you have to get tickets for it. Also, I found the kitchens and the tailor shops very interesting."

Other parents had specific recommendations regarding Plebe Parent Weekend.

A mother from California: "Be sure and take warm clothes—we tend to forget things like that living in Southern California. It can be very cold up there in March or April."

A mother from Pennsylvania: "Take good walking shoes because you are going to be doing a lot of it. For clothing, plan on casual clothes during the day—afternoon clothes are fine for touring the Superintendent's house. However, they have a formal dinner and military ball, and while you see men in suits as well as formal attire, the formal wear looks very elegant. It was interesting to me to see all the clothes and you could almost tell what region people came from—for example, the Southern girls wore lovely full gowns with crinolines and hooped skirts."

When you visit, bring the whole family if you can.

A father from Florida with two sons at the Academy: "The formal dinner dance is a very beautiful affair; however, with my first one, I just took a business suit. I regretted it at the time, although you see others dressed that way. Next spring, when we go up to see our second son, I am going to go formal—it is definitely a black-tie affair."

Parents spoke of two potential problems associated with Plebe Parent Weekend. One is housing, and they strongly recommend that parents go over the list of motels in The *West Point Parent's Almanac* and get their reservations as

254

soon as possible. Closer is generally better in housing—your cadet has to be in by ten o'clock on Wednesday through Saturday nights. You definitely do not want to stay at the Hotel Thayer because your cadet cannot come to your room.

The other problem, for some parents, is a girlfriend problem.

The question that troubles parents is: Should we or should we not take the girlfriend along? (None of the parents mentioned a boyfriend problem.)

Numerous parents commented on the problem and their feelings and experiences were varied. The majority believed that the girlfriend should be left home so the cadet would not be torn between her and the family. They cited the need of the cadet to relax and be nurtured, and not to have additional pressure. However, many qualified this recommendation by saying that if the visit by the girlfriend is really important to the cadet, by all means take her along—that the bottom line is the cadet's happiness.

A few of the parents described good experiences when they took the girlfriend along, but they qualified their comments with such statements as: "She was a jewel," and "She was like a part of the family and very supportive of what he was doing."

Several parents also spoke of compromises. The most common recommendation was to leave the girl home on weekends that were mainly for parents, such as Labor Day Weekend and Plebe Parent Weekend. But, for events like football games or formal balls, the girl should be encouraged, or even helped financially, to make her own visit.

It is not recommended that the girlfriend go by herself on Plebe Parent Weekend. The plebe can only leave the post with relatives or with the relatives of a fellow cadet. He cannot accompany his girlfriend off the post.

DOWNER PHONE CALLS

The worst problem for most parents is the downer phone calls. Typically, the cadet will call home after a few weeks and will be in some state of depression. All the parents say that this is normal behavior and that a parent should expect calls like this. They point out that besides homesickness, the cadets are undergoing a traumatic change in their lifestyle.

Later, as the academic year gets underway, the depression often gets worse because of low grades—which many have never seen during their previous twelve years of schooling. Parents who have lived through many such phone calls had a variety of advice. Here is a sampling:

A father from Florida: "His first calls were not really downers, but I suspected that when we got up there on Labor Day that he would need to unload—which he did. He was very quiet for the whole weekend but before we left I knew he wanted to talk. I said, 'What's wrong? You're not yourself.' He broke into tears and said, 'Dad, this is not a fun place to be. No matter how hard you try you can't control anything—no matter how hard you work, you can't influence the situation.'

"I said—and I have a military background—'Son, that is precisely how they want you to feel. As an Army officer you are not going to be able to control anything but yourself and the soldiers who are, hopefully, trained and disciplined to do what you command. You can't control artillery, air, supplies—and you certainly can't control the enemy.' I think that talk helped; it is important for cadets to understand why they being treated as they are."

A mother and parents' club president from Pennsylvania: "I had those calls and I hear about them all the time. I tell those I counsel to assess the day of the week and the time of day they are calling. Sometimes you find out that the downer calls may coincide with a bad day. My son always used to call on Tuesday evening about eight o'clock. He would be very down, but by the end of the conversation he would get everything out of his system and he would be fine—although we would worry until the next call. We found out later that Tuesday was a long, hard day for him. He was in an advanced scuba-diving class, which he practiced the first thing in the morning; then he had classes all day and hockey afterwards. By eight o'clock, still facing hours of homework, he just wasn't himself—he was exhausted. The Sunday calls were nothing like that—on Sundays he had a whole different outlook on life.

"What do you say if they hate it so much they want to quit? It depends upon the kid, of course, but generally I advise parents to try to get them to finish the year—to give it a fair trial. In fact, I see nothing wrong with a parent arguing strenuously when they believe the kid has not given it a fair trial—at least through the first semester.

"However, if the kid insists on coming home, I think at least one of the parents, if possible, should go there and talk everything over—don't just let them quit without talking them through all their options. I always stress the importance of letting them know that you won't be disappointed in them if they quit—they need to know that they have the complete support of the parents. Many times I think they just need a chance to unload and to talk things out. The worst thing is when the parents get upset and act like it is the end of the world when the kid wants to quit."

A mother from Illinois put the ups and downs this way: "When we would get one of those calls, my husband would talk briefly; then the other son would talk because he was always positive and encouraging. Then, when I picked up the phone, I could hear the change in voice—he just wanted to get out all his misery to me. And I would listen and just mother him to death over the phone—I'd just let him be miserable.

"Later we found out that the pattern of the downer calls was related to the sleep that he got—the more tired and worn down he got, the more down he would be. Also, if he was in the process of doing something he really hated, he would be down. I remember how he was not thrilled with the boxing—he didn't like his nose bleeding every time—that got him down. But now he is fine. He is 38th in his class and is on the regimental staff with a phone in his room."

A father and former parents' club president from Illinois: "One of the worst problems I have seen is when kids get low grades and the parents refuse to accept that. It is hard when they have high SATs and are used to getting good grades in high school. Parents have to realize that it is much harder at West Point and that high grades in high school don't necessarily mean a thing. If parents will accept those low grades as normal, at least for awhile, then they can counsel the cadet and encourage him."

A mother and parents' club president from Kansas: "They're up and down and you just have to expect that. The important thing is to listen but not sympathize—I mean don't side with them against West Point. I think kids who have always had it good are the ones it is hardest on. Those who have been slapped around by life are more likely to rebound when they're low."

A mother from California: "Almost all of them hate it at first and they call home really down. I think you have to encourage them and tell them to just hang in there another week or until Thanksgiving or until Christmas. Keep telling them that it will get easier. I say this because my son would be down one week because things were miserable and I would get off the phone and worry all week. Then, the next week he calls and says, 'Oh mom, you know what happened? I was voted plebe of the week.' So it is up and down, and it goes like that.

"I think the key is to always talk positive—be upbeat, without offending them, of course."

A mother and former parents' club president from Iowa: "You're going to get those calls and my advice is just to be a good listener. Also, realize that they have nobody they can unload on. Their roommates are struggling and don't want to hear a lot of negative things. So who else can they turn to? They need somebody to feel sorry for them. Also, you have to realize that they are going to get low, but that they have to reach that low before they can start going up again."

An Ohio mother: "Our son wanted West Point from the time he knew what it was, but after two weeks there, we got the first call and he said he was thinking of bagging it. Luckily, we have been a family that always communicated so we had some good long talks. The most important thing in these talks is to lead the kid back through the reasons why he wanted it in the first place; then ask if there has been any change in goals. I think you have to be sympathetic but also strong in insisting that they give it the chance that it needs.

"Part of the problem is that they are all bright kids and they try to make logic out of situations that are not logical. They can't accept things at face value—they can't accept standard answers without questioning them. They just have to realize that they must obey without questioning.

"That is a real hard adjustment and a lot of them go through the first few months doubting whether they made the right decision. Parents have to gather their inner strength and somehow convince them that they did make the right decision—support them long enough so the cadet himself can make a decision based on intelligence rather than emotion and two or three weeks without sleep.

"Even at that it was very close with us. He called and said that he had begun the paperwork to get out. At that time you pull out all the stops. I called a friend who had graduated in the 60s and asked him if he had any friends back there. He gave me the name of one and I called him. He picked our son up and had a long talk with him; then he called us. That really helped all of us—keep that option in mind—people like that are more than willing to help.

"Well, someone convinced him to stay through the first home football game—knowing, I guess, that it would be his first chance to have a little fun. After that, and after talking to so many people back there, he would see someone who would say, 'Oh, you're still here,'—like they were proud of him. After that, he started to believe that people there really did care. From then on he picked himself up, was 47th in his class, had stars on his lapels [for a 3.5 average] and began looking forward to the challenges ahead.

"The next year he and another cadet talked to a gathering of candidates. Both of them stressed the importance of visiting West Point before accepting the appointment. But they said, don't just sit and snicker when you see someone getting chewed out, but put yourself in that position—nose to nose—and try to imagine how you are going to cope with that before it happens. It is easy when you see all that happening to someone else. They emphasized that incoming cadets always think that won't happen to them unless they screw up. They don't realize that they DON'T have to screw up—that it is going to happen anyhow—that it is a game that has to be played so the upperclassmen can mold them the way they want them to be. Also they said that a cadet has to be able to sort out the important chewings out from the unimportant—and learn not to dwell on the latter."

OTHER ADVICE

Several parents commented about their cadets attitude and behavior during vacations at home. They advised not to expect a transformation in the way the cadets keep their room. They say that the typical parent expects the West Point standards to rub off and that the cadets will keep their rooms neat and orderly. Instead, the parents say the cadets often regress and are as bad or worse than when they left—that they overreact to what they have been through.

Another problem at vacation time is that the cadets come home, sleep for a day and a half, then venture off and spend more time with their friends than with their family. Parents complained of various degrees of disappointment about this behavior, but all acknowledged that visits with friends ended up having positive value because the cadets see just how much more they, themselves, have matured compared to their friends.

Parents also cautioned not to plan things for the vacationing cadet, especially visits to Uncle Joe and Aunt Millie in full dress uniform! A family picture is okay, they say, but otherwise the advice is to let the cadet sleep, eat lots of whatever they crave, let them zonk on television if they desire, and, in general, keep the vacations as low key as possible.

Cadets become much closer to their roommates and classmates than at civilian colleges so don't be surprised, say parents, when your cadet wants to bring friends home during a vacation. Also, they say that parents should not be disappointed when the cadets announce that they are going to spend their vacation at their friend's home or do some traveling with their friends. Just try to remember that it is those friends who have sustained your cadet and shared long periods of adversity. So it is perfectly natural for them to also want to share some of the good times with their friends.

Another problem parents mentioned was the one-way telephone linkage with the cadets. After the first few weeks, it is relatively easy for the cadet to call home, but it is difficult for the parent to call the cadet.

The parents will be told that any calls concerning their cadet's welfare should be directed to the Company Tactical Officer, or Tac. However, the cadets themselves almost

260

Graduation Day—the day cadets and parents celebrate. But get your motel reservations early!

begged the author to advise parents NOT to call the Tac unless it was something important. Plebes, especially, do not want to draw attention to themselves, and they worry that knowledge of a call from a parent will get around their Company and they will somehow suffer from it.

But, by all means, if there is an emergency, or if the parent really feels that a cadet is having some kind of threatening problem, call the Tac—the number for each company is in the *Parent's Almanac*. And, if you are not satisfied with what the Tac is doing or has told you, you are perfectly within your right to move up the chain of command; after the Tac, call the Regimental Tactical Officer (RTO), and if still not satisfied, call the Brigade Tactical Officer (BTO). You can get those numbers from the West Point switchboard: 914-938-4011.

An alternative to contacting the Tac is to contact one of the chaplains. They have the ability to check out a number of problems without consulting the Tac or anyone else, and at certain times, like when the cadet is in the hospital, they can be a very good source of help. They are especially helpful in handling sensitive matters such as family problems that parents want to keep confidential. To contact a chaplain, just call the switchboard—they are on call 24-hours a day.

One final word of advice—and it comes from the author.

Just as soon as you think your son or daughter is serious about going to West Point, find out if there is a parents' club in your area and JOIN IT! The club members have been through almost every kind of experience. They can counsel you on admissions problems and on most problems you and your cadet might encounter in the four years that he or she will be at the Academy. In addition, many of the older clubs provide a social outlet that a lot of parents will enjoy—particularly as they become more caught up in the West Point spirit. There is an old saying, "Once a West Pointer, always a West Pointer." However, that saying can often be extended to parents as well. Many who were active in clubs when their sons and daughters were at West Point, also like to remain active just to be helpful and to enjoy the fellowship of those who share their love for the place.

ACKNOWLEDGEMENTS

Hundreds of individuals helped with this book, but it all started in the West Point Public Affairs Office—now the Academy Relations Office. The officers in charge of that office, first, Colonel Jack Yeagley, and later, Colonel Nick Hawthorne, cooperated in every way that I asked. My sincere thanks to both of them.

For the two-year period of this inquiry Mrs. Andrea Hamburger of the Academy Relations Office responded to numerous calls and lined up interviews for three different visits. In addition, she served as a guide and trekked with me through wind and rain over much of the West Point terrain. For all of that, thanks Andrea.

Thanks are also due others in the Academy Relations Office. Claire Morris served as a guide and helped arrange interviews with parents' club officers. Major Edward Evans also served as a guide and answered many questions. In the final stages of the project Ray Aalbue coordinated manuscript review and two visits by my son.

The West Point Admissions Office cooperated fully with this project thanks to the Director, Colonel Pierce A. Rushton, Jr. He spent several hours in personal discussions, he read the complete manuscript and made helpful suggestions, and he made every staff member available anytime I wanted to call. My sincere thanks, Colonel Rushton.

Another person in the Admissions Office who spent a lot of time helping me was Major Richard Sutton, the Minority Recruiting Officer. He made himself available in his office and at his home and I want to especially acknowledge his dedicated efforts to help minority candidates.

Others in the Admissions Office who helped with briefings, queries and interviews were Colonel Geoffrey Louis, Colonel Phil Leon, Lt. Colonel Art Mulligan, Major (Ret.) Bruce Turnbull, Captain Robin Carrington, Captain Doug Watson, Captain Steve Naru, Lt. Roslyn Walford and Lt. Gerren Grayer.

Also special thanks to Mr. Joe Dineen in the media section of the Admissions Office who made his photo collection available and who provided helpful advice. In addition thanks to Annebet McEliece who screened the files and located special photos that were requested.

In the Office of the Commandant, Chief of Staff Colonel Seth Hudgins, Jr. was helpful in numerous ways. He handled numerous phone inquiries, arranged interviews with staff members and cadet leaders, reviewed the complete manuscript and, in two long interviews, shared his unique insights of West Point—insights based upon the experiences of his father and his son as well as his own years as a cadet, tactical officer and Chief of Staff.

Thanks also to Lt. Colonel Jim Siket, Major Gary Heumphreus, Major Greg Stone, Major Bill Pokorny and Captain John Turner of the Commandant's Office who generously provided information on Beast Barracks, the Fourthclass Development System and the Honor Code.

The Dean, Brigadier General Roy Flint, gave a long interview, then ordered the academic division to give me access to any professors I wished to observe or interview. My sincere thanks to General Flint and the following professors and administrators for their advice and, in some cases, manuscript review: Colonel Ed Tezak, Colonel Lance Leach, Colonel Pat Hoy, II, Colonel Peter Stromberg, Colonel Frank Giordano, Lt. Colonel Rickey Kolb, Lt. Colonel Bob Schumacher, Lt. Colonel Lee Dewald, Lt. Colonel Ed Mayer, Lt. Colonel George Forsythe, Lt. Colonel Bill Shutsky, Major Linda Shockley, Major Sam Walker, III, Major Francis George, Major Jose Vazquez, Captain Kevin Sheehan, Captain Jeff Nauss, Captain Marty Vozzo, Captain Sharon Daniel and Captain Phil Macklin.

Also special thanks to Brigadier General (Ret.) David Cameron, the retired head of the Mathematics Department who, from his Virginia home, gave a long, interesting interview and reviewed the academic chapters of the manuscript.

Thanks also to Colonel Albert Vanderbush of the Athletic Department for an enjoyable afternoon discussion of the West Point sports programs.

While researching this project, I visited the Military Academy Preparatory School (USMAPS) in New Jersey and observed candidates preparing for West Point. While there I interviewed Dean Harold Beal, Colonel Dean Darling and Captain Kristi Snelling Hicks. I thank them for their helpful information.

Colonel (Ret.) Robert Lamb and the Association of Graduates were also helpful in my inquiry. Especially valuable was the assistance of Colonel (Ret.) Morris Herbert who graciously helped me arrange interviews with ten distinguished graduates and also reviewed the complete manuscript. Colonel (Ret.) Paul Child kindly gave me a tour of the publications department and provided several photos from AOG archives.

Many congressional staffers kindly gave their time to discuss candidates and their problems with the nomination process. I would like to acknowledge the following: Ruth Ann Norris (Senator DeConcini, Arizona), Patty Shay (Rep. Dannemeyer, California), Jeff Subco (Senator Exon, Nebraska), Betty Burger (Senator Grassley, Iowa), Carolyn Kegley (Senator Pryor, Arkansas), Clayton Hodgson (Senator Harkin, Iowa), Shelly Wilkins (Rep. Robinson, Arkansas), Ginger Yates (Senator Bumpers, Arkansas), Susan Gurrekovich (Rep. Clinger, Pennsylvania), Helen Scheurer (Rep. Luken, Ohio), Helen Hiestand (Rep. McEwen, Ohio), Randy Forster (Rep. Hall, Ohio), Jenny Irwin (Rep. DeWine, Ohio), John Seager and Alisa Sokolis (Rep. Kostmayer, Pennsylvania), Grace Garrelli (Rep. Bilbray, Nevada), Carol Leffler (former Rep. Cheney, Wyoming), Valorie Walkins (Senator McClure, Ohio), Melodi Moor (Rep. Bolter, Texas), Karen Mollenauer (Rep. Murphey, Pennsylvania), Sally Testa (Rep. Kasich, Ohio), Donna Faunce (Rep. Smith, Iowa), Karen Parsley (Rep. Daub, Nebraska), Jeanne Zappone (House Speaker Foley, Washington), Susan Wilson (Rep. Feighan, Ohio), Ann Mackey (Senator Ford, Kentucky), Tom Andreason (Rep. Craig, Idaho), Carol Lederman (Rep. Markey, Massachusetts), James Ross (Rep. Watkins, Oklahoma), Paula Noble (Senator Helms, North Carolina), Helen Brindle (Rep. Spratt, South Carolina), Wilma Robertson (Rep. Nelson, Florida), Dixie Loucks (Rep. Brown, Colorado), Sandra Manwill (Senator Garn, Utah), Larry Shannon (former House Speaker Wright, Texas), Marlene Moulder (Rep. Fields, Texas), Mitzie Martinez (Rep. Schroeder, Colorado), Jim Peterson (Senator Nunn, Georgia), Tom Navarro (Senator Wilson, California), Sue Elsenbrook (Senator Bentson, Texas), Celie Nelson (Rep. Rhodes, Arizona), Pam Barbey (Rep. Kyle, Arizona), and Dolores Dunn (Rep. Stump, Arizona).

Also helpful were the many panelists and liaison officers, each with years of experience conducting interviews with candidates. Many thanks to the following: Dennis Hawker, Jeri Smith-Fornara, Mary Jo White, Captain Richard Hartman, John Brandon, Donna Staver, Kelly Tobin, Paul Breon, Lt. Colonel Vic Staub, Al Hoberman, Dave Lesko, Steve Getzow, Paul Shalita, Pauline Riel, Dr. Hiram Carr, General Robert Teater, Colonel Bill Trice, Donna Buol, General James Abraham, Teresa Bloomingdale, Captain Bob Kaufman, June Milson, Ray Walton, Mary Lou Berry, Commander Maury Cartier, Bob Venafra, John Augenstein, Betty Runion, General Irving Reed, Brenda Jenkins, Salvador Porras, Robert Ohashi, Ed Patterson, Tom Sharp, Dr. Gene Woods, Colonel Charles Green, Colonel Jack Dibble, David Matta, Dr. Robert Elliott, Arnet Ward, Colonel Hugh Winn, Lt. Colonel Roy May, Major Mark Grazer and Colonel Pat Patterson.

The West Point cadets were the single best source of information for this book and I would like to thank the following who took precious time from their busy schedules to meet with me and pass on their experiences and advice: Tyler Fitzgerald, Malcolm Schaeffer, Patrick Walch, Paul Westover, Bryan Monteith, Robert Kroning, Frank Polasheki, Greg Louks, Lee Walters, Michael Mammay, Todd Royar, Tim Hess, Daniel Fritz, Tim Decker, Scott Whipp, Dave Wilkie, Chris Easter, Erick Reinstedt, Johnny Wright, Robert Williams, Charles Johnson, Harn Linwood, Dan Albert, Shawn Boland, Tracy Hetterscheidt, Tom Prescott, Cadet Nasir, Yu-Sik Kim, Bill Marshall, John Tiner, Lucie Deile, Keith Purvis, John Fortson, Ed Mathia, Dwight Hunt, Nick Mauldin, Greg Duvall, Michael Ellis, Andrew Sherrard, Mike Novak, Alvin Tiu, Mike Parsons, Warren Daniel, Chris Liga, Rob Proctor, Mike Ash, Scott Mapstone, Tim White, Eric Strong, Christopher Galy, Alex Vernon, Christina Juhay,

John Brunlik, Brian Harkinson, Thom Mukri, Sean Kushner, Bill Campbell, Dave Oksenberg, Ron Campbell and Ken Kamper.

Thanks also to the five women graduates who are quoted in Chapter 21: Captain Kathy Snook, First Lt. Deborah McDonald, First Lt. Maureen Finnessy Collins, First Lt. Ginni Guyton and Second Lt. Joan Littman.

The information in Chapter 22, "Advice for Parents," came from parents who have survived the plebe year along with their cadets. For the helpful advice that they have passed on I would like to thank: Joyce Johnson, Michael Collins, Colonel Ed Bierman, Wayne Morgan, Ellie Green, Mary Lou Illingworth, Jean Vertin, Bill and Shirlie Campbell, Dorothy Littman, Alice Petry, Gene Sullivan, Lynn Hankinson, Mary Jean Houlohan, James and Charlotte Kirby, Cynthia Sparkes, Julie Erwin, Gary Atwood, Tom and Marlene Ellis, Steve and Elizabeth Schmelling, George and Marion Novak, William and Doris Deile, Doris Albert, Jewel Warfield, Dennis and Ruth Clements, Chuck Gorske, Judith Wright, Roger Keuter, Chuck Carr, Jean Lacey and Gail Whatley.

Thanks also to the ten graduates who are featured in Chapter Two, "What West Point Meant To Me:" Lt. General (Ret.) Garrison Davidson, Brigadier General Charles "Monk" Meyer, Colonel (Ret.) Jack Broughton, Colonel (Ret.) William DeGraf, Mr. Denis Mullane, The Honorable Eugene Sullivan, Mr. Joseph Anderson, Major Richard Morales, Mr. Andrew Burke and Captain Mary Finch.

Finally, I want to acknowledge two members of my family who have worked closely on this project. My son, William M. Smallwood, made two visits to West Point, edited all of the copy, and supervised every aspect of production. His help was invaluable and I deeply appreciate it.

My wife, Patricia, accompanied me on one of the visits and helped with the notetaking. In addition, she copy-edited the manuscript and did her usual good job of managing my affairs so I could be free to put all of my effort into this project. For that and much more, thanks Pat.

wls

INDEX

APPENDIX

West Point Leadership Department's Recommended Reading List for Candidates:

1. Once an Eagle, Anton Myrer

2. Killer Angels, Michael Shaara

3. Platoon Leader, James R. McDonough

4. Red Badge of Courage, Stephen Crane

5. The Killing Zone, Frederick Downs

6. The Forgotten Soldier, G. Sajer

7. All Quiet on the Western Front, Erich Remarque

8. A Bridge Too Far, Cornelius Ryan

Recommended List of Videos:

1. Breaker Morant

2. The Boat (Das Bot)

3. Gallipoli

4. All Quiet on the Western Front

5. The Longest Day

6. Hamburger Hill

7. The Karate Kid

8. Platoon

Available from Beacon Books

The Naval Academy Candidate Book...............$7.95
   (ISBN 0-929311-01-9)

The West Point Candidate Book.....................$9.95
   (ISBN 0-929311-02-7)

The Air Force Academy Candidate Book.........$9.95
   (Second Edition - Available Spring 1990)
   (ISBN 0-929311-03-X)

To order, send check plus $1.50 postage and handling to:

Beacon Books
P.O. Box 1322
Mesa, AZ   85201

Or call us with your VISA or Mastercard:

(602) 977-2380   Mon. - Sat. 9-5 MST.

ORDERCARD

THE ACADEMY CANDIDATE SERIES: How to PREPARE • How to GET IN • How to SURVIVE

Indicate Quantities

_____ Naval Academy Candidate Book, 1st Ed. — $7.95

_____ West Point Candidate Book, 1st Ed. — $9.95

_____ Air Force Academy Candidate Book, 2nd Ed. — $9.95
(Available Spring 1990)

Fourth Class Postage and Handling. — $1.50

Total _____

_____ Check if you want your order sent by First Class Mail. I've enclosed an extra $1.50 for First Class Postage. ($3.00 total postage and handling)

**For faster service, phone orders accepted with Visa or Mastercard.
Call 602-977-2380 Monday-Saturday 9-5 MST.**

Note: Because these books are revised frequently, price subject to change without notice.

ORDERCARD

THE ACADEMY CANDIDATE SERIES: How to PREPARE • How to GET IN • How to SURVIVE

Indicate Quantities

_____ Naval Academy Candidate Book, 1st Ed. — $7.95

_____ West Point Candidate Book, 1st Ed. — $9.95

_____ Air Force Academy Candidate Book, 2nd Ed. — $9.95
(Available Spring 1990)

Fourth Class Postage and Handling. — $1.50

Total _____

_____ Check if you want your order sent by First Class Mail. I've enclosed an extra $1.50 for First Class Postage. ($3.00 total postage and handling)

**For faster service, phone orders accepted with Visa or Mastercard.
Call 602-977-2380 Monday-Saturday 9-5 MST.**

Note: Because these books are revised frequently, price subject to change without notice.

ORDERCARD

THE ACADEMY CANDIDATE SERIES: How to PREPARE • How to GET IN • How to SURVIVE

Indicate Quantities

_____ Naval Academy Candidate Book, 1st Ed. — $7.95

_____ West Point Candidate Book, 1st Ed. — $9.95

_____ Air Force Academy Candidate Book, 2nd Ed. — $9.95
(Available Spring 1990)

Fourth Class Postage and Handling. — $1.50

Total _____

_____ Check if you want your order sent by First Class Mail. I've enclosed an extra $1.50 for First Class Postage. ($3.00 total postage and handling)

**For faster service, phone orders accepted with Visa or Mastercard.
Call 602-977-2380 Monday-Saturday 9-5 MST.**

Note: Because these books are revised frequently, price subject to change without notice.

Send book(s) to:

Name: _____

Address: _____

_____

City/St/Zip: _____

Send this order card to:
Beacon Books
P.O. Box 1322
Mesa, AZ 85201

— — — — — — — — — — — — — — — — — — —

Send book(s) to:

Name: _____

Address: _____

_____

City/St/Zip: _____

Send this order card to:
Beacon Books
P.O. Box 1322
Mesa, AZ 85201

— — — — — — — — — — — — — — — — — — —

Send book(s) to:

Name: _____

Address: _____

_____

City/St/Zip: _____

Send this order card to:
Beacon Books
P.O. Box 1322
Mesa, AZ 85201